– extend + deepen freedom, equality + democracy

progressive

nascent
cohort

90

THE FIGHT FOR
THE FOUR FREEDOMS

WHAT MADE FDR AND THE GREATEST GENERATION TRULY GREAT

HARVEY J. KAYE

SIMON & SCHUSTER

New York · London · Toronto · Sydney · New Delhi

90

Simon & Schuster
1230 Avenue of the Americas
New York, NY 10020

First Simon & Schuster hardcover edition April 2014

For information about special discounts for bulk purchases,
please contact Simon & Schuster Special Sales at 1-866-506-1949
or business@simonandschuster.com.

The Simon & Schuster Speakers Bureau can bring authors to your
live event. For more information or to book an event, contact
the Simon & Schuster Speakers Bureau at 1-866-248-3049
or visit our website at www.simonspeakers.com.

Designed by Paul Dippolito

Manufactured in the United States of America

1 3 5 7 9 10 8 6 4 2

Library of Congress Cataloging-in-Publication Data

Kaye, Harvey J.
The fight for the four freedoms : what made FDR and the greatest
generation truly great / Harvey J. Kaye. — First Simon & Schuster
hardcover edition.
pages cm
1. Roosevelt, Franklin D. (Franklin Delano), 1882–1945—Influence.
2. United States—History—1933–1945. 3. United States—Social
conditions—20th century. 4. Civil rights—United States—History—20th
century. 5. National characteristics, American—History—20th century.
6. United States—Politics and government—1933–1945. I. Title.
E806.K39 2014
973.917092—dc23
2013012406
ISBN 978-1-4516-9143-6
ISBN 978-1-4516-9145-0 (ebook)

CONTENTS

THE FIGHT FOR
THE FOUR FREEDOMS

INTRODUCTION

We need to remember. We need to remember what conservatives have never wanted us to remember and what liberals have all too often forgotten.

Now, after more than thirty years of subordinating the public good to corporate priorities and private greed, of subjecting ourselves to widening inequality and intensifying insecurities, *and* of denying our own democratic impulses and yearnings, we need to remember.

We need to remember who we are.

We need to remember that we are the children and grandchildren of the men and women who rescued the United States from economic destruction in the Great Depression and defended it against fascism and imperialism in the Second World War.

We need to remember that we are the children and grandchildren of the men and women who not only saved the nation from economic ruin and political oblivion, but also turned it into the strongest and most prosperous country on earth.

And most of all we need to remember that we are the children and grandchildren of the men and women who accomplished all of that—in the face of powerful conservative, reactionary, and corporate opposition, and despite their own faults and failings—by making America freer, more equal, and more democratic than ever before.

Now, when all that they fought for is under siege and we, too, find ourselves confronting crises and forces that threaten the nation and all that it stands for, we need to remember that we are the children and

I

grandchildren of the most progressive generation in American history. We are the children of the men and women who articulated, fought for, and endowed us with the promise of the Four Freedoms.

On the afternoon of January 6, 1941, President Franklin Delano Roosevelt went up to Capitol Hill to deliver his Annual Message to Congress. Just weeks earlier, he had defeated the Republican Wendell Willkie at the polls and won reelection to an unprecedented third term. But Roosevelt now faced a far bigger challenge, one even more daunting than those he confronted in his first and second terms. Still stalked by the Great Depression, the United States was also increasingly threatened by the Axis powers—Nazi Germany, Fascist Italy, Imperial Japan. And with war already raging east and west, Americans had yet to agree about how to respond to the danger. The President, however, did not falter. He not only proceeded to propose measures to address the emergency. He also gave dramatic new meaning to *All men are created equal . . . Life, liberty, and the pursuit of happiness . . . We the People of the United States . . . A new birth of freedom . . .* and *Government of the people, by the people, for the people . . .*

FDR knew about crises. But he knew as well what Americans could accomplish, even in the darkest of times. Born in 1882, he had grown up privileged, the son of New York Hudson River gentry. Yet long before becoming President, he had suffered serious defeats and setbacks, none more devastating than contracting polio in 1921 at the age of thirty-nine. The disease had left him permanently unable to stand up or walk without assistance. However, supported by his wife, Eleanor, and other family members and friends, he had risen above the paralysis to become the most dynamic political figure in the United States. Moreover, his experiences and encounters in the course of doing so had reaffirmed and deepened his already powerful faith and confidence in God, in himself, *and* in his fellow citizens—all of which had enabled him, in the face of the worst economic and social catastrophes in the nation's history, to defiantly state that "the only thing we have to fear is fear itself" and to go on to proclaim, "This generation of Americans has a rendezvous with destiny." Armed with this faith and confidence, and propelled by the popular energies that his words and actions elicited, he determinedly pursued the initiatives of relief, recovery, reconstruction, and reform known as the New Deal.[1]

Together, President and people severely tested each other, made mistakes and regrettable compromises, and suffered defeats and disappointments. Nevertheless, challenging each other to live up to their finest ideals, Roosevelt and his fellow citizens advanced them further than either had expected or even imagined possible. Confronting fierce conservative, reactionary, and corporate opposition, they not only rejected authoritarianism, but also redeemed the nation's historic purpose and promise by initiating revolutionary changes in American government and public life and radically extending American freedom, equality, and democracy. They subjected big business to public account and regulation, empowered the federal government to address the needs of working people, mobilized and organized labor unions, fought for their rights, broadened and leveled the "We" in "We the People," established a social security system, expanded the nation's public infrastructure, improved the environment, cultivated the arts and refashioned popular culture, and—while much remained to be done—imbued themselves with fresh democratic convictions, hopes, and aspirations.

Standing before the American people and their assembled representatives that early January day, the president surely believed their rendezvous with destiny had come. He told them straightforwardly that Americans were now confronting a "moment unprecedented in the history of the United States"—"unprecedented" because never before had "American security been as seriously threatened from without." And he refused to appease those who threatened the nation's safety or defer to isolationist arguments that the country could avoid war by constructing a "fortress America" behind which it might hide.[2]

Referring to the Axis powers' global ambitions, the President stated: "I find it, unhappily, necessary to report that the future and safety of our country and of our democracy are overwhelmingly involved in events beyond our borders." He knew the defense of the United States and everything for which it stood would soon require it to enter the war directly, but he did not then request a declaration of war. At this moment, he called upon Congress and the people to turn the country into the "Arsenal of Democracy" and to enact a Lend-Lease program that would afford Great Britain and its allies the wherewithal to sustain their struggle against fascist Germany and Italy.[3]

Yet Roosevelt did not leave it at that. Counseling that "When the dictators are ready to make war upon us, they will not wait for an act of war on our part," he warned against those few selfish citizens who "would clip the wings of the American eagle in order to feather their own nests" and enjoined that "We must all prepare to make the sacrifices that the emergency—almost as serious as war itself—demands."

However, convinced that Americans had to equip themselves with not only arms, but also "the stamina and courage which come from unshakable belief in the manner of life which they are defending," he neither called for giving up, nor for suspending, what the men and women of the Great Depression had recently struggled so hard to achieve. Far from it. Instead, he called for strengthening "democratic life in America" by actually enlarging their newly won "social economy," citing as fundamentals "equality of opportunity for youth and others," "jobs for those who can work," "security for those who need it," "the ending of special privileges for the few," "the preservation of civil liberties for all . . ." And he specifically proposed expanding the "coverage of old-age pensions and unemployment insurance," providing "opportunities for adequate medical care," and creating a better system to assure "gainful employment" to all who needed it.

Finally, articulating Americans' grandest ideals and strivings past and present, Roosevelt defined a cause and a generation:

In the future days, which we seek to make secure, we look forward to a world founded upon four essential human freedoms.

The first is freedom of speech and expression—everywhere in the world.

The second is freedom of every person to worship God in his own way—everywhere in the world.

The third is freedom from want—which, translated into world terms, means economic understandings which will secure to every nation a healthy peacetime life for its inhabitants—everywhere in the world.

The fourth is freedom from fear—which, translated into world terms, means a world-wide reduction of armaments to such a point and in such a thorough fashion that no nation will be in a position to commit an act of physical aggression against any neighbor—anywhere in the world.[4]

Isolationists denounced the President's call to turn the United States into the "Arsenal of Democracy" and conservatives rejected his expansive democratic vision. But most Americans responded otherwise. They backed the call to action, affirmed the promise pronounced, and in the wake of Japan's December 7, 1941, attack on Pearl Harbor, made "Freedom of speech and expression, Freedom of worship, Freedom from want, Freedom from fear" the nation's war aims.

In the name of democracy and the "Four Freedoms," 16 million Americans would put on uniforms and pursue a global struggle we would come to call the "Good War"—not for the character of the combat, but for the rightness of the cause and the unity of purpose in which the nation pursued it. With their allies, they would storm beaches, slog through jungles, tramp across icy fields, sail through submarine-infested waters, fly missions over heavily fortified territories, and punch, push, claw, and ultimately power their way to victory. At the same time, their fellow citizens would not only pray for them to return safe and sound, but also go "All Out!" both to provide the arms and materiel required for victory *and* to protect and improve what those millions were defending.

President and people once again were to test each other, make mistakes and compromises, and suffer defeats and disappointments. Nonetheless, they not only prevailed over their enemies, but also, as before, compelled each other to enhance American democratic life in the process. Despite continuing antidemocratic opposition, Americans expanded the labor, consumer, and civil rights movements, subjected industry and the marketplace to greater public control, reduced inequality and poverty, and further transformed the "We" in "We the People." Moreover, they embraced new initiatives to expand freedom, equality, and democracy at war's end.

Roosevelt passed away in April 1945. Germany and Japan surrendered in the months that followed (Italy had done so in 1943). And yet the promise of the Four Freedoms did not expire. Even as the United States began to "take off" in an unprecedented economic expansion and enter into a "Cold War" struggle with the Soviet Union, most Americans set out to make that promise all the more real.

But not all Americans. Not everyone wanted to enhance American democratic life. Conservatives, reactionaries, and corporate bosses had their own ideas for postwar America. Determined as ever to reverse the progressive accomplishments of the Roosevelt years and cancel out the promise of the Four Freedoms, they set themselves anew to suppressing if not extinguishing Americans' democratic aspirations and energies. And they enjoyed successes. By the early 1950s, they had tamed liberals, marginalized progressives and radicals, and stymied the democratic campaigns of labor and the civil rights movement—not to mention effectively effaced FDR's Four Freedoms from public debate.

And yet, for all of their efforts, this powerful minority could not get Americans to forget their hard-won victories or the promise that encouraged them. In fact, as Americans continued to make the nation ever stronger and more prosperous, they also pushed freedom, equality, and democracy forward. Never as quickly or as completely as some wished, but always forward. They built new communities and new churches, schools, and civic associations. They secured higher living standards for themselves and their families. And they not only expanded social security, but also began to enact laws against racial and religious discrimination. And when they were seriously challenged in the 1960s to live up to the promise that so many of them had struggled to articulate and advance, they recommitted the nation to doing so.

The power of Roosevelt's Four Freedoms endured.

Those who marched for civil rights, campaigned to end poverty, organized public-employee unions, pushed to enact health care for the

elderly and poor, demanded equal rights for women, reformed the nation's immigration law, expanded public education and the arts, pressed
for greater regulation of corporate activity to protect the environment,
workers, and consumers, and protested the Vietnam War did not regularly recite those freedoms. But they were inspired and informed by the
struggles and achievements of the President and people who first proclaimed and fought for them—and were most often called to act anew
by veterans of that fight.

Undeniably, the "Age of Roosevelt" and the progressive pursuit of the
Four Freedoms can seem a very long time ago. But even now, after so
many years of conservative political ascendancy and concerted class
war from above—more than thirty years of deregulating corporate activity, reducing the taxes of the rich, assailing labor unions, shuttering
industries, and neglecting the public infrastructure—the democratic
legacy of that generation continues to nourish us. We all live in the
long, long shadow of those men and women, of what they did and what
they afforded us. And in the intervening decades, the Four Freedoms
and what they encompass have actually broadened. Pick any area of
American life. The consequences of that generation's commitment to
the promise of those freedoms are evident. Moreover, our most volatile
political and cultural contests often fall precisely along the fault lines
of those freedoms.

All of which renders it all the more remarkable that we do not
honor those men and women for their progressive struggles and
achievements. That the Right and conservative rich continue, as they
always have, to work at delaying, containing, and rolling back that
generation's greatest democratic accomplishments is not remarkable.
But that liberals and leftists have lost their association with that generation is. How is it that the most celebrated generation in American
history is not remembered for its most enduring accomplishment and
greatest gift to the nation, the embedding of FDR's Four Freedoms in
the very bedrock of American life?

In 1997, the FDR Memorial was unveiled along the Tidal Basin in

Washington, D.C., and in 2004, the National World War II Memorial was opened on the National Mall directly between the Washington Monument and the Lincoln Memorial. At the same time, millions of Americans not only snatched up books like Stephen Ambrose's *Citizen Soldiers*, Tom Brokaw's *The Greatest Generation*, and James Bradley's *Flags of Our Fathers*, but also went to see Steven Spielberg's *Saving Private Ryan*, sat for hours watching programs such as HBO's *Band of Brothers* and *The Pacific* and Ken Burns's PBS documentary *The War*, and turned out for events both grand and intimate commemorating a generation's labors and sacrifices.[5]

The memorials, histories, and public speeches and ceremonies beautifully honor those who prevailed against depression and total war. And yet, even as we have proclaimed our eternal gratitude and promised never to forget them and all that they did, we have failed to remember what made the "Greatest Generation" and its "greatest leader" truly great.

At serious cost to the memory and legacy of that generation, and to our own shared prospects, we have allowed the public telling of their lives and struggles to be drained of its most progressive, democratic, and inspiring content.

Consider that in their otherwise moving works, the Greatest Generation's tribunes, Ambrose, Brokaw, Bradley, Spielberg, and Burns, make no mention of FDR's pronouncement of the Four Freedoms. They utterly ignore how a President and people articulated anew the nation's historic promise in "Freedom of speech and expression, Freedom of worship, Freedom from want, Freedom from fear," and went "All Out!" in their name not only to defend American democratic life, but also to enhance it. And they utterly ignore how a President and people not only saved the United States from economic destruction and political tyranny and proceeded to turn it into the strongest and most prosperous country on earth, but did so by harnessing the powers of democratic government, making America freer, more equal, and more democratic than ever before in the process.

Journalists and columnists of every political stripe compounded our amnesia. Like the storytellers, they, too, wrote and spoke as if the lives and histories memorialized in the FDR and World War II monuments had nothing to do with each other. They made no mention of how Roosevelt and his fellow citizens fought the Great Depression not by retreating from America's finest ideals, but by rejecting the sirens of reaction and defeatism and working to make those ideals all the more real. They made no mention of how those Americans not only proved to themselves that they could transcend their faults and failings and prevail against daunting challenges, but also both reaffirmed what it meant to be American even as they prepared to confront the evils of Nazism, fascism, and imperialism. And they made no mention of how Americans, seared in the manifold failures of the 1920s, made the pursuit of the Four Freedoms their own even before they went to war in Europe and Asia.

Moreover, even as intellectuals and pundits Right and Left marveled at the intensity of their fellow citizens' fascination for the Greatest Generation, they never addressed the democratic significance of it all. Ever attentive to America's democratic impulse, those on the right recognized it and instinctively sought to counter it. Sadly, writers on the left missed it entirely. They not only failed to appreciate the democratic longings that Americans' admiration for the Greatest Generation signaled. They criticized the celebrations and the popular response to them.

Having sought to rein in Roosevelt even before he was elected, the right and conservative rich have been working ever since to roll back the progressive achievements of the generation that embraced the four-time elected President. And knowing the powers of the past in shaping our political and cultural imaginations they have never failed to realize that doing so required suppressing, obscuring, or manipulating and, when possible, appropriating the story of the making of American freedom, equality, and democracy. Echoing their political ancestors of the 1930s, they responded to the renewed interest in Roosevelt by once again vehemently accusing him and his "New Dealers" of imposing policies not simply inimical to American life, but inspired by fascism and communism; of not just failing to end the Great Depression, but of actually prolonging it; and of not simply enlarging the federal government at the expense of individual and corporate enterprise, but of hijacking the Constitution and trampling on American freedoms. Even as they have strenuously endeavored to disassociate the men and women of the Greatest Generation from the progressive achievements of the Roosevelt presidency, they have enthusiastically celebrated the veterans of the Second World War for their patriotism, and laid claim to their legacy in those narrowed terms.[6]

Meanwhile, liberal and progressive intellectuals reacted to what the historian Emily Rosenberg referred to as the "memory boom" with criticisms bordering on condescension. Yes, the Greatest Generation phenomenon entailed lots of commercial and patriotic hype. And yes, both isolationism and racism marked American attitudes and actions in the 1930s and 1940s. But liberal and progressive commentators ignored the democratic legacy and appeal of the men and women of that generation. Indeed, they failed to see that the tribunes of the Greatest Generation were not making too much of what those men and women accomplished, but rather too little—and consequently they did nothing to respond to the right's erasure of a generation's progressive struggles and achievements.[7]

We Americans did not turn to the past in the 1990s because we wanted to escape the present or because we were fooled into doing so. In the wake of a dozen years of Republican presidential administrations and in the midst of the most conservative era since the 1920s, we did so to recall and engage it.

Sensing that the very meaning of America was in jeopardy, we instinctively did what Americans have always done at such moments. We looked back, back to those who most powerfully expressed what it means to be an American, most particularly to those who, confronting crises, made American life freer, more equal, and more democratic in the process.

Some of us did so in the clearest of terms. Responding to the spread of right-wing militia groups and the horrific 1995 attack on the Oklahoma City federal building, the political activist Chip Berlet recalled his father's military service and postwar commitments to urge renewed respect for "civil liberties, civil rights, and civil discourse." He acknowledged that his father, a decorated veteran of the Battle of the Bulge, a lifelong Republican, and an ardent anti-Communist, had his prejudices; and yet, he noted, the same man refused to allow those attitudes to override the ideals for which he had fought. Berlet proudly recounted that his dad, while serving as a Little League coach in their suburban New Jersey town in the 1950s, recruited an interracial team and a Jewish assistant coach and, when acting as the grand marshal of the Memorial Day parade in the early 1970s, insisted on the right of peace marchers to join in the procession. And he proceeded to relate an exchange that he had had with his father not long before he was to die of cancer: "My Dad was determined to don his uniform one last time on Memorial Day. As I helped him dress, I asked him about the war. His only reply was to hand me one of his medals. Inscribed on the back were the words "'Freedom from Fear and Want. Freedom of Speech and Religion.' The four freedoms." As Berlet put it, "My Dad fought fascism to defend these freedoms, not just for himself, but for people of different religions and races, people he disagreed with . . . even people he was prejudiced against. Today, the four freedoms are under attack—in part because we forget why people fought World War II."[8]

Other Americans spoke less politically, though no less meaningfully. In November 2000, when the outcome of the presidential election had yet to be resolved, Lorrie Young, a self-described forty-year-old Southern California homemaker, felt compelled to write a letter to *The San Diego Union-Tribune* telling of her experience after reading *The Greatest Generation*. Wanting more "Americana," and seeing that the San Diego Museum of Art had a Norman Rockwell exhibit under way, she headed downtown to take in the show. Rockwell's famous "Four Freedoms" paintings—works produced in 1943 to visually represent FDR's words—incited much more than admiration in her. Standing before Rockwell's *Freedom of Speech*—the picture of a "Lincolnesque laborer standing in a town hall meeting having his say"—Young said: "The World War II stories I'd been reading about in Brokaw's book hit [me] like a rock. I was embarrassed to be tearing up. But, looking around me, I saw four other people, young and old, in the same state. Some were softly sobbing, some just sat, taking it all in."

As much as Young found herself "overtaken by sadness," she did not speak nostalgically. Responding to the most expressively democratic of Rockwell's works, she did not long for the past. Rather, she voiced her appreciation for those who had fought for the Four Freedoms and her own worries about the state of her America: "It is profoundly sad to realize that so many incredibly brave men and women gave so much to preserve what has become an embarrassment to their offspring and their country. We once stood for courage, strength, dignity and honesty." More than wishing to return to the supposed "good old days," Young expressed a desire to reinvigorate America: "Maybe this exhibit captures a version of our American culture that those of us forty and under missed out on, a time when dignity and integrity were more important than winning at all costs . . . I am ashamed of my ingratitude and wish to give back something to my country—a country where 'the four freedoms' still bring people to tears in a museum."[9]

After the past decade and a half that witnessed not only the tragedy of 9/11 and the nightmare of Hurricane Katrina, but also prolonged wars in Central Asia and the Middle East, the restriction of civil liberties, spying on American citizens, the abuse of human rights, the breaching of the wall separating church and state, massive tax cuts for the rich, the further disabling of labor unions, the targeting of Social Security for privatization, a disastrous financial crisis and economic downturn that we will forever refer to as the Great Recession, massive bank bailouts, the continued widening of wealth inequality, the loss of jobs and homes, and an exasperating politics of obstruction and deference, it becomes all the more critical that we recall the progressive lives and labors of the men and women of the 1930s and 1940s and the President who led them.[10]

We need to remember. We need to remember what we have been trying so hard to remember. But doing so is not easy. We have been led to forget. As powers-that-be have been ever wont to do, our own have regularly sought to shape the telling of the past in favor of controlling the present and future. And sometimes even those who seem most eager to remember the nation's democratic history have contributed to a kind of amnesia. Nevertheless, we Americans cannot afford to forget our democratic history, for as Wilson Carey McWilliams once observed, "a people's memory sets the measure of its political freedom."[11]

Only when we remember what made the Greatest Generation and its greatest leader truly great, only when we restore to our parents and grandparents their democratic lives and labors, only when we redeem the progressive vision and promise of the Four Freedoms, will we really appreciate why we turn to them as we do and begin to honor them as we should. Only then will we understand the democratic imperative that they passed on to us. Only then will we, too, save the nation by making it freer, more equal, and more democratic.

CHAPTER ONE

"We have not yet fully explored the democratic way of life."

Harold Saperstein, Martin Dash, and Akiva Skidell heard President Roosevelt's 1941 Message to Congress and, like so many other Americans, made the Four Freedoms their own. To these young Jewish Americans, "freedom of speech and expression" meant the right to speak even when doing so challenged the prevailing consensus; "freedom of worship" signified the right to pray and live freely and equally as a Jew in an overwhelmingly Christian society; "freedom from want" declared that the pursuit of economic security and opportunity had just begun; and "freedom from fear" meant a determined effort to "end discrimination and persecution." And these young men carried that vision with them into the war—Saperstein as an army chaplain in Europe, Dash as a naval officer in the Atlantic on the destroyer USS *McCormick,* and Skidell as a radio operator in Europe with the 2nd Armored Division.[1]

Discussing her work for "What My Job Means to Me," a 1943 article for the black journal *Opportunity,* Leotha Hackshaw, an inspector of binoculars in an army ordnance plant, stated: "In our own time our President has raised the standard of the 'Four Freedoms.' These freedoms are not new. They have been fought for over and over again. The

Negro has attained one of these and part of another. Freedom from fear and freedom from want he is fighting for now; for under them democracy can reach its fulfillment." And recalling his disappointment that he and his men were assigned to battling forest fires in Washington State instead of the nation's enemies, Walter Morris, a platoon leader in the 555th Parachute Infantry Battalion—the U.S. Army's first black paratroop unit—related that when he seriously confronted the question of what he was doing and why he so wanted to succeed, he realized he was doing it for his "children" and his "children's children," for "I knew . . . in my heart," he said, "that this country, as great as it is, would overcome the stigma of separation and prejudice."[2]

In a letter to his not yet born son—a son whom he would never see, for he was killed in action in France in August 1944—First Lieutenant Wallace Zosel of the 666th Engineers Topographical Company wrote: "I am grateful [you] can grow in the best country in the world, and, believe me, we who are overseas really know how wonderful America really is. True, we . . . have seen many things we would like to have changed, but that is what we hope to do . . . That is perhaps our chief reason for fighting this war . . . Millions of us over here are working, and fighting, and dying because we want America to be a nation of hope for mankind."[3]

How could those young Americans have felt as they did? Anti-Semitism excluded Jews from organizations and activities and expressed itself in acts of violence. Racism segregated people by color and oppressed those of color, sometimes murderously so. Women's lives were limited by "traditional" assumptions and expectations. Business hostility to labor unions led to pitched battles and bloodshed. And an economic depression so severe it had led citizens to speak of the death of the American dream and, possibly, democratic government itself continued to shadow the nation with high unemployment right up until the country's full-scale mobilization for war.

Given all of that, what gave those young men and women these hopes and aspirations they expressed even as they faced a war threatening the very survival of the United States? What sustained their faith in America and led them to believe they could advance the Four Freedoms?

Eager to indict Franklin Roosevelt for hijacking the Constitution and crippling free enterprise, conservatives don't tell us. Eager to arraign him for serving the interests of capital and stifling revolutionary possibilities, radicals don't tell us. And as eager as they remain to defend his record and legacy, liberals don't tell us, either. In fact, even the tribunes of America's "Greatest Generation" and "citizen soldiers," such as Tom Brokaw, Stephen Ambrose, and Ken Burns, never really tell us.

They do not tell us that the men and women and boys and girls of the 1930s witnessed, if not themselves experienced, not just fierce racial and religious oppression, brutal class inequalities and injustices, and the terrible trials and tribulations of the Great Depression, but also the greatest democratic upsurge and transformations since the 1860s, if not the Revolution.

Americans did not simply suffer and endure the Great Depression. They confronted it.

They did so in diverse ways. Critically, they did so by electing a man to the presidency who believed in America's democratic purpose and promise and gave full voice to the progressive imperative and possibilities inherent in it—a President who through his spoken words and a vast host of newly created agencies such as the NRA (National Recovery Administration), AAA (Agricultural Adjustment Administration), CCC (Civilian Conservation Corps), WPA (Works Progress Administration), and NYA (National Youth Administration) articulated Americans' democratic memories and yearnings and mobilized their spirits and energies to pursue not only relief and recovery, but also reconstruction and reform. Moreover, they did so by electing and reelecting a President who spoke to their deepest understandings, hopes, and aspirations and challenged them to fight not just the economic depression but also the order of things that had engendered it—a President who called on them to remake America by advancing and affording themselves a new deal.

And they responded to the challenge with conviction.

They responded not only by backing their President's efforts to publicly regulate industry and commerce and by going to work in their millions in public-works projects to rebuild the country's public spaces, infrastructures, and landscapes, but also—increasingly determined to both secure their rights as Americans and compel FDR to pursue the New Deal faster and further than he might otherwise have done—by speaking their own words and creating or expanding their own alphabet soup of agencies such as the UMW (United Mine Workers), ILGWU (International Ladies' Garment Workers' Union), AYC (American Youth Congress), NNC (National Negro Congress), and CIO (Congress of Industrial Organizations).

Defying historical expectations, fierce conservative, reactionary, and corporate opposition, and the siren calls of demagogues, they and their President initiated progressive changes in American government and public life, changes that radically extended and deepened American freedom, equality, and democracy.

How could those young Americans have felt as they did?

How could they not? They and their fellow citizens had confronted the Great Depression and prevailed. Yes, they had much still to do. However, in contrast to so much of the rest of the world, where dictators had come to rule with iron fists and concentration camps, a generation of Americans had stood up to the crises that threatened them by making the United States not just physically and culturally richer, but at the very same time all the more free, equal, and democratic. That generation—those men and women and those boys and girls—had already begun to prove to themselves that they could not only endure hardship and triumph over adversity, but also mobilize and harness the powers of democratic government to progressively remake America and themselves. Indeed, they had not just reaffirmed the nation's democratic purpose and promise, but also, whether they knew it or not, helped to compose FDR's Four Freedoms peroration.

In 1937, in the immediate wake of FDR's first term and at the very outset of his second, the cultural critic Harold Stearns would remark, "At whatever point you touch the complex American life of today you get a sense of new confidence, new pride, and even new hope." Insisting it had to do with more than "economic recovery," he explained: "It is a dim but growing conviction that our way of life has not yet been tried and found wanting—indeed, a feeling that we ourselves have not even completely attempted it. In a word, we do not believe that democracy has failed us, but that we have not yet fully explored the democratic way of life."[4]

Yet not many years earlier—even before the economy went into free fall—such democratic optimism would have seemed misplaced to most Americans. The Roaring Twenties may be remembered as a time of economic growth and prosperity. And for a certain class of people it was. But it was also a time in which conservatives, reactionaries, and the corporate rich dominated American life, politically, culturally, and economically. It was anything but a time of progressive hopes and dreams.

The United States entered World War I to "make the world safe for democracy," but doing so did not encourage democracy in postwar America. Women gained the vote. However, a vicious Red Scare drove radicals out of the country or to the margins of public life; and racism, nativism, anti-Catholicism, and anti-Semitism—all the favorite isms of the renascent Ku Klux Klan—not to mention Prohibition and a narrow-minded evangelical Protestantism, intensified their hold on public life. At the same time, isolationism replaced internationalism, which the U.S. Senate signaled clearly by rejecting U.S. entry into the new League of Nations.

America was ethnically and racially diverse—and it had become all the more so with the arrival of millions of immigrants from eastern and southern Europe, east Asia, and Mexico in the years before the war. But the country continued to be dominated by "White Anglo-Saxon Protestant" elites. As the columnist Joseph Alsop would later observe: "The nation's culture was a WASP culture. The nation's economy was WASP-dominated . . . Even the nation's politics were WASP politics." And that politics included stemming the tide of immigration. In 1924, Congress enacted restrictive immigration acts that banned Asian newcomers altogether and set quotas effectively limiting the annual number of new Europeans to 150,000 and those from beyond "Nordic" Europe to 15,000.[5]

Moreover, governed by Republican presidents, Americans seemed uninterested in the turn-of-the-century leftist politics that had inspired challenges to the ruling classes of the corporate mogul-dominated "Gilded Age"—leading the former president and now Chief Justice William Howard Taft to happily state in the wake of Calvin Coolidge's 1924 presidential election victory: "This country is no country for radicalism. I think it is the most conservative country in the world." And not only conservatives thought so. Heading into self-imposed Parisian exile along with many another intellectual and artist—placing American culture all the more in the hands of those eager to market it or, like the renowned social critic H. L. Mencken, debunk it—the same Harold Stearns who would write so optimistically fifteen years later lamented in 1922: "We have no heritage or traditions to which to cling except those that have already withered . . . and turned to dust."[6]

Ever more concentrated, corporate enterprise reigned supreme in this so-called New Era of the 1920s. Business boomed, wealth accumulated, and labor union rolls shrank from 5 million to fewer than 3.5 million members. President Calvin Coolidge declared, "The chief business of the American people is business," and capital's publicists, preaching the wonders of technological innovation, promoted a "cult of prosperity."[7]

Prosperity, however, did not characterize everybody's life. Inequality widened and economic insecurity intensified. Agriculture never recovered from its postwar price depression, sending many not just deeper into debt, but also into town for work—which, along with industrial mechanization, served to swell the urban labor supply, suppress wages, and keep living standards low for most workers and their families.[8]

Sensing that workers wanted to organize unions, their organized bosses did everything they could to prevent it from happening. Presumably, the very things that had impressed the socialist Sidney Hillman, Russian-Jewish leader of the Amalgamated Clothing Workers union, had impressed them. Moved by the skill and savvy of his co-unionists, most of them, like himself, immigrants, Hillman said in 1914: "To see these people, only a few years ago from lands where factories were unknown, meeting to discuss problems of the rights and wrongs of shop discipline, of changing prices, of the rightfulness of discharge is a thing to fill one with hope for the future of democracy." But whereas for Hillman this fresh democratic energy had signaled the coming of "the Messiah," for capitalists it portended the arrival of the Antichrist.[9]

Harnessing the wartime rhetoric of "Americanism"—"100% Americanism"—and the fears of the Red Scare, the business classes denounced unions and their demands as "anti-American." As they saw it, collective bargaining between management and labor and the creation of "closed shops" in which all workers were obliged to join the union denied individual rights and equal opportunity. John Edgerton, the president of the National Association of Manufacturers, exclaimed: "I can't conceive of any principle that is more purely American, that comes nearer representing the very essence of all those traditions and institutions that are dearest to us than the open shop principle."[10]

Seeking to dissolve the ethnic communal ties that limited their own prerogatives, businessmen not only promoted conservative renditions of "Americanism" in the public arena. They also instituted "Americanization" classes in the workplace and underwrote such campaigns in the schools. Moreover, hoping to prove that unions were unnecessary—as well as obviate the desire for state welfare programs they could not control—many adopted the American Plan of "welfare capitalism," paternalistically providing their employees with small pensions, paid holidays, and company-approved social activities.[11]

Still feeling insecure, however, bosses employed private police and spies, demanded that workers sign contracts promising not to join a union, and even resorted to setting up "company unions" to deter independent efforts. And if workers did organize and stage actions, companies did not hesitate to recruit both strikebreakers and head-breakers and to secure court injunctions with their implicit threat of force by police or state militia. Forever favoring property and contracts, judges refused to recognize labor organizing as a matter of free speech and assembly. In 1922, Chief Justice Taft, the "labor law architect of the New Era," expressed the sentiment of the ruling elites when he noted, "we have to hit" organized labor.[12]

It's not that those elites rejected democracy. They just didn't want *more* of it. Nor did they reject government. Again, they just didn't want more of it. The War Department's *Manual of Citizenship Training* clearly reflected their thinking. It not only warned that immigration from "central, eastern, and southern Europe" presented a "grave danger" to "our constitutional form of government and the blessings of liberty we enjoy." It also laid down that "the United States is a Republic, not a democracy," presented the former as "the culmination of civilized government," and made clear that citizenship guaranteed "Unrestricted possession of property."[13]

While instructors were to teach that "The mission of America is to demonstrate that a people can govern themselves," the history they were to impart simply affirmed the existing order. Introducing "Great Americans," the manual referred to Thomas Jefferson as a "radical democrat." Yet, lest anyone get the wrong idea, it explained that, "Living to-day, he undoubtedly would be found . . . giving voice in protest against the present tendency—marked as well in his time—of *too much government*." And though it praised Abraham Lincoln for "saving the Union," it effectively ignored emancipation.[14]

The governing elites' real hero was neither Jefferson nor Lincoln, but Alexander Hamilton, whose policies as the nation's first Treasury Secretary subordinated democracy and laboring people to commercial growth and the formation of a powerful mercantile and financial elite. Celebrating his vision and legacy in 1923, President Harding dedicated a prominent statue of Hamilton in front of the Treasury Building.

Democracy deferred to capitalism nationally. But down south it also bowed to a species of feudalism. White supremacy and racial apartheid ordered society by law, custom, and terror. Three-quarters of the region's 30 million citizens lived essentially in poverty. Cotton was king and peonage was common. And while land and mill owners gave lip service to liberty and democracy, they maintained, with impunity, one-party, specifically Democratic Party, regimes that, through poll taxes, all-white primaries, and intimidation, disfranchised most blacks as well as a good majority of poor whites.[15]

The governing elites had reason to be anxious. They had subdued America's democratic impulse, not discharged it. Though in retreat, unions soldiered on, committed to advancing not only workers' material interests, but also a more democratic conception of what it meant to be an American. Labor activists of the 1920s set forth an "Americanism" that insisted upon workers' rights to both free speech and assembly and an "American standard of living" in which higher wages provided good housing, medical care, and education, and shorter hours afforded time for family, civic affairs, self-improvement, and recreation.[16]

While committed to "voluntarism"—the principle of not relying on government for protection—the craft unions of the American Federation of Labor (AFL) advocated active citizenship and support for candidates who "uphold the cause of labor." Though handicapped by their own prejudices, they officially opposed bigotry, and a few major unions, like the United Mine Workers (UMW), International Ladies' Garment Workers' Union (ILGWU), and Amalgamated Clothing Workers of America (ACWA)—all three, industrial unions—pursued interethnic and even, in many places, interracial labor solidarity.[17]

Unionists, African Americans, and immigrants also kept alive an alternative national history to that promoted by the powers that be. In his 1925 book, *The Miners' Fight for American Standards*, the UMW president John L. Lewis praised industrial capitalism's productivity and the prosperity it provided, but called on the ideals of the "Fathers of the Republic" and the nation's long history of "progressive" movements to decry the "substitution of the dictatorship of ownership for constitutional government."[18]

Proffering an equally radical vision of America's making, the president of the black Brotherhood of Sleeping Car Porters, A. Philip Randolph, told a crowd of 60,000 at the 1926 Sesqui-Centennial Exposition in Philadelphia that "despite the cynicism of certain political historians on the reconstruction period of Negro history, an unbiased examination will reveal that black freedom gave to the South its first glimpse of democratic institutions." And after proclaiming that blacks ever since "have fought nobly in the ranks of white workers" and served ably as "the carriers and preservers of democracy," he prophesied that their "next gift to America will be in economic democracy." Meanwhile, bearing "memories" of Emancipation and Reconstruction and an "expansive view" of democracy, 100,000 southern blacks every year pursued America's promise by heading north in the "Great Migration."[19]

Most immigrants wanted to become American. In the predominantly working-class Slovak communities, activists contended that their people's "love of liberty and democracy" would naturally make them good Americans; but they also insisted, "If there is any Americanization to be done, we will do it ourselves." And though unable to celebrate their participation in the nation's founding, Slovaks celebrated their role in the country's industrialization, "building railroads, working in the mines, steel mills . . ."[20]

Others, higher up the social ladder, sought to sustain Americans' democratic memory and imagination as well. In popular works such as *The Rise of American Civilization, Jefferson and Hamilton: The Struggle for Democracy in America*, and *Main Currents in American Thought*, "Progressive scholars" such as Charles and Mary Beard, Claude G. Bowers, and Vernon Louis Parrington reminded their fellow citizens that the battles of the Founding era made the United States "not only a republic, but a democratic republic" and that American history has entailed a perennial contest between "the rights of man" and "the rights of property."[21]

Diverse middle-class and better-off folk joined groups such as the American Civil Liberties Union (ACLU), the National Association for the Advancement of Colored People (NAACP), the League of United Latin American Citizens (LULAC), the National Consumers' League (NCL), and the Women's Trade Union League (WTUL), seeking to defend freedom of speech, secure the rights of minorities, and enact laws to abolish child labor, protect women workers, and guarantee all employees living wages, decent hours, and the right to organize unions. While they did not constitute a movement, they were not without consequence. The NCL and WTUL, for example, engendered a progressive women's network and the latter afforded a venue in which women as different as the future First Lady Eleanor Roosevelt and the Polish-Jewish immigrant and union organizer Rose Schneiderman could work together and become good friends.[22]

Liberal politicians such as Senators George Norris, Robert F. Wagner, and Robert M. La Follette (followed by his son Robert Jr.)—respectively, a Nebraska Republican, a New York Democrat, and a Wisconsin Progressive—also continued to challenge the status quo by speaking in favor of both labor's rights and public initiatives for the public good. And in 1928, New York's governor, Al Smith, enthused immigrants and ethnics, both Catholic and Jewish, by becoming, despite southern suspicions, the first Catholic ever to secure the Democratic presidential nomination.[23]

The very notion of a renewed progressivism made conservatives nervous. Secretary of Commerce and Republican candidate for president in 1928, Herbert Hoover ardently believed in private enterprise and local initiative, but, renowned as the "Great Humanitarian" for his refugee relief work in the First World War, he was no Social Darwinist, no advocate of "survival of the fittest." Still, perceiving in Smith's candidacy the dangerous potential of a new, possibly ethnic-based politics, he was not beyond accusing the Democrats of abandoning "the principles of our American political and economic system" for "state socialism" simply for proposing in their platform that the federal government address the existing joblessness, develop the nation's water resources, and invest in public works.[24]

Bolstered by continued "prosperity" and anti-Catholicism, Hoover won. But in the very same speech in which he charged the Democrats with being un-American, he twice boasted that Republican administrations, and the "American system," had brought the country "nearer to the abolition of poverty, to the abolition of fear and want, than humanity has ever reached." Those words would soon come back to haunt him, as the fruits of conservative governance would come to haunt the nation.[25]

CHAPTER TWO

"Never were we more aware of America."

I n 1909, Herbert Croly wrote in *The Promise of American Life*: "We may distrust and dislike much that is done in the name of our country by our fellow countrymen; but our country itself, its democratic system, and its prosperous future are above suspicion." Indeed, Americans believed that democracy served to ensure not only the persistence of prosperity, but also the possibility of more and more Americans sharing in it. Thus, Croly spoke for many of them when he warned: "In case the majority of good Americans were not prosperous, there would be grave reasons for suspecting that our institutions were not doing their duty."[1]

Twenty years later Americans confronted just such circumstances in the extreme.

In October 1929 the stock market crashed and the Great Depression proceeded to devastate American life. Factories, businesses, and banks closed. Close to 15 million workers went jobless, many more were reduced to part-time labor, and those who were employed suffered lower wages, the loss of benefits, increased hours, and "speed-ups." Savings were wiped out. Families were evicted from their homes. Farmers saw their incomes drop still further and one-third of them would lose their homesteads—a tragedy made all the worse when drought struck the Great Plains and turned vast stretches of the region into the "Dust Bowl." While union rolls shrank still further, welfare rolls skyrocketed, draining municipal treasuries and overwhelming charities. Hundreds of thousands of Americans took to the road in search of work. People went hungry. Marriage and birth rates declined. Crime increased. Fear of losing one's job, one's home, one's everything, became a common concern and, for many, a terrible reality. To this day, three images stand out: "the bread line, the apple peddler, and the shantytowns."[2]

Blacks and other minorities suffered most. They not only lost their jobs along with millions of other Americans, but prejudice helped direct the remaining jobs to whites. One of every two African-American workers ended up unemployed. Horrifically, lynching increased down south. And in the Southwest, nearly 350,000 Mexicans were deported or repatriated in the first few years of the new decade.[3]

With good cause Americans called the new shantytowns "Hoovervilles." As pressure intensified for governmental action, Hoover resisted, fearing direct federal intervention would undermine the "American system" he believed in. In terms of policy, that belief translated into the hope that the economy would right itself before local resources ran out and the next elections came. Eventually, he did act, but it would be too late to save his presidency.[4]

With the federal government reluctant and slow to respond, people took to the streets in protest and, sometimes, took the law into their own hands. Recruiting the jobless into councils, leagues, and committees, respectively, Communists, socialists, and progressives organized marches to demand work or relief and rallied neighbors to physically prevent families from being evicted from their houses and apartments. Joining together in the Farmers' Holiday Association, midwestern agrarians not only turned out to block foreclosures on neighbors' homes and holdings, but lobbied state governments to regulate agricultural prices. When that failed, they tried to push up prices themselves by withholding produce from the market and blocking shipments by the uncooperative. And in 1932, twenty thousand out-of-work World War I veterans from all around the country—white and black, quite a few accompanied by wives and children—made their way to Washington, D.C., in hopes of securing early payment of the "veterans bonus" that Congress had approved in 1924 for disbursement in 1945.[5]

Authorities met many demonstrations with violence. In March 1930, New York City police brutally attacked a rally of thirty-five thousand people organized by the Unemployed Councils. In March 1932, Dearborn, Michigan, police opened fire on a "Hunger March" of three thousand outside Ford's River Rouge plant, killing four and wounding fifty others. And on July 28, 1932, General Douglas MacArthur ordered fully armed cavalry and infantry troops to storm the "Bonus Marchers'" encampments and drive the veterans and their families out of the capital, killing several and bloodying hundreds.[6]

The unemployed were acting not simply out of desperation. They were also essentially fighting for what would come to be articulated as the Four Freedoms. They believed in America's promise and they wanted to redeem it. They rallied, marched, and petitioned to try to get the nation's economic and political elites to acknowledge and act in favor of that promise. As one journalist reported, Dearborn's Hunger Marchers—citizens "white, black and brown"—were "ordinary Americans" seeking a "redress of grievances." Organized by Detroit's Unemployed Council, they demanded not just jobs and assistance. They also demanded, among other things, an end to Ford's "spying on workers," a shorter workday for the still-employed, and "the right to organize." But their assemblies and petitions were answered with truncheons and bullets.[7]

With the governing elites declaring America's political development accomplished, Americans began to ask whether democracy could meet the worsening crisis. Reporting on the refugees from the Bonus March, the left-wing writer Malcolm Cowley quoted one veteran to testify to the not just desperate but supposedly scornful mood overtaking the country: "I used to be a hundred-percenter, but now I'm a Red radical. I had an American flag, but the damn tin soldiers burned it. Now I don't ever want to see a flag again. Give me a gun and I'll go back to Washington."[8]

Communists fantasized revolution and, nightmarishly, so, too, did many among the nation's elites, some of whom now spoke openly, if not longingly, of the need for a strongman—someone like Italy's Fascist chief, Benito Mussolini—to take charge before all hell broke loose. Warning of the peril facing "American civilization," *Vanity Fair* editorialized in its June 1932 issue, "Appoint a dictator!" And after surveying the many and various calls for authoritarian initiatives emanating from the ranks of the rich and important, even the editor of the *American Political Science Review* wondered aloud if "Perhaps we shall have a dictator. Perhaps we shall go fascist. Who can guarantee that we may not even some day go communist?"[9]

The incipient insurgencies captured press attention; but most Americans remained politically passive. Anne O'Hare McCormick of *The New York Times* remarked in August 1931 that "Un-American as it sounds, we are all waiting, waiting for something to turn up." A year later, she feared that "The contemporary American . . . has lost his early zest for citizenship." More pointedly, the cultural critic Gilbert Seldes admonished: "We had for twenty years been overthrowing the burden of libertarian ideals; we were not the country of free speech or free press or free assembly; we were not the country of the rights of labor; we were not free of religious prejudice; we were not interested in social justice . . ."[10]

Seldes reflected the profound pessimism that gripped many, but hardly all, Americans. Referring to popular efforts around the country to pull together and share skills and resources—events that did not grab headlines—McCormick perceptively noted: "Something is happening . . . the citizen is not so much dead as dazed. And not so much dazed as painfully coming to life . . . They call it nationalism, but in that they are mistaken. It is what might be named Americanism."[11]

Indeed, Americans were beginning to stir and they were doing what generations before them had done in times of grave national crisis. They were looking back—back to those who had first articulated the nation's ideals and fought to advance them. And in doing so they were beginning to remember who they were and what they were about.

Bearing the Stars and Stripes, rebellious farmers recalled their rebellious forefathers. One of them told a reporter: "They say blockading the highway's illegal . . . Seems to me there was a Tea-party in Boston that was illegal too." The Conference on Progressive Labor Action, led by the former minister A. J. Muste, developed an "American Approach" to organizing and issued a "Declaration of Workers and Farmers Rights" modeled after the Declaration of Independence. And returning to their campuses after delivering aid to striking Kentucky miners, young New York Communists grabbed hold of not the *Communist Manifesto*, but the U.S. Constitution to defend the strikers' cause in terms of American "civil rights and liberties."[12]

Radicals were not alone in reaching back. Under the auspices of the Woman's National Democratic Club, thirteen leading liberal politicians and intellectuals published *Democracy at the Crossroads*, a manifesto of sorts in which they declared, "In a true republic the rights of man must come first" and "There can be no breadlines in a democracy." Insisting on a "right to work" and the need to raise workers' purchasing power, Senator Robert Wagner of New York urged federal investment in public works. And reminding Americans that "democracy did not come . . . without a struggle," the historian Claude Bowers made the case for a new politics of social justice that, starting with "unemployment insurance and old-age pensions," would afford working people a "sense of security."[13]

Yet the finest testimony to a continuing belief in the nation's historic purpose came from a contingent of Bonus Marchers who, driven from Washington by General MacArthur's assault, had made their way to New York. There, along the city's Hudson River shoreline, they built a multiracial and cooperative Hooverville and—flying the Stars and Stripes over nearly every hut—named it "Camp Thomas Paine," after the revolutionary pamphleteer who first called for an independent and democratic America.[14]

With the 1932 elections in view, McCormick declared, "Never were we more aware of America." Moreover, she wrote, Americans were beginning to develop a "consciousness, still hardly more than a subconsciousness, that we have in our hands the magnificent makings

of a new society, a really new economic era. It waits only for the liqui-
dation of our biggest frozen asset, the active and responsible citizen."[15]

Of course, McCormick had qualified her argument with a mighty
big "if," since by her own formulation most Americans were apparently
still "waiting for something to turn up." And yet it would turn out that
Americans had been waiting not for "something," but for someone—
someone who shared their continuing faith in America and could
speak to and engage their democratic memories and yearnings.

On the evening of October 31, 1932, Herbert Hoover told a campaign
rally of 22,000 Republicans in New York's Madison Square Garden:
"This campaign is more than a contest between two men. It is more
than a contest between two parties. It is a contest between two philoso-
phies of government." And Hoover went on to portray his new Democratic opponent, Franklin Roosevelt, as a dangerous radical, "proposing
changes and so-called new deals which would destroy the very foundations of the American system of life."[16]

Roosevelt's life spoke of the Establishment, not radicalism. The
only child of Hudson Valley aristocrats, educated at Groton and Harvard, and related to Theodore Roosevelt—both on his own and by way
of marrying TR's niece Eleanor—FDR had practiced corporate law and
served as a New York state senator, Assistant Secretary of the Navy in
the Wilson administration, Democratic candidate for vice president in
1920, and governor of New York twice.

And yet Hoover was not so wrong in viewing his opponent as he
did. While Roosevelt was no socialist, he was, in a very American
way, a radical. He utterly rejected the idea that the political and social
order ruled and revered by the Republicans, with the collusion of so
many Democrats, represented the pinnacle of American progress and
the "culmination of civilized government." To FDR, that very "order"
presented the foremost "danger" to a more fundamental America—the
America the Founders had envisioned as a grand experiment in popular
self-government and which generations of Americans, native-born and
immigrant, had labored to make ever more free, equal, and democratic.

Unlike so many of his station, Roosevelt did not fear Americans' democratic impulses. He feared what might happen if they were too long thwarted, with Fascist Italy and Communist Russia as prime examples. He told his friend John Kingsbury in 1930: "There is no question in my mind that it is time for the country to become fairly radical for a generation. History shows that where this occurs occasionally, nations are saved from revolution." While Roosevelt was not interested in fomenting a revolution, he was dedicated to pursuing America's promise. "Democracy is not a static thing," he said. "It is an everlasting march."[17]

Roosevelt described himself as "a Christian and a Democrat," coyly adding at times, "a little left of center." But he meant what he said. Raised Episcopalian, he took his religion seriously. While no saint in either his private or public life, he attended church, relished hymn singing, read the Bible, subscribed to Christian moral teachings—which required, as he had learned at Groton, service to "God, the nation, and humanity"—and believed in "an external guidance." Still, he was neither dogmatic nor chauvinistic about his faith. He hated religious intolerance and believed strongly in freedom of worship.[18]

Inheriting his party affiliation as well, FDR took it no less seriously. Whatever "Democrat" meant in a coalition that encompassed northern liberals, western progressives, and southern conservatives and reactionaries, he continually pressed the "party of the people" to become the "party of liberal thought, of planned action, of enlightened international outlook, and of the greatest good to the greatest number of our citizens."[19]

Roosevelt revealed his "progressive and liberal" beliefs from his first days in the New York senate in 1911, and he continued to do so in the years to come. Winning the governorship in 1928, he laid out his political vision in his first inaugural address. Pushing beyond the simple dichotomy of individualism versus collectivism to describe the advances New York had already made, he declared his aims were "To secure more of life's pleasures for the farmer; to guard the toilers in the factories and to insure to them a fair wage and protection from the dangers of their trades; to compensate them by adequate insurance for injuries received while working for us; to open the doors of knowledge to their children more widely; to aid those who are crippled and ill . . ."[20]

Friends and scholars alike have speculated on the origins of Roosevelt's political ideas and allegiances. Knowing FDR from his days as a state senator and, then, by way of serving as his Industrial Commissioner in Albany and Secretary of Labor in Washington, Frances Perkins offered the most moving explanation. Recollecting a young man who had "little, if any, concern about social reforms . . . and a deafness to the hopes, fears, and aspirations which are the common lot," she said that he matured somewhat during his years in the Wilson administration. Yet the real change, she insisted, came in his battle with polio: "The man emerged completely warmhearted, with humility of spirit and with a deeper philosophy. Having been to the depths of trouble, he understood the problems of people . . ." Moreover, Perkins noted, his convalescence involved continuing "liberal education," dispensed by Eleanor, even as she herself became more active in politics and reform efforts.[21]

Whatever their precise origins, Roosevelt's "politics" were motivated not simply by ambition, but also by a powerful faith in America and in his fellow citizens—all of it firmly grounded in a deeply felt sense of history. In 1938, the progressive writer Max Lerner predicted that Roosevelt "will be remembered . . . as a man who, without being of the people . . . was able to grasp and to some degree communicate what the common man dimly felt." What made that possible was not only that FDR was "wholeheartedly a democrat," and not only that FDR constantly wanted to know what Americans were thinking, but also that he imagined them possessing the same democratic memories, impulses, and longings as he did.[22]

Experience—especially his 1920 bid for the vice presidency as the running mate to the Democratic presidential nominee, James Cox—had taught Roosevelt that political struggle entails a struggle for American memory, a struggle over the meaning and making of America. When Republicans questioned Cox's and his "Americanism" during the campaign because the two Democrats had called for the United States to join the League of Nations, FDR retorted that his opponents were trying to "take out an exclusive patent on the American flag and all the great accomplishments of our history." Even more affirmatively, he set himself in defeat to preparing a new history of the United States, for the existing texts, he said, "lacked movement" and failed to show "The nation was clearly going somewhere right from the first." And though he would soon discover that unlike his heroes Teddy Roosevelt and Woodrow Wilson he was not "a writing man," he would not allow literary failure to deter him from seeking other ways of cultivating a more progressive American narrative.[23]

In 1925, FDR essentially revealed his view of not only American history, but also his own possible place within it, when he reviewed Claude Bowers's *Jefferson and Hamilton* for the *New York Evening World*. He celebrated the book, which presented the 1790s contest between Jefferson and Hamilton and their followers as a struggle between democratic and aristocratic visions of government, for providing a vision of Jefferson's ideas that Americans could use to address the "often essentially similar problems that still lie unresolved before us." Roosevelt himself discovered in Bowers's work a truly "radical-democratic" Jefferson whom he could brandish against those conservatives, both Republican and Democratic, who made the Virginian out to be a proponent of limited government. Citing the accelerating concentration of capital ownership and how it threatened American democratic life, FDR told the attendees of the 1930 Jefferson Day dinner in New York, "If Thomas Jefferson were alive he would be the first to question this concentration of economic power."[24]

In his embrace of the landed Founder who believed so fervently in America's democratic prospects and possibilities, Roosevelt was projecting the man he wished to become and the history he hoped to make: "Jefferson's faith in mankind was vindicated; his appeal to the intelligence of the average voter bore fruit; his conception of a democratic republic came true." In fact, FDR said: "I have a breathless feeling . . . as I wonder if . . . the same contending forces are not again mobilizing. Hamiltons we have to-day. Is a Jefferson on the horizon?" Defeating Hoover in 1932, he would endeavor to answer his own question.[25]

By 1936, Roosevelt had good reason to imagine himself another Jefferson. While he had yet to lead Americans out of the Great Depression, he had mobilized them to undertake not simply relief and recovery, but also reconstruction and reform—indeed, to pursue progressive, if not revolutionary, changes in the nation's constitutional order, the state of the public weal, and the "We" in "We the People."

Most historians deny Roosevelt had radical transformations in mind. They contend that while he brought exceptional verve and determination to the presidency—as well as an uplifting voice and a winning smile—he brought along no comprehensive plan to address the depression. They further insist that his vision of the New Deal projected not struggle but the formation of a "concert of interests" to pursue the "common good."

Roosevelt himself would never speak of the New Deal as a break with America's past—that is, its historical as opposed to immediate past. He spoke of it in seemingly conservative terms. In a June 1934 message to Congress he would say: "Our task of reconstruction does not require the creation of new and strange values. It is rather the finding of the way once more to known, but to some degree forgotten, ideals and values." And reiterating that point in a Fireside Chat a few weeks later, he added: "I believe that what we are doing today is a necessary fulfillment of what Americans have always been doing—a fulfillment of old and tested American ideals . . . All that we do seeks to fulfill the historic traditions of the American people."[26]

It was more than mere rhetoric. Roosevelt set out to engage Americans' democratic memories and yearnings, to rally their spirits and energies to confront not only the depression, but also the order that had spawned it. He wanted to renew the narrative and politics that projected the nation as a continuing effort to extend and deepen freedom, equality, and democracy. As he would explain in his 1936 Brotherhood Day radio address: "I do not look upon these United States as a finished product. We are still in the making." And in an address at a World War Memorial dedication ceremony in St. Louis later that year, he would say: "A true patriotism urges us to build an even more substantial America where the good things of life may be shared by more of us, where the social injustices will not be encouraged to flourish."[27]

In his 1932 presidential campaign, Roosevelt clearly registered his determination to institute radical changes. Calling for "plans . . . that build from the bottom up and . . . put their faith once more in the forgotten man at the bottom of the economic pyramid," he promised "bold, persistent experimentation." Recognizing Americans' pronounced need for "work and security," citing the imperative of a "more equitable distribution of the national income," and insisting that "economic laws are not made by nature [but] by human beings," he "pledged" a "New Deal" that would include overseeing financial transactions, developing public-works projects, rehabilitating the nation's lands and forests, easing the burdens of debt-ridden farmers and homeowners, raising workers' purchasing power, and establishing a system of "old age insurance." And decrying how economic advances—aided by government largesse to railroads and other private companies—had led to the "concentration of business" in the hands of a class of "financial Titans" and the decline of economic opportunity and freedom for the majority of Americans, he proposed an "economic declaration of rights, an economic constitutional order" to renew the nation's original "social contract" as articulated in the Declaration's guarantee of "life, liberty, and the pursuit of happiness." In the plainest of terms, he said: "Every man has a right to life; and this means he has also a right to make a comfortable living . . . Our Government . . . owes to everyone an avenue to possess himself of a portion of [America's] plenty sufficient for his needs, through his own work."[28]

FDR's conception of political change emphasized legislation more than activism, but Roosevelt intended Americans to understand he wanted more than their votes. Accepting his party's nomination in Chicago in July 1932, he stated: "Let us all here assembled constitute ourselves prophets of a new order of competence and courage. This is more than a political campaign: it is a call to arms. Give me your help, not to win votes alone, but to win in this crusade to restore America to its own people." Addressing a Sunday gathering in Detroit that October, he delivered a sermon on his "philosophy of social justice through social action." And speaking in St. Louis a few weeks later, he celebrated laboring peoples' historic struggles as if to alert their descendants to what they, too, might have to do: "You American farmers and

American workmen are entitled, by all the fundamental rights that you have acquired in generations of fighting, to a free and untrammeled election day . . . The man who tries . . . to chip away these rights is an untrustworthy leader in business or politics." [29]

Hearing labor's own aspirations echoed in those arguments, both the Mine Workers' John L. Lewis, a Republican, and the Clothing Workers' Sidney Hillman, a Socialist—the former, "behind the scenes," the latter, openly—backed Roosevelt. And with the ballot-box support of not only Democrats, but also many Republicans and, most promisingly, first-time voters and working people of all ethnic identities and religious persuasions, he won a landslide victory and laid the groundwork for a new Democratic Party electoral coalition. [30]

CHAPTER THREE

"The people were ready, really, to take action."

Taking office on March 4, 1933, in the midst of a deepening financial crisis, Roosevelt did not only seek to reassure Americans that "the only thing we have to fear is fear itself." Reiterating his understanding that "This Nation asks for action, and action now," he also called on them to reclaim the "temple" from the "money changers" and exercise military-like "discipline" to fight the depression. And he then quickly set himself and his newly appointed cabinet members to the urgent task of turning rallying cries and campaign promises into legislative proposals and government policies and programs. But what ensued entailed far more than a package of public policy initiatives.[1]

FDR and his "New Dealers"—the thousands of men and women who eagerly enlisted to build and staff the expanding federal departments and newly created agencies of what would forever be known as the New Deal—were setting out on a grand democratic experiment of renewal and transformation. The Harvard economist Gardiner Means, who left academe for a post in the Department of Agriculture, would say they were struggling to "find a way to make things work." And the Treasury Department economist Edward Bernstein observed that that "spirit of innovation and experimentation was what made the New Deal click." There were precedents, but most of what they did was improvisation. They came up with ideas, plans, and projects. They tried things out. They did not, they would not, they could not, stand still. Everything seemed to be at stake and everything seemed possible.[2]

Moreover, Americans had heard in their new President's words more than simply a promise that government action was forthcoming. They heard a call to action. And their democratic impulses surged. They were not only ready to work at lifting themselves up. They welcomed the prospect of a grand experiment and intended to be more than the subjects of it. Taking up his post with the Federal Emergency Relief Administration in Birmingham, Alabama, the young New Dealer John Beecher would recall that he encountered not resignation but readiness: "The ferment I discovered . . . was just tremendous. The people were ready, really, to take action."[3]

Indeed, the majority of Americans would enthusiastically embrace the progressive possibilities that they believed FDR's words projected. They would take up the jobs and labors that the New Deal created. They would organize themselves—as workers, as consumers, as citizens—to demand their rights. And they would make America freer, more equal, and more democratic.

President and people alike would overreach, make mistakes, and antagonize powerful interests and each other. But they did not often retreat—and they would repeatedly draw on their early improvisations and experiments to carry out renewed efforts and ensuing initiatives. They did not win everything they fought for. But they won far more than they had first imagined possible. And in the course of improvising, experimenting, working, and struggling, they would not only progressively transform the nation and themselves. They would also ready themselves for their rendezvous with history.

In less than a year and a half, Roosevelt not only secured passage of an extraordinary body of legislation. He also strengthened existing government agencies and established an unprecedented host of new ones, including the Federal Emergency Relief Administration (FERA), National Recovery Administration (NRA), Agricultural Adjustment Administration (AAA), Civilian Conservation Corps (CCC), Public Works Administration (PWA), Tennessee Valley Authority (TVA), Civil Works Administration (CWA), Securities and Exchange Commission (SEC), Federal Communications Commission (FCC), Federal Deposit Insurance Corporation (FDIC), and Home Owners Loan Corporation (HOLC).[4]

The nearly universal desire for action afforded FDR and the New Dealers significant space in which to act. However, powerful forces compelled them to make critical compromises. Businessmen were unpopular, but they still commanded industry and commerce, and while not necessarily averse to government action to instigate economic recovery, they opposed paying for it or allowing government to interfere in their managerial prerogatives. Democrats now reigned in Congress, but southerners headed key committees and, as much as they might want to send federal dollars down to Dixie, they opposed legislation that might undermine the South's racial regimes. Moreover, Roosevelt and his colleagues were themselves so determined to pursue relief, recovery, reconstruction, and reform all at the same time that they sometimes burdened key initiatives with competing objectives.

The National Industrial Recovery Act (NIRA), establishing the NRA, provides a case in point. Modeled after World War I arrangements, the NRA was supposed to help revive manufacturing and commercial activity, raise workers' purchasing power, *and* promote cooperation between capital and labor. To encourage business participation and prevent cutthroat competition, it suspended antitrust laws and created industry-wide councils of business leaders that were to issue codes regulating production, prices, and wages. To improve workers' incomes and conditions of labor, as well as secure AFL approval (the crisis had already weakened the Federation's attachment to voluntarism), it called for establishing Labor and Consumer Advisory Boards and stipulated in Section 7(a) that workers had "the right to organize and bargain collectively through representatives of their own choosing." And to create a universal standard for the industry-specific codes to follow, the NRA director, Hugh Johnson, secured agreement on a temporary "blanket code" that abolished child labor and set both a national minimum wage (30–40 cents an hour) and a maximum number of work hours (35–40 a week). FDR himself projected even more progressive possibilities when he said, on signing the NIRA into law: "no business which depends for existence on paying less than *living wages* has any right to continue in this country."[5]

The economy and many workers' lives did improve, but the NRA would fail to produce either dramatic growth or class harmony. Hastily drafted codes inevitably caused trouble. Even more damaging, corporate executives—at the expense of small business interests and consumers—continually called the shots in writing the codes and regularly fixed prices higher than warranted. And still determined to resist unions, many of them took advantage of the vagueness of Section 7(a) to organize "captive" or company unions in their workplaces.[6]

The New Dealers had more success improving the state of agriculture. Instituting a system in which farmers voluntarily reduced their planted acreage and limited their production of basic commodities in return for government-guaranteed prices and subsidies (paid for by taxes on food processors), the AAA raised both agricultural prices and incomes. However, while midwestern family farmers saw real gains, many thousands of southern tenants and sharecroppers, black and white, saw no benefits when landowners refused to share government payments with them. Worse, when those landowners reduced their cultivated acreage, their renters and croppers were shoved off the land and into the ranks of the jobless and homeless.[7]

Nevertheless, Roosevelt and his New Dealers were initiating a revolution in American government and public life. Subjecting capital to public regulation, providing relief on a grand scale, and pursuing social- and industrial-democratic policies and programs, they were not just increasing the size and operations of government, but also, as FDR had envisioned, redrawing the nation's constitutional order. So thoroughgoing an evolution of America's purpose and promise had last been attempted after the Civil War, and prior to that only at the country's founding.[8]

In the radical belief that citizens had to be secured against the powers of the state, the Founding Fathers had appended the Bill of Rights
to the Constitution in 1791. Standing on their forebears' shoulders,
the New Dealers were now seeking to expand the reach of those fundamental civil and political rights and to augment them with social and
economic rights. In a message to Congress in 1934, Roosevelt declared:
"the security of the home, the security of livelihood, and the security
of social insurance are . . . a minimum of the promise we can offer to
the American people. They constitute a right which belongs to every
individual and family willing to work." At the same time, he and his
colleagues sought to reposition government itself to serve as a defender
of Americans against those who might attempt to obstruct or disable
them in the exercise of their rights. In a September 1934 Fireside Chat,
Roosevelt said: "I believe with Abraham Lincoln, that 'The legitimate
object of government is to do for a community of people whatever they
need to have done but cannot do at all or cannot do so well for themselves in their separate and individual capacities.'"[9]

In that spirit, FDR and the New Dealers heavily invested in public-works projects, not only to quickly provide jobs for the jobless, but
also to radically transform and improve the nation's public infrastructure and public spaces. Here, too, they felt empowered by American
ideals and precedents, but more than their nineteenth-century prede-
cessors they were committed to "using government to foster economic
development" in ways that would "benefit . . . 'the people' rather than
'the interests.'" Enlisting a total of 3 million young men between 1933
and 1942, the CCC would "plant more than 2.3 billion trees . . . on 2.5
million acres of previously barren, denuded or unproductive land . . .
slow soil erosion on 40 million acres of farmland . . . and develop 800
new state parks." Employing 4.5 million people during the harshest
months of 1933–34, the CWA "built or improved 500,000 miles of
roads, 40,000 schools, over 3,500 playgrounds and athletic fields, and
1,000 airports." And affording work to a total of 8.5 million people between 1935 and 1943, the WPA of the ensuing "Second New Deal"
would upgrade 600,000 miles of rural roads, lay 67,000 miles of city
streets, erect 78,000 new bridges and viaducts, construct 40,000 public

buildings, and build several hundred airports. Concurrently, the PWA would underwrite construction of thousands of miles of roadways and an equally remarkable number of public buildings and structures such as schools, libraries, hospitals, post offices, state and municipal offices, bridges, and water and sewer systems—35,000 projects altogether—including the Boulder, Grand Coulee, and Bonneville dams out west, the Lincoln Tunnel and Triborough Bridge in New York, Skyline Drive in Virginia, and the Los Angeles water supply system. The TVA would realize a dazzling scheme of dams, reservoirs, environmental works, and community enterprises providing hydroelectric power and economic development to the long-neglected people of the Tennessee Valley region. And the Rural Electrification Administration (REA), created in 1935, would in just a few years enable the formation of more than 400 local power cooperatives, bringing affordable electricity to nearly 300,000 farms and rural households that corporate utilities had refused to serve. FDR's "public works revolution" dramatically enhanced the state of the public weal and—placing the needs of the commonwealth above those of corporations—rendered powerful testimony to the possibility of pursuing public action for the public good.[10]

Mobilizing Americans not only in the millions, but also in all their diversity, the New Dealers were beginning to transform the nation in yet another fundamental way. Recognizing that racism, anti-Catholicism, and anti-Semitism, not to mention sexism, obstructed reform and denied the hopes and prayers of millions, many a New Dealer worked at reconstituting the "We" in "We the People." Which was no easy task, especially regarding race. Southern officials, despite federal directives to the contrary, were to blatantly discriminate against blacks in distributing federal relief; southern businessmen effectively licensed themselves to pay African Americans less by securing regional wage differentials in the NRA codes; and southern congressmen unashamedly wrote discrimination into the new laws and programs—not only the NIRA, but also the later Social Security and National Labor Relations acts—by excluding from their coverage farm and household workers, who were predominantly black or, as in the Southwest, Latino. Moreover, Washington remained a segregated city.[11]

Nevertheless, the New Dealers made critical advances. FDR himself brought to D.C. a cohort that included Frances Perkins as Secretary of Labor, the first woman ever to hold a cabinet-level appointment; Henry Morgenthau, Jr., as Treasury Secretary, only the second Jew ever to do so; Harold Ickes as Interior Secretary and PWA director, who, though white, had led the NAACP in Chicago; Harry Hopkins, who as FERA, CWA, and then WPA director would work strenuously to assure the well-being of the poor, indeed, to advance the idea "that relief was a matter of right . . . not charity"; and, of course, Eleanor Roosevelt as First Lady, who by her actions would break the mold of presidential wives and, through her many speeches and writings, ardently advocate the causes of women, labor, blacks, and the young. Together they further signaled that more than WASP men could govern the nation by enlisting thousands of Catholic and Jewish lawyers and professionals— most notably, the law-writing team of Tom Corcoran and Ben Cohen— to draft the new legislation and policies and head up the new agencies and programs.[12]

In that same vein, while FDR did not push civil rights legislation, he spoke out against racial violence and endorsed efforts to integrate government and the New Deal. In the same 1936 radio address in which he said, "We are still in the making," he also stated: "it is well for us to remember that this America of ours is the product of no single race or creed or class." And at historically black Howard University, he would say: "As far as humanly possible, the Government has followed the policy that among American citizens there should be no forgotten men and no forgotten races. It is a wise and truly American policy."[13]

Some of his foremost New Dealers shocked and outraged southern sensibilities far more by their actions. Mrs. Roosevelt hosted black friends such as the NAACP head Walter White and the educator Mary McLeod Bethune, along with many other African Americans, at the White House. Secretary Ickes desegregated the Interior Department cafeteria, insisted that PWA-project contractors hire skilled black workers, and recruited African Americans to policymaking and administrative positions. And on assuming direction of the new WPA in May 1935, Harry Hopkins moved aggressively to enforce Roosevelt's executive order banning discrimination from its operations—which included appointing Mary McLeod Bethune to direct the Office of Minority Affairs of the new National Youth Administration, from which post she "led" FDR's so-called Black Cabinet.[14]

Furthermore, intent upon preparing Americans to stand strong and united to fight the Great Depression and, if history demanded it, European fascists and Japanese imperialists, Roosevelt himself proceeded to articulate a more inclusive vision of the American nation. Addressing the Federal Council of Churches in late 1933, he decried "lynch law" as a "vile form of collective murder," urged the faithful to teach "the ideals of social justice," and made clear his belief that government's role in religious matters was to "guarantee" Americans, both "Gentile and Jewish," the "right to worship God in their own way." In fact, with events abroad and at home in mind, he regularly reaffirmed the country's fundamental commitment to religious freedom. When antagonists attacked him, claiming that his ancestors were Jews, he refused to dignify anti-Semitism: "In the dim distant past," he said, "they may have been Jews or Catholics or Protestants—what I am more interested in is whether they were good citizens and believers in God—I hope they were both."[15]

Recognizing the impossibility of doing so, Roosevelt did not seek to eliminate the immigration quota system. But he radically recast the official view of "non-Nordic" Europeans by rhetorically weaving them into a shared American narrative. Speaking in predominantly Catholic and blue-collar Green Bay, Wisconsin, in August 1934, he told a huge outdoor crowd:

> [T]hroughout Europe—your ancestors and mine—had suffered from the . . . unjust Governments of their home land, and they were driven by deep desire to find not alone security, but also enlarged opportunity . . . [They were] a mixed population, differing often in language . . . external customs and . . . habits of thought. But in one thing they were alike. They shared a deep purpose to rid themselves forever of the jealousies, the prejudices, the intrigues and the violence . . . that disturbed their lives on the other side of the ocean.

Still, he said, the story did not end there: "the average man had to fight for his rights . . . against those forces which disregard human cooperation and human rights in seeking that kind of individual profit which is gained at the expense of his fellows." Indeed, linking the new "great national movement" to the struggles of their forebears, FDR left the story open-ended.[16]

African Americans heard their story in his words. Recalling how she would race around to find someone with a radio "so as not to miss anything the president might say," the black Georgian Viola Elder stated how she imagined herself seated with him in conversation "in his living room." And based on fieldwork in rural Mississippi in the mid1930s, the sociologist Hortense Powdermaker observed: "Roosevelt has become the representative and symbol of [southern black] hopes. When he first spoke of the forgotten man, most . . . in the community thought he meant the Negro. Some still think so, and feel that with crop diversification and Federal relief, the forgotten man has begun to be remembered." Furthermore, she wrote, "Although they have no voice in the government, and find no security through its legal institutions, government activities arouse their lively interest and something close to confidence," and for these Negro men and women, "the Federal administration has combined the rather incongruous elements of paternal benevolence and revolutionary change."[17]

Despite its shortcomings, the early New Deal afforded southern blacks a lifeline and the new Civil Works Administration of 1933–34 provided higher wages than some had ever received. That very spring, the blues singer Joe Pullum would express the sense of liberation that so worried propertied southern whites:

> CWA, *look what you done for me:*
> *You brought my good gal back, and lifted Depression off-a-me.*
> *I was hungry and broke, because I wasn't drawing any pay.*
> *But in stepped President Roosevelt, Lord, with his mighty CWA.*[18]

New Deal initiatives would also promote a richer, more democratic Americanism. While the NRA, with its "Blue Eagle" symbol and "We Do Our Part" slogan, was rallying popular support for its efforts by way of campaigns and parades that portrayed economic regulation and industrial democracy as patriotic pursuits, the CCC was beginning to recondition not only America's landscape, but also the first of its ultimately 3,000,000 young recruits (200,000 of them African Americans). Laboring outdoors, eating good meals, and receiving proper medical care, FDR's "Soil Soldiers" would grow fitter, larger, and healthier. The experience would transform them more than physically, however. Offering courses in vocational skills and conservation, dispatching them to locales far from home, and—though camps were segregated by race—bringing them together in all their variety to remake the environment and themselves, it would sow new understandings of teamwork and citizenship. Bud Wilbur, an upstate New Yorker, said of his CCC company in Nevada, "There were Jewish kids, Italian kids, Irish kids, and probably the best mix of nationalities you could find," and the enrollee James Danner told FDR in 1936 of how "second-generation Poles, Slovaks, Italians, Hungarians, all are . . . finding a new pride in saying, 'We are Americans!'"[19]

The New Dealers clearly aimed to empower laboring people. The AAA sought to cultivate "grassroots democracy" by providing for local referenda to set production quotas and land-use planning committees that farmers themselves were to elect—both of which afforded southern black landowners opportunities to vote for the first time ever. Responding to AFL demands, and hoping to counter the power of capital through "industrial democracy" rather than by severely increasing the power of the state, Senator Robert Wagner of New York, the "Legislative Pilot of the New Deal," insisted the NIRA include Section 7(a) guaranteeing workers the right to organize, and when it proved unenforceable, he would take the lead in advancing a more authoritative law. And not only did the NRA exhort shoppers to buy only at those stores displaying its "Blue Eagle" symbol (indicating they had signed on to the program), but as it became ever more apparent that even those businesses were not holding down their prices, administration officials such as Assistant Secretary of Agriculture Rexford Tugwell began to call on middle-class consumer advocacy groups to "organize" more aggressively and popularly in order to more effectively pressure industry and government. FDR himself praised the "impulse among consumers to enter the industrial market place equipped with sufficient organization to insist upon fair prices and honest sales." Moreover, he would admit in 1935: "New laws, in themselves, do not bring a millennium."[20]

By 1936, Roosevelt had mobilized the nation. Indeed, reinvigorating popular hopes, aspirations, and energies, he had also unleashed a great democratic surge in which workers, farmers, women, minorities, intellectuals, students, and others were challenging the propertied and powerful in favor of extending and deepening freedom, equality, and democracy.

Working people, in particular, embraced FDR. Forever recalling how he "lifted their spirits" and restored their belief in themselves, they carried his image in demonstrations and hung it in their homes, often right alongside one of Jesus. Broadway lyricists and Mississippi Delta blues artists alike composed songs in his honor. Black families named their children Franklin and Eleanor. Speaking for laboring men and women of every race and region, a white South Carolina millhand wrote that Roosevelt is "the first man in the White House to understand that my boss is a son of a bitch." Yet the relationship involved more than appreciation and affection.[21]

Rexford Tugwell would observe years later that somehow "ordinary" people understood Roosevelt better than anyone and, doing so, they "adopted" him as their "champion." There was, however, even more to it. Doing so enabled them to act in their own behalf in dramatic, new ways. Hearing talk of "fulfilling American ideals," action "from the bottom up," and "economic rights," they rallied to FDR's New Deal by joining together to reclaim—or, for the first time, lay claim to—America. Responding to a Fireside Chat invitation to tell him of their "troubles," workers, who made up 46 percent of all of those who wrote, sent him millions of letters. And agreeing with him or not, their words regularly confirmed that they understood that America's greatness depended not simply on his actions, but also on their own determination and solidarity—or, as the black labor leader A. Philip Randolph would declare, that "Freedom is never given. It is won."[22]

In fact, American workers moved even faster than the President to take up the struggle—and they were prepared to take it further.

Signed into law in June 1933, the NIRA—titled labor's "Magna Carta" by AFL president William Green—instigated almost 2 million workers, skilled, semiskilled, and unskilled, to flood into the labor movement. Referring to it as "a virtual uprising . . . for union membership," an AFL executive council memo observed that workers themselves "held mass meetings and sent word they wanted to be organized." Viewing it as "a picture of the opening of the gates of freedom," the Plumbers and Steam Fitters' head, Thomas Burke, jubilantly wrote: "Men who never dared consider joining a union now come forward openly, eagerly and joyously." And the Russian-Jewish immigrant and ILGWU organizer Rose Pesotta would warmly recall that the "Unorganized workers who had never before raised the question of their rights . . . and who had accepted whatever they were given as inevitable, suddenly awakened to the fact that they were part of a great democratic nation."[23]

In just one year's time the UMW leapt from 50,000 to 300,000 members; the ACWA from 60,000 to 120,000; and the ILGWU from 40,000 to 200,000. Making it all the more challenging, the industrial unions remained committed to interethnic and interracial labor solidarity, even in the face of workers' own persistent prejudices. Pesotta, for one, would proudly recall the sense of unity she felt when, at the 1933 ILGWU convention, she and her union brothers and sisters moved the entire gathering from one hotel to another rather than tolerate "Jim Crowism."[24]

Industrial labor organizers and activists promoted anew labor's "Americanism" of democratic rights and material security. And those ideals inspired workers in every region and in all their diversity to embrace the New Deal, sign union cards, and carry the Stars and Stripes into action. Rose Pesotta would recount hearing young Mexican dressmakers in Los Angeles speak of how those ideals made them want to become "American citizens"—and notably, 1934 saw a "marked acceleration in initial requests for naturalization papers" from the Mexican-born.[25]

Craft unions expanded, too, as hundreds of thousands of semiskilled workers in the steel, rubber, auto, textiles, and other mass-production industries sought admission. Blinkered by their own prejudice, most AFL leaders remained skeptical of semiskilled "ethnics," thereby compounding the challenge of incorporating their vast numbers to their skilled brotherhoods. Pressed to do something, and hoping thereby to restrain the newcomers' exuberant militancy, they set up temporary "federal unions" under their own direct authority—all of which served to anger their industrial-union colleagues, frustrate the workers themselves, and enable fast-acting corporate managers to corral eager-to-be-organized employees into company unions that, doubling their memberships to 2.5 million, actually grew faster than labor's own.[26]

With or without the federation's approval, workers acted. A total of 2,500,000 of them carried out work stoppages in 1933–34, turning some into large-scale events. Led by radicals, Toledo autoworkers, Minneapolis teamsters, and San Francisco longshoremen staged strikes that spring and summer which—meeting with violence from bosses and local officials, but garnering the active support of other unions and unemployed councils—resulted in city-wide battles in Toledo and Minneapolis and a general strike in San Francisco that shut down the entire Bay Area and every port on the West Coast. Then, in September, 400,000 textile workers from New England to the Deep South, proudly bearing the American flag, struck for their democratic rights and to secure improvements in wages and working conditions. However, they, too, encountered—in locales as different as Rhode Island and the Carolinas—business intransigence and the use of deadly force by guards, local police, and state militias.[27]

Though Section 7(a) of the NIRA did not cover agricultural workers, they, too, organized. In California, 50 thousand Mexican, Filipino, and Anglo migrant farm laborers and cannery workers united to confront employers and police, who viciously answered their demands with terror and force. And in Arkansas and surrounding states, thousands of courageous tenants and sharecroppers, black and white to-

gether, joined the Christian-inspired and socialist-organized Southern
Tenant Farmers' Union (STFU) seeking redress for their treatment by
planters and the AAA.[28]

Labor led the democratic surge, but more than workers asserted
themselves. Upper midwestern family farmers backed the Wisconsin
Progressive and Minnesota Farmer-Labor parties, both of which promised to back the New Deal.[29]

Spurred by labor's new energies and the Roosevelt administration's
calls for consumer activism, middle- and working-class women mobilized. National Consumers' League activists not only lobbied for additional regulation of food prices, but also aligned themselves with both
black groups fighting the racism of the new industrial codes and unions
demanding enforcement of the NIRA's Section 7(a). And New York
housewives, ever more vocally protesting rising prices, organized into
neighborhood "councils" and gave birth to a national "housewives
movement" when, in response to soaring meat prices, they initiated
boycotts of butcher shops in the spring of 1935 that quickly spread
across the country and came to include women of every background.[30]

Meanwhile, in contrast to the 1920s, writers and artists were now
feeling, as the composer Aaron Copland would recall, "the desire to be
'American.'" And they set out, as the writer Alfred Kazin put it, "to recover America *as an idea.*" Even Communist intellectuals, who had previously scorned both liberal democracy and other leftists, took up the
project in 1935 after receiving welcomed new party directives from Mos-
cow. They, too, now worked to form a broad antifascist "Popular Front"
and a "cultural front" to promote the causes of labor and democracy.[31]

Some intellectuals took to the road to witness and document developments. Others turned to the past. No one expressed the radical-
democratic spirit of the day better than the worker and labor organizer
turned poet Carl Sandburg, whose book *The People, Yes* was as affirmative and embracing as its title. But whether reporting on the state
of the nation and the "forgotten man" or recovering America's progressive tradition, all were giving voice to experiences and ideas long
suppressed by conservatives or mockingly dismissed by debunkers that
might further energize the nation's democratic impulse.[32]

Black political-intellectual life also experienced a new ferment. Still attached to the party of Lincoln, most African Americans voted for Hoover in 1932. But as the New Deal began to take off, black leaders saw new possibilities emerging. The NAACP president Joel Spingarn, himself white, convened an August 1933 gathering of the most promising young black intellectuals to discuss how they might now address the needs of African Americans. Known as the Second Amenia Conference, the meeting revealed a division between those who favored continuing the specific quest for civil and political rights and those like the radical Howard University social scientists Abram Harris, Jr., E. Franklin Frazier, and Ralph Bunche who wanted to develop an approach linked to labor and the Left. Both strategies would be pursued, but somewhat separately. Led by its new executive secretary, Walter White, and its chief counsel, Charles Hamilton Houston, the NAACP would challenge racism and segregation by lobbying for federal antilynching legislation, by suing southern states to honor the "equal" in "separate but equal," and by demanding an end to the "all-white primaries" and poll taxes that effectively disfranchised black citizens. And seeking to secure social and economic changes as well, more radical figures such as Harris and Bunche joined with A. Philip Randolph and others to organize the National Negro Congress (NNC) in 1935.[33]

Southern blacks faced great danger in confronting white authority. And yet many did so. Thousands enlisted in unions like the STFU and UMW. Some not only bravely banded together in "political clubs," but also daringly tried, as early as 1934, to participate in the all-white Democratic primaries of South Carolina, Georgia, Alabama, and Texas. Meanwhile, 400,000 others headed north, where they quickly registered to vote and fervently contributed to making blacks a significant urban political force.[34]

Traditionally conservative, college students in the tens and, soon, hundreds of thousands also mobilized and began to stage demonstrations in favor of causes from antimilitarism to civil rights and civil liberties. Pioneering the Popular Front, the Socialist Student League for Industrial Democracy (SLID) and the Communist National Student League (NSL) joined with dozens of other young people's organizations in 1934 to create the American Youth Congress (AYC), which would come to include a politically diverse and both multifaith and multiracial array of youth organizations representing a total membership of 4.5 million. While openly critical of the President for not providing adequate employment and educational opportunities (ironically, FDR himself had urged "American youth of all parties" to "Unite and Challenge!"), its leaders would find a real champion in the First Lady.[35]

Most Americans did not march or protest. But the majority—that is, of those who could vote—showed their support for Roosevelt at the midterm elections of 1934 by going against historical expectations and giving him and his party even larger majorities in both houses of Congress.

CHAPTER FOUR

"Our allegiance to American institutions requires the overthrow of this kind of power."

I n 1932, Roosevelt had declared that democratic leadership is a process of education and he would "go no further than America is ready to follow." And yet, as the story of a delegation of activists that had come to Washington seeking his support indicates, by 1934 even the educator had to be educated, if not occasionally pushed. As the editorialist I. F. Stone related it: "When they were finished the President said, 'Okay, you've convinced me. Now go on out and bring pressure on me.'"[1]

What FDR articulated was a simple truth about progressive political advances. A great democratic leader and a great democratic people realize democracy's expansion by inspiring and encouraging, challenging and compelling, and enabling and propelling each other to transcend themselves and the status quo. And that is exactly what happened in mid-1930s America.

In the face of both conservative reaction and populist demagoguery—

each in its way determined to constrain that expansion—Roosevelt would come to place himself, as the columnist Max Lerner wrote, "at the head of the urban and agrarian masses" and together they would pursue an even more radical "Second New Deal." President and people would enact Social Security, create the WPA, reinforce workers' rights, raise taxes on the rich, and increase public regulation of capital. These were not policies and programs gifted to a generation of Americans and their descendants, but gained through concerted effort. They were earned. They were won.[2]

Circumstances called for the redoubled effort. As much as the 1934 elections gave FDR and his New Dealers reason to rejoice, the nation's recovery was in trouble. The economy and employment were growing, but not fast enough. Unemployment stood at 17 percent. Consumers and small businesses were hurting. On the Great Plains, "dust storms" devastated the land and drove farmers west to California, and down south, renters and croppers were suffering expulsions. Labor unrest not only intensified; it also inhibited industrial recovery as corporate hands resisted New Deal regulations and workers' organizing efforts by clutching all the tighter to the reins of industry.

The vast majority of Americans supported the President. Indeed, liberals and leftists wanted him to enlarge and accelerate the New Deal by expanding relief and strengthening the National Recovery Administration, and union leaders were demanding a firmer commitment to securing workers' rights. But a determined and powerful minority of political conservatives, southern reactionaries, and business leaders remained steadfastly opposed to everything Roosevelt represented—and such people, who saw America's promise as already achieved, wanted not just to push the President. They wanted to topple him.

Rousing the "forgotten man" had made FDR enemies. Herbert Hoover was one. In *The Challenge to Liberty*, the first of many such attacks the former president would issue against Roosevelt, Hoover compared the New Deal with communism and fascism, declaring it nothing less than a threat to "our American heritage . . . and the achievements of the American System."[3]

Not only political conservatives hated Roosevelt. Even though profits were up, increasingly businessmen hated him, especially those of the corporate elite, who saw FDR as a "class traitor." They saw the progressive politics he championed as imperiling their liberties, their powers, their "freedoms," principally the freedom to control property, manage people, and exclude those unlike themselves.[4]

Determined to block FDR's reelection, resist the laws that circumscribed their authority, and restore the system they revered and ruled, the corporate moguls and their allies gathered in groups such as the National Association of Manufacturers (NAM), the U.S. Chamber of Commerce, and the newly formed American Liberty League. Ready to pursue class war from above, these corporate bosses—as U.S. Senate committee hearings chaired by Senator Robert La Follette of Wisconsin were soon to reveal—not only retained teams of lawyers. They also recruited spies and thugs and set up their own weapons arsenals. At the same time, hoping to win the battle of public opinion, they generously underwrote massive pro-business public relations campaigns. Endeavoring to counter the stories propagated by "labor, the socialistic-minded, and the radical" that had led Americans to "misunderstand industry," NAM initiated a major drive to "tell industry's story." And the Liberty Leaguers went all out against FDR and the New Deal.[5]

Organized in 1934 by prominent capitalists such as the brothers Irénée, Lammot, and Pierre of the DuPont Corporation, Alfred Sloan, Jr., of General Motors, Sewell Avery of Montgomery Ward, Ernest T. Weir of Weirton Steel, and Howard Pew of Sun Oil, the Liberty League declared its mission to be to "teach the necessity of respect for the rights of persons and property." Wrapping its campaign in rightwing renditions of American history and "Americanism," it produced radio broadcasts and distributed several million books, pamphlets, leaflets, and bulletins not only promoting "business civilization," but also portraying the New Deal and its "equalitarianism" as dire threats to the nation's constitutional order and values of individualism, small government, and the sacredness of property. Moreover, the Liberty Leaguers darkly charged, President Roosevelt was seeking to create nothing less than a dictatorship.[6]

While the League would spend a great deal of money spreading its message in print and on the airwaves in hopes of attracting middle- and working-class people to its cause, it would remain a club of the well-off. And yet, quite different forces—forces that had the potential to splinter FDR's electoral support—gave the League's leaders hope that they could defeat "that man in the White House" in 1936.

Populist figures who had originally backed the President were now denouncing him and, advancing their own schemes for recovery and reform, building sizable organized followings in the process. Promising to make "Every Man a King," Louisiana's Senator Huey Long, the machine politician and presidential hopeful, had set up the Share Our Wealth Society and gathered considerable adherents in and beyond the Deep South. Haranguing "Wall Street bankers" and demanding currency reform, the Canadian-born, Detroit-area priest and radio personality Father Charles Coughlin—who would later become infamous for his anti-Semitic and pro-fascist diatribes—had established the National Union of Social Justice and secured millions of listeners and subscribers across the northern tier of states. And proposing that the government stimulate demand by paying the elderly $200 a month, a sum they would be required to spend almost immediately, Francis Townsend, a retired California doctor, attracted nearly 3 million members nationwide to his Townsend Clubs.[7]

Separately, Long, Coughlin, and Townsend merely influenced public opinion. However, joined together in a third party with Long as their likely candidate, these three "Pied Pipers" posed a real threat. Though they could not capture the presidency, they might draw enough votes away from Roosevelt to afford a Republican victory. In fact, many liberals and leftists perceived in their "demagogic" and "messianic" politics the makings of an American fascist movement—a view anxiously articulated by Sinclair Lewis in his 1935 bestseller *It Can't Happen Here*.[8]

What the popular followings of Long, Coughlin, and Townsend certainly demonstrated was that Americans wanted more aggressive action—both to fight the Depression and to address the systemic inequalities and injustices that plagued their lives. And Roosevelt knew it. In fact, he was already looking at how he might both speed up relief and recovery and step up reconstruction and reform.

Envisioning "cradle to the grave" coverage, FDR in June 1934 had set up a Committee on Economic Security chaired by Secretary of Labor Frances Perkins, the task of which was to draft a proposal for the president's promised social insurance program. And that fall, looking to both create jobs and bring an end to relief payments (a practice he had never liked), he began to consider revamping the NRA and asked the Civil Works Administration director, Harry Hopkins, Interior Secretary Harold Ickes, and Treasury Secretary Henry Morgenthau to draw up plans for a new grand initiative that could rapidly employ the unemployed and accelerate the improvement of America's public infrastructure and environment.[9]

In January 1935, FDR laid out his new agenda in his Annual Message to Congress. Referring to the 1934 election results as "a clear mandate from the people that Americans must foreswear that conception of the acquisition of wealth which, through excessive profits, creates undue private power over private affairs and, to our misfortune, over public affairs, as well," he proceeded to outline plans for a "social security system" encompassing unemployment insurance, old age insurance, and benefits for dependent children and the handicapped. But he did not stop there. He also declared for a vast new array of public-works projects. And with the passage that spring of his requested $4.9 billion Emergency Relief Act, the President would create the Works Progress Administration and both the Rural Electrification and Resettlement Administrations, the latter two of which were designed to address the needs of poor farmers.[10]

Roosevelt also responded to the needs and demands of organized labor.

The union movement struggled in its pursuit of better wages and working conditions, hobbled both by schisms between craft-union leaders and mass-production laborers and by corporate bosses finding ways around the NIRA's Section 7(a). And as strikes continued around the country, some successful, some not, working Americans were looking to the President for action. Having previously hesitated to do so, FDR now endorsed Senator Robert Wagner's proposed National Labor Relations Act (the NLRA or "Wagner Act"), which would clarify workers' rights, outlaw corporate harassment and company unions, and set up a new, more authoritative National Labor Relations Board.[11]

Conservatives and capitalists vehemently opposed the WPA, Social Security, and the NLRA. Speaking for his corporate peers, GM's Alfred Sloan insisted that unemployment insurance would end up "destroying initiative, discouraging thrift, and stifling individual responsibility." And signaling their shared intentions, he said of the Wagner Act: "Industry, if it has any appreciation of its obligations to future generations, will fight this proposal to the very last."[12]

No doubt thrilling Sloan and his ilk, the Supreme Court decided that May, in *Schechter Poultry Corp. v. United States*, that key parts of the NIRA were unconstitutional. Nevertheless, Congress proceeded to pass not only the Social Security and Wagner Acts, but also the Banking Act of 1935, which strengthened the Federal Reserve System; the Public Utilities Holding Company Act, which broke up holding companies in that industry; and the Revenue Act of 1935, which imposed new taxes on corporations and the wealthy.

However much congressional reactionaries and racists limited the coverage of Social Security and the NLRA, and however much congressional conservatives weakened the Revenue Act, this Second New Deal quickened the nation's democratic impulse. In October 1935, John L. Lewis convened a meeting of seven like-minded union heads to form the CIO—the Committee for Industrial Organization, which in 1938 would become the independent Congress of Industrial Organizations—whose declared objective was to organize workers in the mass-production industries. In December 1935 the Socialist Student League for Industrial Democracy (SLID) and the Communist National Student League (NSL) formed the American Student Union (ASU) with a platform that advocated "equal educational opportunity and economic security for all young Americans," an end to "intolerance and segregation," support for the labor movement, and guarantees of free speech on campus for faculty and students. And in February 1936, the National Negro Congress, with the union leader A. Philip Randolph as its president, held its founding convention with representatives of five hundred black organizations in attendance.[13]

The New Deal advanced not only economic and industrial democracy, but also cultural democracy. Outraging conservatives and the corporate rich, WPA initiatives included the Federal Art, Theater, Music, and Writers' Projects. Employing tens of thousands of out-of-work actors, musicians, artists, writers, technicians, and others ("Hell," Harry Hopkins said, "they've got to eat just like other people!"), these four programs, jointly dubbed "Federal One," would remain small items in the WPA's overall budget, but they would stand out in its operations. Engaging Americans in venues from big cities to small towns, adults and children alike, their performances and productions and classes and workshops cultivated interest and activity both in the arts and in history and current affairs. The plays of the Federal Theater Project attracted a total audience of 30 million. The endeavors of WPA artists included creating nearly 2,600 public murals depicting Americans past and present—and in all their diversity—striving and struggling to secure the nation's promise. And the labors of the Writers' Project extended from preparing the American Guide Series, a small library's worth of volumes on the country's forty-eight states and major cities that detailed every aspect of their environments, histories, cultures, and economies, to collecting folklore and oral histories, including the testimonies of more than two thousand former slaves. All of which further affirmed to many that the lives and voices of the people were being taken seriously.[14]

The WPA would nurture cultural democracy as well, through its National Youth Administration (NYA). Stressing the value and imperative of universal education, the NYA provided work relief to several million sixteen- to twenty-five-year-olds—men and women equally—to enable them to stay in school or enroll in job-training programs. Though it would never receive enough funds to cover all of those who needed support, the NYA aided 4,000,000 young Americans—1,500,000 high school students, 620,000 university students, and 2,600,000 other unemployed young people—with African Americans constituting more than 10 percent of the students and an even

economic   cultural   4 democracy
industrial   social + industrial
THE FIGHT FOR THE FOUR FREEDOMS   61

greater percentage of those receiving training (not to mention that the NYA director, Aubrey Williams, made it a point of hiring black staff to work in both the North and the South). And while not due to NYA activities alone, for the first time, as the historian Kriste Lindenmeyer has written, "most seventeen-year-olds attended high school and more went on to college than ever before."[15]

Collectively, people and government, each pushing or pulling the other, had deepened the New Deal. Its critics saw all the more the stakes and grew all the more determined.

The lines of interest were clearly drawn by 1936. And with the presidential election on the horizon, FDR—flanked by conservatives on his right and demagogues on his left—remained the most popular choice. To vote for a second Roosevelt term would mean casting a ballot for continuing the New Deal. To vote otherwise—for the Republican nominee or a third-party candidate—would be to repudiate progressivism. Most Americans knew what they wanted. Labor mobilized in support of the President. And FDR was poised to win.

But Roosevelt wanted to do more than win. His conservative and corporate antagonists were right. He intended revolution—though not of the sort they were asserting. He hated both communism and fascism, and by no means did he want to destroy capitalism. He wanted to advance a *third* New Deal that would move the nation ever more progressively toward social and industrial democracy. And to do that he needed not just to win, but, especially given the Supreme Court's constitutional conservatism, to win *big*. Indeed, he envisioned building a new Democratic Party coalition of urban working people, Catholic and Jewish immigrants and ethnics, *and* African Americans, while somehow holding on to traditional southern Democrats—a coalition that would allow him, as he had envisioned in 1930, to make the country "fairly radical for a generation." Moreover, despite the persistent hostility of the American press (not so much the reporters as their publishers and editors), FDR felt increasingly confident that the majority of Americans wanted America's progressive transformation to continue.

Roosevelt himself set the stage for a "Revolutionary" campaign in his 1936 Annual Message to Congress that January. Referring to the rise of fascist dictators and the suppression of political and religious freedom in Europe and Asia, he observed that tyranny threatened Americans at home as well: "Within our borders, as in the world at large, popular opinion is at war with a power-seeking minority . . . an economic autocracy." Then—reciting the names of "Thomas Jefferson, Andrew Jackson, Theodore Roosevelt, and Woodrow Wilson," and recalling that he himself had come to office seeking to "restore power to those to whom it rightfully belonged"—he warned that those "financial and industrial groups" that had "abdicated" in 1933 were now seeking a "restoration of their selfish power." And he said, "Give them their way and they will take the course of every autocracy of the past—power for themselves, enslavement for the public."[16]

But that was just the start. The Democratic National Convention was to be held that year in Philadelphia, and FDR would make the most of it.

On the evening of June 27—with July 4th just a week away and thoughts of Jefferson and his Revolutionary words in the air—Roosevelt went before the 100,000 conventioneers and supporters gathered at Franklin Field, a baseball stadium, and the millions more listening via radio, and proceeded to deliver the most radical speech ever given by an American president. Reflecting that "Philadelphia is a good city in which to write American history," he said: "This is fitting ground on which to reaffirm the faith of our fathers; to pledge to ourselves to restore to the people a wider freedom; to give to 1936 as the founders gave to 1776—an American way of life."[17]

As his words suggested, reaffirmation required more than restoration. "In 1776," he declared, "we sought freedom from the tyranny of a political autocracy—from the eighteenth century royalists who held special privileges from the crown." Yet industrialization and the advance of "modern civilization," FDR continued, had engendered a "new despotism" of "economic dynasties" and "industrial dictatorship," an "economic tyranny" ruled by a class of "economic royalists" who "sought to regiment the people, their labor, and their property" and now "reached out for control over Government itself." To defend democratic life, he averred, Americans had to enlarge it: "Today we stand committed to the proposition that freedom is no half-and-half affair. If the average citizen is guaranteed equal opportunity in the polling place, he must have equal opportunity in the market place."[18]

"These economic royalists," Roosevelt noted, "complain that we seek to overthrow the institutions of America." But, he retorted, "What they really complain of is that we seek to take away their power." And they were right, he confessed, for "Our allegiance to American institutions requires the overthrow of this kind of power." Then, making it absolutely clear he would cede American history and its greatest symbols to no one, he added: "In vain they seek to hide behind the Flag and the Constitution. In their blindness they forget what the Flag and Constitution stand for. Now, as always, they stand for a democracy, not tyranny; for freedom, not subjection; and against a dictatorship by mob rule and the overprivileged alike."[19]

"There is a mysterious cycle in human events," the President told his fellow citizens. "To some generations much is given. Of other generations much is expected. This generation of Americans has a rendezvous with destiny."[20]

Americans gave Roosevelt a resounding victory that November. Capturing all but two states, he received nearly 28 million votes versus 16.7 million for the Republican nominee, Alf Landon, and the fewer than 1 million for William Lemke, the nominee of the Union Party, formed by the forces of Long, Coughlin, and Townsend. No presidential candidate had ever before managed such a triumph. FDR had not only won. He had also effected a historic realignment of Jews and blacks to the Democratic Party. Indeed, picking up the votes of 83 percent of southern white Protestants, 81 percent of northern Catholics, 85 percent of Jewish Americans, and 71 percent of African Americans, he had won "big" and secured his new electoral coalition.[21]

With those results, and Democrats now holding 76 seats in the Senate and 331 in the House, a "Third New Deal" seemed assured. But it was not to happen. Eager both to counter the Supreme Court's conservative majority *and* to turn the Democratic Party into an even more progressive party, Roosevelt would undertake, first, an ill-conceived effort to increase the number of justices on the Court and then, in 1938, an ill-fated campaign to purge the party of its most reactionary elements—the latter of which saw the President himself going down to Georgia and openly declaring the regimes of the South the nation's number-one political problem by equating its "feudal system" with the "Fascist system" and stating, "If you believe in the one, you lean to the other."[22]

Roosevelt failed to accomplish either objective and ended up instigating the formation of an anti–New Deal congressional coalition of Republicans and "Dixiecrats" that thereafter would stand in the way of new progressive legislative initiatives. Still, he remained the hero of working people north and south, black and white. As one Floridian put it in a letter to the White House: "Your inspiring frank address . . . gives the working classes of the South new hope." And when the New York City Boys Athletic League asked fifty thousand children who they thought was the "most loved man in the world," while 22, 15, and 15 percent, respectively, said God, Washington, and Lincoln, 39 percent of them named FDR. Those affections and the trust, hopes, and aspirations they reflected mattered powerfully and they would matter all the more when those same young men and women, led by the President they loved, took up arms in defense of the nation and in favor of the Four Freedoms.[23]

The New Deal would change. But it would not come to a halt. The CCC, WPA, and other public-works agencies continued to enhance the country's natural and built environments. The WPA's Federal One projects and National Youth Administration continued to promote a more democratic Americanism. And in 1938, the President secured passage of the Fair Labor Standards Act (FLSA), which abolished child labor and established both a minimum wage and overtime pay for at least one in four American workers.[24]

Moreover, not only did the Supreme Court decide in 1937 that both the Social Security and Wagner Acts were constitutional, but, despite his failed effort to "expand" the court, Roosevelt would soon get to appoint seven new justices and elevate the "Honorary New Dealer" Harlan Fiske Stone to Chief Justice. All of which initiated nothing less than a "Constitutional Revolution" in which the Court increasingly gave priority to democratic or "human rights" over "property rights."[25]

In fact, Roosevelt himself returned all the more frequently in 1937 to the theme of his 1932 Commonwealth Club address. Deploring the persistence of "want and fear," he not only implored Americans to push Congress to expand the Social Security program to cover those left out in 1935, he also started to once again project the idea of augmenting Americans' civil and political rights with a set of social and economic rights, such as the right to housing and health care.[26]

At the same time, Roosevelt continued to speak proudly of America's racial, ethnic, and religious diversity, and press ever more forcefully for the rights of all citizens. Addressing the conservative "White Anglo-Saxon Protestant" Daughters of the American Revolution (DAR) convention in 1938, he said: "Remember, remember always that all of us, and you and I especially, are descended from immigrants, and Revolutionists"—adding, "We look for a younger generation that is going to be more American than we are." And not long after, he sent a public "Greeting" to the NAACP on the occasion of its twenty-fifth annual conference in which he praised the organization for "bringing about that cooperation and understanding between the races so essential to the maintenance of a vital democracy" and stated that "no democracy can long survive which does not accept as fundamental to its very existence the recognition of the rights of its minorities."[27]

The President's commitments were more than rhetorical. Recognizing that Congress would not act to progressively advance the rights of workers and minorities, he appointed the former Michigan Governor Frank Murphy as his Attorney General in 1939 and directed him to take the initiative by creating a Civil Liberties Unit in the Justice Department. A committed small-*d* democrat, Murphy had stunned GM's bosses during the pioneering Flint sit-down strike of 1936–37 by calling out the National Guard to protect not the company, but the workers. And in 1940—not long before Roosevelt was to name him to the Supreme Court—Murphy told his fellow citizens:

Go down in the subway of the great metropolis, walk the crowded streets . . . what do you see? Not Englishmen or Italians alone, or Gentiles or Jews alone, or white people or blacks alone . . . You see the children of every race and every nation and every creed. You see America and America's future. If you are disheartened by what you see . . . then America's future and your own will not be happy. But if you see them all as being of the stock that built this great nation . . . if you look at them as servants of democracy, then our future is bright and full of hope.[28]

Meanwhile, popular democratic energies surged anew.

Empowered by the Wagner Act, the CIO launched major organizing drives in the mass-production industries and workers enlisted in labor's ranks even more enthusiastically than they had before. Some companies avoided trouble and signed contracts; others resisted, but then relented; and still others waged bloody war against their employees, as happened in Chicago when police fired on protesting Republic Steel workers and their families on Memorial Day 1937, killing and wounding dozens. But this time workers responded to corporate intransigence with the "sit-down strike," a new, more spirited tactic in which they didn't just picket but, aided by mothers and wives, occupied the factories—none more spiritedly and famously than the GM autoworkers in Flint, Michigan. And with progressive writers and artists now promoting labor's cause nationally, the union movement, led by the CIO's United Rubber Workers, United Steel Workers, and United Auto Workers, doubled its numbers in 1937 by enlisting 3 million new members.[29]

The AFL would eject the CIO unions in 1938. However, compelled to compete with them, the former would not only now commit itself to organizing industrial labor, but also eventually surpass its rival in membership numbers. And despite a damaging recession in 1938 (caused by FDR's determination to "balance the federal budget" when deficit spending by government remained crucial to combatting the continuing depression), 8 million workers would belong to unions by 1940, including—due to the determination of the CIO in particular—500,000 blacks and 750,000 women. Undeniably, racism and anti-Semitism persisted, and in some places intensified, but not everywhere. As one African-American steelworker observed: "I'll tell you what the CIO has done. Before everyone used to make remarks about, 'That dirty Jew,' 'that stinkin' black bastard,' 'that low-life Bohunk,' but you know I don't hear that stuff anymore."[30]

A new story of America was definitely in the air, encompassing not only labor and class, but also ethnicity, race, and gender. Working with both the private Service Bureau for Intercultural Education and the WPA, the U.S. Office of Education produced *Americans All, Immigrants All* in 1938–39. A program of twenty-six weekly, half-hour national radio broadcasts, it recounted the country's development through the experiences of nearly every "nationality" that came to this country and contributed to its development and the making of American democratic life. The show was heard by millions of Americans— including schoolchildren—either directly on the radio or on specially produced recordings. In fact, many people listened together in groups and "hundreds of organizations" from ethnic and religious societies to union locals and patriotic clubs like the American Legion and DAR wrote to the producers requesting additional materials.[31]

The WPA itself created two series of radio plays, *Women in the Making of America* and *Gallant American Women*, which told of women's activism in and contributions to U.S. history and gave special attention to the campaigns of radicals such as Lucretia Mott and Sojourner Truth for equality and democratic rights. And the Communist songwriters Earl Robinson and John LaTouche composed "Ballad for Americans," an uplifting, twelve-minute-long, multiethnic, multifaith, and multiracial call-and-response telling of American history that became—following a nationally broadcast performance by Paul Robeson and the American People's Chorus in 1939—not only the "anthem" of the progressive cultural front, but also a major American "hit" (which even the Republicans wanted performed at their 1940 party convention!).[32]

African Americans, too, intensified and expanded their struggles. Under the slogan "Don't Buy Where You Can't Work," civil rights groups in the northeast organized boycotts of stores that refused to hire blacks. Even in the racially regimented South, protests intensified. The Southern Tenant Farmers' Union grew to 30,000 members. African Americans in southern cities formed more "voting clubs" to challenge the laws and practices that prevented them from casting their ballots. And with encouragement from the White House, prominent southern liberals, black and white together, joined by the First Lady herself, gathered in Birmingham, Alabama, in November 1938 to found the Southern Conference for Human Welfare (SCHW) and proceeded to launch an anti–poll tax campaign that looked toward undoing the region's reactionary regimes by restoring the franchise to the masses of poor blacks and whites who had lost it with the ascendance in the 1890s of Bourbon and Jim Crow politics. Plus, the NAACP scored a critical victory that year in its pursuit of the "equal" in "separate but equal" when the Supreme Court ruled in *Gaines v. Canada* that Missouri "could not give whites a legal education . . . and deny that right to blacks." The Court did not overturn segregation, but everyone knew the decision represented a critical precedent.[33]

The democratic surge could also be seen and heard in the new "swing music" that, with its big-band orchestras led by progressives such as Benny Goodman and Duke Ellington, not only roused the spirits of young people of every sort and region of the country, but also broke the "color line" in both their songs and performances.[34]

Eleanor Roosevelt herself campaigned all the more vigorously for social justice and the rights of women, young people, minorities, and labor—in fact, Mrs. Roosevelt joined a journalists' union, the American Newspaper Guild, when she began to write her "My Day" column in 1936. Even more famously, she not only resigned in protest from the Daughters of the American Revolution when it refused in 1939 to permit the world-renowned African-American contralto Marian Anderson to perform before an integrated audience in Constitution Hall in Washington, D.C., she also worked with Interior Secretary Ickes to arrange an open-air concert by Anderson at the Lincoln Memorial on Easter Sunday, which drew an integrated crowd of 75,000. And belying the continuous ranting of her conservative critics, the more the First Lady campaigned, the more popular she became. A poll conducted by

George Gallup of the American Institute of Public Opinion in early 1939 showed that 73 and 62 percent of American women and men, respectively, approved of the First Lady's activities.[35]

All of which did not go unanswered. Corporate executives, along with political conservatives and reactionaries, invested fresh resources to contain, if not reverse, the new democratic surge. Business groups responded to heightened consumer activism by creating their own "shadow" consumer organizations bearing names such as the Crowell Institute on Consumer Relations. And though the Liberty League itself disbanded, the National Association of Manufacturers launched another huge public relations campaign to advance among America's middle classes a more favorable image of business.[36]

Projecting private enterprise—which capitalists now took to calling "free enterprise"—as "The American Way" to prosperity, billboards across the country portrayed happy families enjoying the best of American industry. Plus, fearful that the President and his progressive enthusiasts were enlivening Americans' historical memories and imagination in dangerous ways, NAM also published *Young America,* a magazine distributed to many of the nation's public schools, which sought to counter their influence. And the DuPont Corporation renewed its sponsorship of *Cavalcade of America,* a radio series that presented plays on the nation's past intended to emphasize "the qualities of American character which have been responsible for the building of this country"—which usually meant highlighting the inventiveness, innovativeness, and beneficence of the nation's industrial pioneers and leaders.[37]

Corporate ideological initiatives included more direct and aggressive actions than simply roadside billboards and radio broadcasts, however. Convinced that progressive ideas held too powerful a sway in America's classrooms, NAM commissioned the Columbia University banking professor Ralph Robey to conduct an investigation of the nation's social-studies textbooks. And outfitted with Robey's six-hundred-page report, the organization, with the assistance of the American Legion, waged a public war on works that lacked the "right kind of patriotism."[38]

Congressional reactionaries mobilized, too. Headed by Representative Martin Dies of Texas, an infamous nativist, anti-Semite, and racist who actually admired Hitler for his "philosophy of Aryan racial purity," they gained control of a House committee originally created to investigate Nazi subversives and sympathizers and turned it into what would become the infamous House Un-American Activities Committee (HUAC). Duly authorized, Dies and company, intent upon portraying the New Deal as "un-American," pursued a political inquisition against the Roosevelt presidency and the Left and incited something of a "Red Scare" when they began to call administration officials and labor and progressive leaders to testify about the presence and possible influence of not fascists, but Communists, in their agencies and organizations.[39]

No doubt with just such reactionary machinations in mind, Roosevelt warned in a November 1938 election-eve radio broadcast:

> As of today, Fascism and Communism—and old-line Tory Republicanism—are not threats to the continuation of our form of government. But I venture the challenging statement that if American democracy ceases to move forward as a living force, seeking day and night by peaceful means to better the lot of our citizens, then Fascism and Communism, aided, unconsciously perhaps, by old-line Tory Republicanism, will grow in strength in our land.[40]

But FDR also knew that Americans had come to believe—as Harold Stearns had observed in 1937—"that we have not yet fully explored the democratic way of life." Reflecting the spirit and determination of the day, the civil liberties attorney Arthur Garfield Hays argued in *Democracy Works* that democracy was most essentially about "the right to make a fight." Citing Jefferson, Adams, and Paine, the poet Archibald MacLeish wrote in "America was Promises":

> *Believe*
> *America is promises to*
> *Take!*

America is promises to
Us
To take them
Brutally
With love but
Take Them.

Oh believe this!

And echoing the labor leader A. Philip Randolph, the editors of Chicago's black newspaper, *The Defender*, declared: "Democracy is never given. It must be taken."[41]

Like Roosevelt, Stearns, Hays, MacLeish, and the editors of *The Defender* were reacting to as much as encouraging the average American's embrace of the nation's quickening progressive impulse. The degree to which that impulse both permeated down and percolated up is registered in the declarations of the National Congress of Spanish Speaking Peoples ("El Congreso"), a coalition of 136 union locals and Latino organizations formed in 1938 to promote the mutual causes of labor and civil rights. As the historian George Sanchez has noted, the young Mexican Americans who belonged to El Congreso—despite the abuses they endured and the criticisms they voiced—were eager to "fight for American democracy" against fascism and imperialism. By no means, he explained, did they think the United States "represented a society of equality." But as their own words testify, they cherished America, for they saw in its democracy "a chance for change." In democracy, they said, "voices can be lifted. Songs can be sung. You can belong to a union, a club, to a church. And through that union, that club, or that church you can ask for a chance." And in the wake of Pearl Harbor, after urging everyone, young and old, to cooperate in the war effort, they declared: "We are also children of the United States. We will defend her!"[42]

CHAPTER FIVE

"We look forward to a world founded upon four essential human freedoms."

E leven months before Japan's attack on the United States' Pacific naval base at Pearl Harbor violently pulled America into the war, FDR delivered his 1941 Annual Message to Congress. In that speech—the Four Freedoms speech—he not only made clear the intensifying Axis threat to the nation, dismissed isolationist arguments that the United States could and should remain neutral in the already-raging war, and urged his fellow citizens to turn the country into the "Arsenal of Democracy" and enact a Lend-Lease program to aid Britain. He also translated his previous eight years in office and Americans' resurgent aspirations and energies into the terms that would give historic purpose to the five years of global struggle to come. He cautioned against those who would try to take advantage of the crisis for personal gain, insisted on the need to enhance American readiness by building upon the progressive initiatives of the 1930s, and articulated the vision that became the cause of a generation.[1]

The President and his advisors had spent days on the speech before he delivered it on the afternoon of Monday, January 6. But he had spent much longer on it than that. He knew he had strong public support for what he was to say. Only weeks before, he had won reelection to an unprecedented third term. The response to his Fireside Chat of December 29, in which he first advanced the "Arsenal of Democracy" idea, had been extremely positive. Even longtime critics of the New Deal such as Frank Kent of *The Baltimore Sun* acknowledged that "the President has voiced what the great bulk of Americans have in their hearts." And polls showed that approximately two-thirds of the American people wanted to aid Britain even if it meant going to war as a consequence.[2]

However, FDR knew as well that up until only a short time ago most Americans wanted no direct involvement in overseas conflicts. As he prepared his speech, the task before him was to present their achievements in a way that sharpened appreciation of what they had accomplished while conveying just why European fascism and Japanese imperialism imperiled everything they believed in and held dear. At the same time, he recognized that even now, with Germany occupying Europe and Japan overrunning East Asia, there were many Americans, including some very prominent ones, who would vehemently reject what he was proposing. Among their number were quite a few of those gathered at the Capitol, who would not applaud for no other reason than their profound dislike of everything he and the New Deal represented.

The 1941 Annual Message went through seven drafts before Roosevelt felt it was ready for delivery. As his chief of staff Samuel Rosenman later recounted: "The President himself had dictated five pages, and worked on it very hard through the various drafts . . . filling each of them with his handwritten corrections and insertions."[3]

The Four Freedoms had been taking shape in FDR's mind for some time. He had spoken of them in various ways for a numbers of years. But not until the writing of the fourth draft did he state them precisely. Rosenman clearly recollected that moment. It was the night of January 1. The speechwriting team of Harry Hopkins, Robert Sherwood, and Rosenman himself, along with the White House secretary Dorothy Brady, was sitting with the President in his study going over the third rendition of the address when, just as they neared the end of it, Roosevelt exclaimed that he had "an idea for a peroration." Then, "[after] a long pause—so long that it began to feel uncomfortable," the President said, "Dorothy, take a law." And he proceeded to dictate, "We must look forward to a world based on four essential human freedoms . . ." Indeed, Rosenman said, "the words seemed now to roll off his tongue as though he had rehearsed them many times to himself."[4]

Roosevelt fully grasped that when he went up to Capitol Hill to deliver his Message five days later, he would be addressing not just the members of Congress, but the American people as a whole. And it surely must have seemed that all of the political campaigns and struggles and legislative victories and defeats of the previous two terms had led him to what he was about to do.

Anticipation of what the President was going to say ran high. Despite the January cold, hundreds had gathered outside the Capitol building. They would not hear Roosevelt speak. They just wanted to be there. Inside, the House chamber was full to overflowing. Representatives and senators, cabinet officers and diplomats, the First Lady and other dignitaries awaited the President's words. And as *Time* magazine reported, FDR did not delay: "The President leaned heavily on the rostrum, threw open the big black leather binder, straightway began his message . . ."[5]

Speaking without hesitation, Roosevelt proceeded to expound upon the profound crisis and mortal dangers facing the United States and to explain how the nation could not only confront them but prevail in doing so. Rejecting as utterly foolish the isolationists' argument that Americans should simply hunker down behind great defensive walls, he rallied his fellow citizens around a dynamic image of America serving as the great Arsenal of Democracy. And dismissing conservatives' claims that the crisis required Americans to suspend or give up their hard-fought-for social and economic advances of the past eight years, he argued that an effective industrial and military mobilization required them to not simply sustain their achievements, but to extend and deepen them. *Time* would observe, "Mr. Roosevelt spoke clearly as ever, but there was no lightness in his voice, no touch of humor.

As he went on, his big head thrown back, his voice gained depth and strength, and emotion." And his words garnered fervent applause—at times, thunderous applause.[6]

Finally, the President proclaimed his vision of what Americans might actually realize in the struggle that lay before them: "In the future days, which we seek to make secure, we look forward to a world founded upon four essential human freedoms. The first is freedom of speech and expression . . . The second is freedom of every person to worship God in his own way . . . The third is freedom from want . . . The fourth is freedom from fear . . ." And, he confidently averred: "That is no vision of a distant millennium. It is a definite basis for a kind of world attainable in our own time and generation."

The vision was global. But Roosevelt rooted it firmly in American experience and aspiration: "Since the beginning of our American history we have been engaged in change—in a perpetual, peaceful revolution—a revolution which goes on steadily, quietly, adjusting itself to changing conditions without the concentration camp or the quicklime in the ditch. The world order which we seek is the cooperation of free countries, working together in a friendly, civilized society."

The historic rendezvous of which he had spoken in 1936 had arrived: "This nation has placed its destiny in the hands and heads and hearts of its millions of free men and women, and its faith in freedom under the guidance of God . . . there can be no end save victory."

Headlining its coverage "Roosevelt Rallies Democracy for Finish Fight on the Axis," *Newsweek* called the speech a "challenge to the world." And welcoming his abandonment of "unrealistic and dishonorable . . . neutrality," *The New York Times* editorialized not only that FDR's "message is a confession of deep faith, a summons to duty and a call to action," but also that it clearly "has the endorsement of the vast majority of our people, and that they will approve whatever measures are needed to put it into practice." All recorded as well that while most of the Republicans present did not applaud (*The New York Post* columnist Samuel Grafton figured "a few Democrats" did not do so, either, on hearing "freedom from want"), ardent isolationists made quite a bit of noise afterward. That was to be expected, for the President, to the great

applause of most Americans, had essentially called the country to war
in the name of the Four Freedoms.[7]

From the time he first took office in 1933, Roosevelt had been concerned about the threat that Hitler, Mussolini, and Japan's rulers posed
to world peace. And ever since his days in the Wilson administration,
FDR had hoped that the United States would participate in international collective-security arrangements to counter just such ambitions.
However, in his failed 1920 vice presidential campaign, and again early
in his presidency, he had learned that Americans were leery of foreign
alliances.[8]

Americans did not like Hitler, Mussolini, or the ruling clique in
Japan. But neither did they like the idea of going to war against them.
When Japanese planes attacked and sank the USS *Panay*, anchored
near Nanking, China, killing two U.S. seamen and wounding thirty
more, Americans demanded nothing more than an apology and indem-
nity. Imagining that they were protected by geography, Americans had
little interest in fighting wars on distant shores. Besides, they already
were fighting the Great Depression.[9]

Roosevelt, convinced that his countrymen would think otherwise if
they perceived the real dangers threatening American shores and values, set himself to "educating" them to the perils of too great a reliance
on isolationism. His goal wasn't to incite fear and anxiety, but rather—
as in his efforts to recruit them to the labors of the New Deal—to remind them who they were and what that both afforded and demanded.
In an October 1937 Fireside Chat, he said, "I want our democracy to
be wise enough to realize that aloofness from war is not promoted by
unawareness of war. In a world of mutual suspicions, peace must be affirmatively reached for. It cannot just be wished for. It cannot just be
waited for." And after observing in his 1938 election-eve radio remarks
that "the flares of militarism and conquest, terrorism and intolerance
[in other lands], have vividly revealed to Americans for the first time
since the Revolution how precious and extraordinary it is to be allowed
this free choice of free leaders for free men," he stated. "The rest of the

world is far closer to us in every way than in the days of democracy's founders—Jefferson, Jackson, and Lincoln. Comparisons in this world are unavoidable. To disprove the pretenses of rival systems, democracy must be an affirmative, up-to-date conception."[10]

America's work in the world, the president was reminding Americans, was far from over. Assuming the burden of that work did not mean they had to give up the New Deal. The converse was true. In his April 14, 1938, Fireside Chat, Roosevelt explained, "Democracy has disappeared in several other great nations . . . not because the people of those nations disliked democracy, but because they had grown tired of unemployment and insecurity, of seeing their children hungry while they sat helpless in the face of government confusion, government weakness through lack of leadership in government." Yet, he continued, "We in America know that our own democratic institutions can be preserved and made to work. But in order to preserve them we need to act together, to meet the problems of the Nation boldly, and to prove that the practical operation of democratic government is equal to the task of protecting the security of the people." And in a speech to the National Education Association convention later that spring, he declared: "If the fires of freedom and civil liberties burn low in other lands, they must be made brighter in our own."[11]

The task FDR and a cohort of similarly concerned citizens set themselves was daunting. The vast majority of Americans were disgusted by the blatant criminality and brutality of the Axis regimes; what direction that disgust took the nation was an entirely different matter. The public-opinion researcher Jerome Bruner would term American ambivalence "nightmarish."[12]

Americans did not trust Europe's, let alone Asia's, rulers. White Americans had "escaped" the Old Country and, while they might feel affection for the lands of their ancestors, they had little confidence that Europe or any other continent could be progressively transformed. And black Americans, given the record of western European imperialism and colonialism in Africa, had even less reason to care about Europe's destiny.

Furthermore, the memory of World War I, which had cost 116,000 American lives, had left Americans mistrustful, even downright cynical, about foreign "entanglements." After all, what President Wilson had claimed would be a war to "make the world safe for democracy" had been followed by Fascist and Communist dictatorships, continuing imperialism, and economic depression. Books bearing titles such as *The Merchants of Death* and *Iron, Blood and Profits* deepened their cynicism, along with their isolationist sentiments. As, too, did the 1934 Senate hearings on the munitions industry chaired by the North Dakota Senator and ardent isolationist Gerald Nye. In the course of nearly one hundred sessions and two hundred oral testimonies, the latter gave disturbing credence to charges that financial capitalists and munitions manufacturers had conspired to "dupe" the country into war in 1917.[13]

Deep social divisions made unifying the country for action against fascism and imperialism all the more challenging. Decrying supposed Jewish power and influence, the pro-Nazi "Radio Priest," Father Charles Coughlin, not only drew a loyal following, but incited young Irish-Catholic youths of the Christian Front, a new paramilitary organization, to assault Jewish children and elderly people on the streets of Boston and Brooklyn. However, the Boston Irish had no corner on anti-Semitism. Congress, the State Department, the U.S. Army, and the American Legion—as well as the nation's premier colleges and universities—contained many a Jew-hater who would successfully oppose legislative efforts by Senator Robert F. Wagner to lift immigration quotas in order to permit greater numbers of refugees fleeing Hitler to enter the country. And similarly, white supremacists, spouting "states' rights" and racial epithets from the corridors of Congress to the courthouses of Dixie, stiffened their resistance to African-American demands for justice and equality, which included blocking passage of antilynching bills.[14]

Moreover, not only did harsh conflict between capital and labor persist. The labor movement itself was splitting into the AFL and the CIO. And while capitalists were hardly pacifists, the war that most of them hoped to see would have pitted Nazi Germany against the Soviet Union. In fact, some of America's largest companies, such as GM, Ford, DuPont, and Alcoa, had licensing and production agreements with Germany's biggest corporations.[15]

Also, as Roosevelt well knew, many German and Italian Americans, while by no means pro-fascist, sympathized with their nations of origin; Irish Americans remained strongly anti-British; and the Catholic faithful, whatever their qualms, generally did not dissent from the Vatican's support for conservative and even fascist movements battling secular and anticlerical leftists.

Most Americans looked out from their shores, saw a world edging ever closer to war, and had good reasons for wanting to stay out of it. Indicative of the nation's prevailing popular isolationism, little more than rhetoric and a heroic volunteer brigade of 2,500 Americans could be mustered in support of the Spanish Republic while Mussolini and Hitler transparently used the civil war as training ground for conflicts to come.[16]

Roosevelt was not without his own doubts about responding aggressively to German, Italian, and Japanese aggression. He dreaded the prospect of war: "I have seen war . . . I hate war." He also wondered if he could trust the British and French, given their own imperial interests and repeated willingness to appease Mussolini and Hitler—which would include giving way to Italy's conquest of Ethiopia and signing the now-infamous September 1938 Munich agreement that compelled Czechoslovakia to cede the Sudetenland to Germany, paving the way for Hitler to occupy all of the country six months later.[17]

Despite reservations, Roosevelt also knew, as with the New Deal, that the stakes were too high to cede the initiative to isolationists or detractors. And with the outbreak of war in Europe in September 1939, the fall of France in June 1940, and Germany's ensuing "Blitz" against Britain, he steadily regained command of foreign policy. Even as he headed into the 1940 presidential campaign, he not only convinced Congress to revise the Neutrality Act and expand the American military. He also created a "war cabinet" with the Republicans Henry Stimson and Frank Knox serving, respectively, as Secretary of War and Secretary of the Navy; embargoed steel and scrap-iron sales to Japan; donated old destroyers to Britain in exchange for Caribbean bases; and even secured passage, though just barely, of the Selective Service Act—not to mention, secretly gave the go-ahead to explore the making of an atomic bomb, in order to beat Germany to it.[18]

Seeing that the country was moving to a war footing, isolationists and "non-interventionists" rallied in the summer of 1940 around the banner of the America First Committee, a group organized by several leading midwestern businessmen. Described by the journalist and historian John Egerton as a "motley assortment of pacifists, anti-Semites, pro-Nazis, and laissez-faire capitalists," the Committee nonetheless gained a reported membership of 850,000 that, along with a few liberal oddities, included such notable mouthpieces as the former ambassador to Britain Joseph P. Kennedy and the aviation hero Charles Lindbergh. Convinced that Britain would soon collapse under the Blitz, Kennedy contended that the United States should not waste its efforts trying to save it, and Lindbergh, an anti-Semite who had accepted honors from Hitler's Third Reich, echoed Kennedy's assertion. And all the while, reactionary newspapers such as the *Chicago Tribune*, the New York *Daily News*, and those of the Hearst chain propagated America First positions in their editorial pages, and senators such as Burton K. Wheeler of Montana and Gerald P. Nye of North Dakota advocated them in Congress.[19]

Nevertheless, FDR had reason to feel encouraged. The America First Committee did not represent majority opinion. In fact, Americans' already resurgent democratic impulses quickened all the more and their sense of their own precarious international position, as well as their sympathy for Britain, was intensifying. The poet and playwright Stephen Vincent Benét gave voice to these sentiments, answering fascist assertions that "Democracy is dead and finished" and fascism "is the wave of the future" with the declaration, "freedom . . . is new," "democracy . . . goes forward," indeed, "Democracy is the Revolution."[20]

Sympathies notwithstanding, Americans were reluctant to go to war. They were understandably fearful of the consequences, and yet they were equally mindful of the risks, both abroad and to the democratic accomplishments of the past seven years.

Democratic talk, both inspired and anxious, pervaded American culture and references abounded to the Founding Fathers—not just

Washington and Jefferson, but also the radical-democratic author of *Common Sense* and *The Crisis*, Thomas Paine—and to the Great Emancipator and wartime president, Abraham Lincoln. Finding audiences were new literary anthologies like *The Democratic Spirit* and *A Treasury of Democracy*; biographical collections such as *American Heretics and Saints* and *They Worked for a Better World*; and treatises such as *The Course of American Democratic Thought* and *The Prospects of American Democracy*. Edward Bernays, the "father of public relations," not only authored *Speak Up for Democracy: What You Can Do—A Practical Plan of Action for Every American Citizen*, but also persuaded organizations like the Boy Scouts, the YMCA, and the Elks to take up the project. And while colleges and civic groups held forums on the "Foundations of Democracy" and "Democracy and National Unity," schoolchildren studied *Democracy Readers*, celebrated "Democracy Days," and performed "Democracy" plays.[21]

From the launch of *PM*, the independent-left, New York daily newspaper that openly advanced an "anti-fascist, pro-labor, pro–New Deal outlook," to the release of Hollywood films like the populist director Frank Capra's *Mr. Smith Goes to Washington* (1939) and *Meet John Doe* (1941), advocates for both continuing the New Deal and preparing to meet the reactionary menace abroad rallied the public.[22]

"Intercultural" activists, led by the writer Louis Adamic, created the Common Council for American Unity to develop ideas of "cultural" or "ethnic" democracy; the National Conference of Christians and Jews (NCCJ) promoted the "Judaic-Christian ideal of brotherhood" through publications, classroom programs, and annual "Brotherhood Days"; and the American Jewish Committee and B'nai B'rith's Anti-Defamation League (ADL) championed "freedom and democracy for all." Similarly motivated, a cohort of renowned playwrights that included William Saroyan, Robert E. Sherwood, Stephen Vincent Benét, Orson Welles, and Archibald MacLeish formed the Free Company and proceeded to produce ten original radio dramas to "remind" Americans of the promise of the Bill of Rights. And remarkably, all three major Baptist Conventions—Southern, Northern, and National (African-American)—approved an "American Baptist Bill of Rights" in 1939 in which they declared: "Believing religious liberty to be not only an inalienable human right, but indispensable to human welfare, a Baptist must exercise himself to the utmost maintenance of absolute religious liberty for his Jewish neighbor, his Catholic neighbor, his Protestant neighbor, and for everybody else."[23]

These diverse initiatives expressed the widespread sense Americans had that they shared something special, something that overwhelmed their differences, something that, while rooted in the meaning of America, had been cultivated anew by their New Deal labors and struggles, something to be assured for future generations—liberty, equality, democracy.

Exclaiming that the "U.S. was singing, as it had not done in years, of pride in its past, of hope in the future," *Time* reported in July 1940 that 13,000 people turned out to Manhattan's Lewisohn Stadium to hear a concert dedicated to "Democracy" that, while celebrating America, shined a light on its continuing injustices as well. The New York Philharmonic debuted *Challenge 1940* by the Oklahoma-born composer Roy Harris; "white and Negro choirs and musicians" performed *And They Lynched Him on a Tree*, a cantata written by Katherine Garrison Chapin with music by the black composer William Grant Still; and Paul Robeson sang everyone's favorite, "Ballad for Americans." The magazine also reported that sales of Kate Smith's recording of "God Bless America" had leapt dramatically since the outbreak of war in Europe. And in that same spirit, the NCCJ organized an "I Am an American Day" at the New York World's Fair that October that was attended by more than 125,000 people—the grand climax of which was a two-and-a-half-hour pageant featuring the thousand-member chorus of the International Ladies' Garment Workers Union. Narrated by a figure dressed as Walt Whitman, the pageant presented critical moments from American history and a rousing performance of *I Hear America Singing*, a cantata based on Whitman's poems.[24]

In May 1940, prominent antifascists led by the Kansan William Allen White, the famed publisher-editor of the *Emporia Gazette*, founded the Committee to Defend America by Aiding the Allies. And that October, members of the Committee, joined by a host of progressive figures such as Louis Adamic, A. Philip Randolph, the *Nation* editor Freda Kirchwey, and the poet Carl Sandburg—as well as Eleanor Roosevelt—created the Council for Democracy (CFD). Sponsoring lectures, rallies, and two weekly radio programs, *Speaking of Liberty* and *Americans All,* the CFD, headed by the news commentator Raymond Gram Swing, criticized prejudice and promoted unity to combat fascist subversion. Though White's committee itself never exceeded ten thousand members, it increasingly reflected popular opinion. Tuning in to CBS radio to hear Edward R. Murrow's eyewitness reports—"This is London"—from the Blitz-besieged capital, Americans in growing numbers now backed aid to Britain.[25]

As Americans prepared themselves for the global defense of democracy and the ideals of the past eight years, forces were already in play that would be given full expression in FDR's Four Freedoms speech. More and more prominent and progressive voices such as the writers Archibald MacLeish, Max Lerner, Lewis Mumford, and Samuel Grafton came out for entering the war against fascism and for pursuing the struggle in an avowedly *radical-democratic* fashion. MacLeish, whom FDR named Librarian of Congress in 1939, insisted that the defense of democracy demanded renewed democratic initiatives: "For democracy is never a thing done. Democracy is always something that a nation must be doing . . . Democracy in action is a cause for which the stones themselves will fight."[26]

At the same time, figures very close to Roosevelt were now talking publicly about enhancing or augmenting the Bill of Rights along the lines he himself had begun to lay out in 1937. Solicitor General Robert H. Jackson, whom FDR would appoint Attorney General in 1940 and name to the Supreme Court the following year, told the National Lawyers Guild in 1938, "We too are founders . . . We too are makers of a nation . . . We too are called upon to write, to defend and to make live, new bills of right." Indeed, he said, the "economic bill of rights" that liberals were crafting would encompass "collective bargaining for labor . . . the ending of starvation wages and sweatshops, the right of the willing to work, the right to a living when work is not available, the right to some shelter from the cruelties of impoverished age."[27]

Dedicating the "Plaza of Four Freedoms" at the New York World's Fair on April 30, 1939, with the President and First Lady seated nearby, Mayor Fiorello La Guardia directed everyone's attention to the four towering statues arrayed around the pool at the plaza's center that were designed to symbolize the four freedoms of the First Amendment: Religion, Speech, Press, and Assembly. Saying he did not think Americans would ever want to live under a government that denied those freedoms, La Guardia bluntly stated that they "cannot be fully enjoyed without economic security," and then prophesied: "soon there will be a fifth . . . the right to live properly and decently and happily, and to give to your children a chance to enjoy the other four freedoms."[28]

And the political scientist Charles E. Merriam revealed, in a lecture at the University of Chicago in November 1940, that the administration was already working on the possibility of expanding the Bill of Rights. Serving as vice chair of the National Resources Planning Board (NRPB)—created by FDR to devise policies and programs that government might institute to rebuild the economy, address citizens' needs, and prevent another depression—Merriam explained that "we undertake what was declared but not done . . . when life, liberty, and the pursuit of happiness were set forth as the rights of man." And he predicted that the "modern bill of rights" would encompass "the right to a job, the right to economic security, the right to a fair share of the gains of the civilization in which one participates."[29]

But the administration's foremost advocate for extending and deepening Americans' fundamental freedoms was surely Mrs. Roosevelt. In her 1940 book, *The Moral Basis of Democracy*, she not only asked Americans to consider what democracy meant to them and what they were willing to do to sustain it. She also reminded them of the revolutionary origins of American democratic life, decried the fact that "We [still] have poverty which enslaves, and . . . prejudice which does the same," *and* spoke of what needed doing to better realize the nation's historic purpose and promise. Here, too—almost a year before FDR enunciated his Four Freedoms—she began to articulate the "Four

Equalities" that would soon become the hallmark of her speeches and writings in these years: "Equality before the law; Equality of education; Equality of opportunity to earn a living; Equality to express oneself and participate in government."[30]

The President, however, did not leave such talk to others. Campaigning in Cleveland, Ohio, just before Election Day 1940, he rejected fascist claims—if not also conservative, reactionary, and corporate hopes—that the democratic story had run its course: "We have seen a rebirth of American democracy in America" and "It is the destiny of this American generation to point the road to the future for all the world to see." He celebrated Americans' labors: "You provided work for free men and women . . . You used the powers of government to stop the depletion of the top soil . . . decline in farm prices . . . foreclosures of homes and farms. You wrote into law the right of working men and women to bargain collectively . . . You turned to the problems of youth and age . . . You made safe the banks . . . You advanced . . ." And he challenged his fellow citizens with a vision of what they might yet accomplish:

> I see an America where factory workers are not discarded after they reach their prime . . . I see an America whose rivers and valleys and lakes are protected as the rightful heritage of all the people. I see an America where small business really has a chance to flourish and grow . . . I see an America of great cultural and educational opportunity . . . An America where the wheels of trade and private industry continue to turn . . . where the legitimate profits of legitimate business are the fair reward of every businessman . . . An America where the workers are really free and . . . can take their proper place at the council table with the owners and managers of business . . . An America where those who have reached the evening of life shall live out their years in peace and security . . . I see an America devoted to our freedom—unified by tolerance and by religious faith—a people consecrated to peace, a people confident in strength because their body and their spirit are secure and unafraid.[31]

FDR won reelection to a third term. But his triumph was shadowed by the question of what was to be done. He had promised American mothers in the 1940 campaign that unless the country was attacked, he would not send "[their] boys . . . into any foreign wars." Moreover, he knew the country was not yet prepared for military action, physically or otherwise. And yet, action was imperative.[32]

Just days later, Stephen Vincent Benét addressed the American Academy of Arts and Letters on the task of writers in the face of the world crisis. Urging an appreciation of the "deep-rooted, inarticulate thing that democracy is in the lives and hearts of our people," he exhorted his colleagues to engage American memory and imagination: "We can call upon the great men, the great words of our own past . . . for in looking back . . . we can see at what a price, by what endurance and fortitude, the freedom we have inherited was bought." But, Benét explained: "We need new words also—and great ones—to match the present, to build for the future that must be . . ." Then, with a nod to Paine, he said: "I do not know by whom these words will be made. They will not be made by the summer soldier or the sunshine patriot. And yet, if we believe in freedom—if we believe in life itself—they must be made." Benét was not alone in thinking so.[33]

When the President delivered his 1941 Annual Message to Congress in January, one might have imagined that he or she heard Washington, Jefferson, and Lincoln in his words, for Roosevelt spoke directly to American historical memory and imagination. But he did not quote those "great men." And yet, articulating Americans' historic ideals and aspirations in words old *and* new—"Freedom of speech and expression . . . Freedom of worship . . . Freedom from want . . . Freedom from fear . . ."—he charged a generation with fresh purpose and promise. That day, through those words, FDR gave voice to the widely held presumption, the boon of the lived experience of the New Deal, that the American experiment was unfinished, its ideals expressed in action not remembrance, that venerating the country's past demanded rededication to the Founding spirit of expansive, restless, at times exuberant, democracy.

Not everyone would call the Four Freedoms "revolutionary," as the economist Eliot Janeway did, or proclaim that "the people of the United States through their President have given the world a new Magna Carta of democracy," as William Allen White did. But most Americans took them seriously, if not for the world, at least for the United States. Not only would they commit themselves to the nation's defense, soon to become officially the war effort. They also accelerated their pursuit of the vision FDR had projected. They did so not because it was FDR's vision, but because it accorded with their own vision of country and themselves.[34]

While they still did not want the country militarily engaged (as the historian Robert A. Divine has noted: "rarely do people respond positively to a simple query about entering a major conflict"), the great majority not only backed Lend-Lease even at the risk of war, but believed the United States would soon "get into the war." More critically, an October 1940 Gallup poll of "young men and boys" had shown that 76 percent of them were ready to serve if called. And most critically, by October 1941, 67 percent of all Americans would say they were "ready to risk war with Japan rather than allow her to become more powerful," and more than 70 percent that "it is more important to defeat Hitler than to stay out of the war."[35]

That spring and summer the President spoke often of the Four Freedoms. He also called on the words of Washington and Paine, though tellingly, he now made Lincoln, "the war president," his primary presidential reference. And to the outrage of isolationists, he severely tested the limits of a president's war-making powers by steadily positioning the nation for more than defense.[36]

In March, Roosevelt secured further increases in military spending and signed the Lend-Lease Act. In April, he extended America's "security zone" into the mid-Atlantic. In May, he declared an "unlimited national emergency." In July, he ordered the occupation of Iceland and cut off oil exports to Japan. And in August, he secured renewal of the Selective Service Act and met with British Prime Minister Winston Churchill off the Newfoundland coast to both develop a war strategy and issue the Atlantic Charter.[37]

The Atlantic Charter signed by FDR and Churchill did more than move the United States much closer into a formal alliance with Great Britain. It also made the pursuit of the Four Freedoms and a democratic world order central to that developing alliance—which represented a significant diplomatic victory for Roosevelt because Churchill, a Conservative, was ever determined to hold on to the British Empire. The Charter directly challenged that assumption. In fact, the Charter committed the two nations both to assuring "the right of all peoples to choose the form of government under which they will live" and to seeking "for all, improved labor standards, economic advancement and social security." As the historian Elizabeth Borgwardt has put it, the Charter projected nothing less than "a New Deal for the world."[38]

Meanwhile, the President also took steps to both defend and promote democratic life at home. Responding to the rising inflation generated by the military buildup, he created the Office of Price Administration (OPA) in April 1941 under the direction of the liberal economist and veteran New Dealer Leon Henderson. Though assigned the job of supervising and regulating prices, Henderson had no enforcement authority. However, corporate bosses knew that if they failed to comply with OPA-ordered price controls they might not only look bad in the eyes of the public, but also lose out on military contracts. Moreover, hoping to enhance the power and influence of the OPA, Roosevelt and Henderson set out to secure popular backing for its efforts by setting up a Consumer Division with consumer activist Harriet Elliott as its head. And Elliott quickly reached out to consumer organizations in favor of initiating grassroots activities that would come to include offering consumer-education programs, staffing "consumer information centers," and "watching prices" at local stores. While the OPA had little immediate success in controlling inflation, its Consumer Division garnered the active support of both the consumer and labor movements and laid the foundations for more authoritative interventions and grander grassroots mobilizations to come.[39]

Roosevelt next set up the Office of Civilian Defense (OCD) under the direction of Fiorello La Guardia and assigned it responsibility not only for "Planning and implementing programs . . . to protect civilian life and property in the event of an emergency," but also for "Promoting activities designed to sustain the national morale and creating activities and opportunities for constructive civilian participation in the defense program." Plus, to assure the latter, as well as cultivate the vision of the Four Freedoms through popular initiatives, he created the Civilian War Services Division (CWS) within the OCD and named the First Lady herself to head it.[40]

Propitiously, the American Junior League of America (AJLA) had contacted Mrs. Roosevelt immediately after FDR delivered the 1941 Annual Message, to propose the creation of a "national network of Volunteer Bureaus" and, with its aid, along with that of hundreds of other civic, religious, labor, fraternal, and youth groups, the CWS established Bureaus all around the United States, carried out a nationwide survey of community needs and services, and enlisted the labors of nearly 5 million people to serve in shorthanded community agencies. At the same time, the CWS spurred local institutions not only to reinvigorate their efforts in providing traditional social services, but also to organize new programs, including courses on everything from nutrition and physical fitness to civil liberties. Americans in their millions responded to the nationwide call to participate. The OCD itself recruited 6 million volunteers specifically for civil defense work.[41]

La Guardia himself suggested that to enhance popular morale and unity Americans should commemorate the upcoming 150th anniversary of the Bill of Rights. Relishing the idea, FDR quickly garnered the endorsements of numerous organizations and state and city governments. With congressional approval, December 15, 1941 was proclaimed "Bill of Rights Day." And in both speeches and writings—as well as in *We Hold These Truths*, a radio play produced by Norman Corwin that was heard by 60 million Americans—many a liberal public figure and union leader drew a direct line from the four freedoms of the First Amendment to FDR's Four Freedoms.[42]

In May 1941, the administration also launched its campaign to sell Defense Bonds and Stamps (soon to be renamed "War Bonds and Stamps"). Recruiting labor unions, farmers' groups, civic organizations, and women's, youth, and ethnic-heritage associations to help sell them, the Treasury Department made the bonds and stamps not only widely available for purchase (including via payroll savings plans), but also readily affordable by working people. Additionally, it created school programs to encourage saving and good citizenship; sponsored the *Treasury Star Parade*, a weekly radio show emphasizing the need to make sacrifices in defense of democracy and unite against America's fascist enemies; and staged several star-studded national "Bond Drives" in the course of the war years. All told, 85 million people would eventually purchase nearly $186 billion worth of the bonds and stamps.[43]

However, the imperative to prepare for war set limits to what Roosevelt could do in favor of democratic activism. New Dealer and close associate Harry Hopkins would say of him: "You can see the real Roosevelt when he comes out with something like the Four Freedoms. And don't get the idea that those are any catch phrases. *He believes them!* He believes they can be practically attained." So, too, did most Americans. However, circumstances would compel the President to make compromises to assure the cooperation of industrialists, the votes of southern congressional Democrats, and the unflagging loyalty of the nation's military elite.[44]

Often more anti–New Deal and antiunion than antifascist, corporate executives in key sectors such as automobiles and aviation were hesitant to convert from civilian to military production. And fearing that the defense effort would subject them all the more to government controls and the demands of labor, they staged what the journalist I. F. Stone cleverly termed a "capital sitdown strike"—which was surely one of the things FDR had in mind when he warned of those who "would clip the wings of the American eagle in order to feather their own nests." With Secretary of War Stimson's words—"If you are going to try to go to war, or to prepare for war, in a capitalist country, you have got to let business make money out of the process or business won't work"—echoing in his ear, the President moved to engage the "economic royalists" rather than further antagonize them. He never gave them full control, but to offset their antipathies and anxieties he basically handed over the industrial mobilization to men of their class. Moreover, he not only gave in to their demands for tax breaks to underwrite the new plants and equipment that were urgently needed to meet the nation's immediate military needs. He also allowed major defense contracts to go to companies, such as Ford and Bethlehem Steel, that were still refusing to recognize their workers' unions.[45]

Roosevelt deferred to racists as well. Responding to organized African-American pressure during the 1940 election campaign, he had directed the military to enlist blacks in proportion to their numbers in the country's total population, increase the abysmally small number of black army officers, and create a flight school for blacks at Alabama's Tuskegee Institute that would train the pilots of the 99th Pursuit Squadron, the renowned "Tuskegee Airmen." However, the power of southern congressmen, as well as the opposition of the country's military leaders (including Secretary of War Stimson), discouraged FDR from immediately doing more. Southern Democrats favored military preparedness, but not at the expense of white supremacy and the separation of the races. Bowing to Jim Crow, the President sanctioned the segregation of the armed forces in the autumn of 1940 and effectively licensed the Navy and Marines to continue to exclude African Americans, other than as messmen, and the Army to continue to assign them to all-black noncombat "service companies."[46]

Diverse Americans, however, would not wait for the President to elaborate upon the Four Freedoms. To rally "those forces who believe that the struggle for democracy at home and the fight against the foreign foes of democracy is one struggle on two fronts," progressive (but anti-Communist) intellectuals led by James Loeb and Reinhold Niebuhr—with the endorsements of labor leaders such as A. Philip Randolph and Walter Reuther—created the Union for Democratic Action (UDA) in April 1941. UDA chapters formed around the country, members staged public "gatherings" outside the halls where isolationists met, and that fall a "School for Democratic Action" opened in New York.[47]

The CIO and AFL alike firmly backed a strong defense and the social-democratic vision of the Four Freedoms, but the CIO's leaders were also eager to extend and deepen "industrial democracy," and with that objective in mind they proposed plans for labor's direct participation in guiding the mobilization. Philip Murray, the new president of the labor congress, called for creating "industrial councils" that would reorganize America's defense industries so as to make labor an equal partner with business and government in coordinating production and give workers a real voice in the production process. And Walter Reuther, the head of the United Auto Workers' General Motors Department and a major UAW Detroit local, issued a plan to rapidly convert automobile plants into military aircraft factories that he projected would enable the country to produce a phenomenal "500 planes a day" if labor was treated as an equal in the project.[48]

FDR's Four Freedoms speech also led the labor movement to undertake direct democratic action—and 1941 would witness 4,300 strikes involving 2.4 million workers and see union membership increase by 1.5 million. Strengthened by industry's growing demand for labor, the UAW and the United Steelworkers of America (USWA)—as FDR had hoped—won major victories, starting at Ford and Bethlehem Steel. Moreover, workers secured wage increases both at the newly organized firms and at previously unionized ones such as General Motors, U.S. Steel, and General Electric.[49]

Labor's renewed aggressiveness led FDR to set up the National Defense Mediation Board (NDMB) in March 1941, but in some instances neither the National Labor Relations Board nor the new NDMB could secure industrial peace. A walkout for higher wages by a Communist-led UAW local at North American Aviation in Southern California severely curtailed production of fighter aircraft and compelled the President—under intense pressure from corporate bosses, Congress, and the Secretary of War—to order armed troops to occupy the plant in June 1941.[50]

While African Americans had plenty of reason to be cynical about the talk of defending democracy, most had no intention of remaining marginal to the struggle, even if they first had to "fight for the right to fight." Nine days after hearing FDR proclaim the Four Freedoms, A. Philip Randolph called for African Americans to march on Washington to "fight for jobs in National Defense . . . struggle for the integration of . . . the armed forces . . . [and] demonstrate for the abolition of Jim Crowism in all Government departments and defense employment." Scheduling the event for July 1 and talking publicly of a turn-out of 10,000 (with hopes of far more), Randolph set up the March on Washington Movement (MOWM). Aided by the Brotherhood of Sleeping Car Porters, he secured the support of nearly every major national black organization and innumerable local black churches and civic groups. Soon thirty-six chapters were established around the country and huge rallies were held in New York, Chicago, and St. Louis—leading the Chicago *Defender* to predict the march would be "the greatest crusade for democracy ever staged by America's black minority."[51]

In Washington anxiety was rising. Worried about the hostile reaction of southern congressmen and the military, and even more so about the likelihood of violence, the President sent the First Lady, a friend of Randolph's, to try to dissuade him and his allies from proceeding with their plans. She failed.

FDR then invited Randolph, along with Walter White of the NAACP, to meet with him at the White House on June 18.

At the meeting Randolph and White no longer insisted upon the integration of the military, realizing such a request would be futile at this time. But they continued to demand an executive order banning discrimination in defense industries and vocational training programs. Urging them to cancel the march, Roosevelt tried to assuage them with personal promises. But they would not be moved. Asking Randolph exactly how many marchers he anticipated, Randolph replied, "One hundred thousand," which White immediately affirmed. And seeing no alternative, FDR responded—in perhaps the classic instance of "you've persuaded me, now make me do it"—by proceeding to issue the desired executive order and establish the Fair Employment Practice Committee (FEPC) to oversee compliance with it. In return for which, Randolph, though he would not disband the movement, called off the march.[52]

MOWM was a "Negroes-only" initiative. But other, related efforts were not. In July 1941, southern progressives black and white, supported by both labor federations and several national civic groups, organized the National Council to Abolish the Poll Tax to try to secure the vote for the 11 million southerners disfranchised by the tax (60 percent of whom were white). And that fall the federal government launched a weekly radio show, *Freedom's People*, which highlighted African-American contributions to the nation's advancement past and present. Featuring guest artists such as Paul Robeson and Josh White, the show's producers made their message brilliantly clear by closing every episode with: "Onward they march—13 million Negro citizens of the United States, sharing the labor, accepting the responsibilities of our Democracy. Knowing the weight of chains—the helplessness of bondage—they are today a mighty force for freedom. To them liberty is a precious thing. For—truly—they are Freedom's People."[53]

A generation of Americans had struggled against extraordinary odds and opposition to not only right the country's economic ship, but also do so while expanding democracy, liberty, and equality on every front. Their labors were history making and transformative, but it now seemed as though they had been just preparatory, and in every sense they remained incomplete. The challenges ahead—made clear by the constant media reminders of the European war—were tremendous. And yet Americans did not turn away. Indeed, younger cohorts were coming up alongside older—young men and women who would soon not only shoulder the burdens of war most directly and intimately, but also expand their elders' accomplishments in ways unforeseen nine years earlier. New Deal Americans of every age recognized that their rendezvous with destiny had come.

On December 4, 1941, the *Chicago Sun* made its first appearance on the streets of the Windy City. Intended by its owner Marshall Field III to provide a liberal alternative to the reactionary and isolationist *Chicago Tribune*, the new *Sun* firmly declared itself committed to "the Four Freedoms of President Roosevelt and all the other freedoms vouchsafed to American citizens by the Constitution and the Bill of Rights." And just a few days later it and every other newspaper in the country would bear banner headlines declaring that on Sunday, December 7, Japanese planes had attacked Pearl Harbor and killed 2,500 Americans.[54]

CHAPTER SIX

"How can Hitler win against men such as these!"

The Nazi Propaganda Minister Joseph Goebbels had said, "Nothing will be easier than to produce a bloody revolution in North America. No other country has so many social and racial tensions . . . We shall be able to play on many strings there." But contrary to Nazi expectations, while those tensions would flare in nasty and even murderous ways, Americans did not fall apart.[1]

On the day after the December 7 attack on Pearl Harbor, Americans turned up en masse at recruitment centers, and by war's end 16,000,000 in all—one of every eight Americans, not only men, but also 350,000 women, indeed, young Americans of every class, race, and ethnicity—were to answer the call to military service.

At the same time, the civilian labor force, which had already grown by 5 million since 1939, grew by another 5 million to a 1943 wartime peak of 55 million, with women comprising upwards of one-third of the total number (inspiring Redd Evans and John Jacob Loeb's popular song, "Rosie the Riveter"). All the more determined to turn the United States into the Arsenal of Democracy, American workers would create nothing less than a production miracle and send the Total National Income soaring from $97 billion in 1941 to $161 billion in 1945. Massively outproducing their enemies and heavily supplying their allies, they manufactured 5,800 merchant ships, 1,600 naval vessels, 80,000 landing vessels, 300,000 aircraft, 635,000 jeeps, 100,000 tanks and armored cars, 2.4 million trucks, 15 million guns, and 40 billion bullets. And though the number of farmworkers decreased as folks headed off to industry and the military, food production increased by 32 percent.[2]

Moreover, millions of Americans bolstered the war effort and strengthened American civil society by contributing their energies on the Home Front. The new United Services Organization or "USO"—created jointly by the Young Men's Christian Association, Young Women's Christian Association, National Catholic Community Services, National Travelers Aid Association, National Jewish Welfare Board, and the Salvation Army—signed up 1.5 million volunteers to entertain the troops and provide them with a "home away from home." The Office of Civilian Defense doubled its volunteer rolls to 12 million by 1943 and that same summer Americans provided one-third of the vegetables consumed in the United States by planting 20 million "Victory Gardens." Even in the final year of the war, 7.5 million people would volunteer for the Red Cross.[3]

Samuel Hynes, who served as a Marine Corps pilot in the Pacific, would look back and write that the "Second World War . . . was our most democratic war . . . Every American family was involved in some way—a son or father in uniform, a daughter in a munitions factory, a wife building ships." Or as Ernest Montoya, a combat veteran of the 32nd Infantry Division, recalled: "Everybody had somebody in it." And so it was. Even the Roosevelts' sons were serving.[4]

Americans naturally worried about what they had gotten into, especially at the outset, when they suffered terrible setbacks and losses on every front. But the great majority remained resolute. In September 1942, the director of Princeton University's Office of Public Opinion Research (OPOR), Hadley Cantril, found America "remarkably unified," and, noting the high level of popular support for the idea of national service in industry, he said the public was "ahead of Congress [and the Administration] in its willingness to sacrifice to beat the Axis." A year later, after traveling the entire country recruiting field staff for OPOR, the pollster Selden Menefee would report in the critically acclaimed book *Assignment: U.S.A.* that despite fractures of class, race, ethnicity, and religion, Americans were "fighting this war wholeheartedly—with less flag-waving and fanfare than we had in World War I, but with more unanimity and a clearer sense of purpose." As Senator Daniel Inouye of Hawaii, a Congressional Medal of Honor recipient who served in the all-Japanese-American 442 Regimental Combat Team and lost his right arm in the conflict, recalled years later: "We stood as one. We spoke as one. We clenched our fists as one."[5]

With the United States now directly engaged in the conflict, Roosevelt created a host of new agencies to oversee and coordinate the war effort, including the War Production Board (WPB), the War Manpower Commission (WMC), the Office of War Information (OWI), and the Office of Economic Stabilization (OES). And while he essentially left corporate executives in charge of production, he took steps not only to defend labor against its congressional and business enemies, but also to enable unions to continue to grow and improve working people's material lives.

The AFL and the CIO had each issued a "No Strike Pledge" in the wake of Pearl Harbor. Nevertheless, FDR knew he, too, had to act to sustain industrial peace and to tame capital. Scrapping the NDMB, he established the National War Labor Board (NWLB) in January 1942 and accorded equal representation at all levels of its operations to business and labor. Assigned responsibility for settling war-industry disputes and setting war-industry wages, the NWLB not only announced the "Little Steel Formula," which granted labor a 15 percent cost-of-living increase to cover the rate of inflation since January 1941 and effectively set a pattern for all industries. It also announced a "Maintenance of Membership" policy whereby unions that honored the "No Strike Pledge" would automatically enroll new workers as members for the duration of their existing contracts, unless those workers themselves opted out in their first two weeks on the job. And propelled by the Maintenance of Membership rules in the war industries and organizing campaigns elsewhere, unions would expand their ranks during the war from 10 million to 15 million—with women's memberships increasing from 800,000 to 3 million.[6]

In the course of 1942, Roosevelt also secured enactment of legislation strengthening the Office of Price Administration's authority to ration essential items such as fuels and foodstuffs *and* fix rents and prices. Inflation would persist, but less severely than it would have otherwise. And as much as corporate profits would increase during the war, class inequalities would actually decrease due to the administration's taxation and wage-and-price-control policies as well as to the concerted efforts of the expanding labor and consumer movements. While the top fifth of family incomes would grow by 20 percent, those below them grew even faster, the bottom two-fifths by more than 60 percent. As the labor historian Nelson Lichtenstein has noted: "Working people ate better and worried less . . . infant mortality declined by more than one-third . . . [and] life expectancy surged ahead by three years for whites and by five for African Americans."[7]

FDR did not ignore African Americans, either. They themselves made sure of that. As Eubie Blake sang, "We Are Americans Too." In early 1942 the *Pittsburgh Courier* launched a national "Double V" campaign, declaring "The first V for victory over our enemies from without, the second V for victory over our enemies from within. For surely those who perpetrate these ugly prejudices here are seeking to destroy our democratic form of government just as surely as the Axis forces." That same year, young black activists in Chicago organized the nonviolent but direct-action Congress of Racial Equality (CORE); fifty-eight traditionally "conservative" southern black ministers and educators issued the "Durham Manifesto," calling for "an end to the poll tax, the white primary, police brutality, voter intimidation, and exclusion from juries and unions"; and NAACP membership soared, soon to rise from 50,000 to 450,000.[8]

The President had little, if any, chance of addressing racial injustices legislatively given the South's power in Congress. But it didn't stop him from occasionally trying—or from finding other means of doing so. While the Fair Employment Practice Committee investigated discrimination in the war industries, the new Civil Rights Section of the Department of Justice redeemed the Civil Rights Act of 1866 and started to investigate and prosecute cases of lynching, police brutality, and coerced agricultural labor. And in 1942, FDR himself actively backed liberal efforts in Congress, first, to abolish state poll taxes and, then, to pass a "Soldier Vote" bill that would not only assure military men and women absentee ballots, but also exempt southern GIs from their respective states' poll taxes. The former passed in the House by a 254–84 vote, but was killed by a southern filibuster in the Senate. The latter actually passed in both the House and the Senate, but not until southern representatives had made sure the ballots were state-administered, which effectively undermined the process and limited the vote. African Americans were rightly disappointed, but that the contest was occurring at all inspired hope.[9]

Determined to win "not just the war but also the peace to come," liberals and progressives in and out of the Roosevelt administration remained anxious about their fellow citizens' commitments and determination. Speaking at the University of Virginia in late 1942, Attorney General Francis Biddle posed the question that seemed to haunt the liberal imagination: "Do the people of our land fight only to win the war—or to use the war for great and democratic ends?"[10]

War may have transcended the nation's political and social divisions, but it did not erase them. Following the lead of Eric Johnston, the president of the U.S. Chamber of Commerce, some executives did accommodate themselves to the New Deal and organized labor, though by no means unreservedly so. Most industrialists, however, remained adamantly hostile to the progressive developments of the 1930s and utterly scornful of the Four Freedoms. Thomas J. Wallner, the head of the Southern States Industrial Council, "warned" in September 1942: "America is losing the war for one fundamental reason and only one; our government—meaning primarily the President of the United States—still stubbornly persists in the attempt simultaneously to fight a foreign war and wage an internal economic revolution—and wars are not, never were and never can be won that way." And W. P. Witherow, the president of the National Association of Manufacturers, drew a distinction before his corporate associates that would echo down through the decades: "I am not making guns or tanks to win a people's revolution . . . I am making armaments to help our boys save America."[11]

It wasn't just that corporate America did not want the status quo; they actively sought the status quo *ante* the New Deal. In the months and years to come, they would block a truly democratic mobilization, campaign to limit the powers of labor and the rights of working people, and oppose price regulation and controls. And their efforts were to gain all the more traction in the wake of the 1942 midterm elections, when low voter turnout on the part of millions of working people—who were heading into service or moving around the country to take up defense jobs—gave Republicans forty-seven new House seats and ten new Senate seats.

While the President's party would retain nominal control of Congress, the conservative congressional coalition increased decisively. On the first day of the new 78th Congress, Representative Charles Gifford of Massachusetts, a leading Republican, called on his colleagues to "win the war from the New Deal," and Representative Eugene Cox, a Georgia Democrat, declared, "Government by bureaucrats must be broken, and broken now." Max Lerner would write: "There is an Unholy Alliance in Congress between the Republicans and the Tory Democrats. That alliance ramifies further into the press, the big advertising and publicity organizations, and the corporate 'peak associations' like the NAM. It reaches into the reactionary wing of the Administration itself . . . The object was to smash FDR and the New Deal."[12]

Nor did racial hostilities abate. With southern whites and blacks migrating north and west to industrial centers, and northern whites and blacks heading south to military bases, racial antagonisms not only intensified in places, but also at times threatened to weaken, if not disrupt, the war effort. This was especially the case when whites staged "hate strikes" against the entry of blacks into long-segregated workplaces and even more so when "race riots" broke out in cities around the country in the summer of 1943—the worst of them in Los Angeles, where ugly press reports incited sailors and marines to beat up young Latino and black "zoot suiters"; in Mobile, where white shipyard workers brutally assaulted black co-workers when management followed the FEPC's orders and promoted several of the latter to skilled jobs; and in Detroit, where, on a terribly hot night in late June, the incessant racist rants of Klansmen and pro-fascists finally succeeded in provoking whites to attack their black fellow citizens, leaving twenty-five blacks and nine whites dead.[13]

Anti-Semitism persisted as well. But even more tragically, Roosevelt himself once again bowed to military advisors when, in February 1942, he ordered the "relocation" of 120,000 Japanese Americans to internment camps in the nation's interior. It was an act that Max Lerner called "the most glaring instance of military injustice to civilian Americans in our nation's history."[14]

Further disconcerting liberals, polls suggested that Americans were not speaking of the war in the idealistic terms expected and that many could not readily explain the country's war aims. And ensuing studies revealed that significant numbers of them could neither precisely name the Four Freedoms nor even clearly identify the Bill of Rights. In May 1942, Archibald MacLeish, now director of the Office of Facts and Figures (a forerunner of the soon-to-be-created Office of War Information), observed that although Americans apparently "know very well *why* [we] are fighting" and "what we are fighting *against*," they do not yet know "what we are fighting *for*."[15]

While liberals and progressives were right to worry about both conservative and corporate ambitions and the state of the nation's race and ethnic relations, they underestimated the majority of their fellow citizens' democratic commitments and determination.

To be sure, Americans had cause to be confused about their country's war aims. Declaredly fighting for democracy, they were allied with not only the greatest colonial power in modern history, Great Britain, but also one of the modern world's most brutal regimes, Stalin's Russia. And most people could not help but see that congressional Republicans and southern Democrats seemed as eager to make war on the New Deal and Four Freedoms as to beat the nation's enemies abroad.

Moreover, while many an official and critic worried about the relative absence of flag-waving and song-singing, they were failing to recall how the last war had made most Americans circumspect when speaking of what they now hoped to achieve. As Lieutenant John Mason Brown of the U.S. Navy wrote while serving aboard a troop transport in the Atlantic: "We were not fooled and did not fool ourselves. We were not romantics filled with cape-and-sword twaddle. The last war was too near for that." [16]

That Americans were not expressing themselves as brashly or idealistically as had their 1917 counterparts did not mean, however, that they didn't know what was at stake. Lieutenant Brown put it in the most intimate of terms: "We knew the horrors of war, all right . . . Yet we were prepared to make all sacrifices. There was nothing else for us to do. The leaving of our families was part of our loving them." [17]

As Max Lerner noted, Americans "entered the war despite an isolationist tradition and despite all the powers and principalities of reaction which tried to keep them out. They accepted conscription very early in the struggle, and with it they accepted the democratic principle in the military services." In sum, "Our young men went to fight on foreign soil, because that was the only way to preserve their country and their values." [18]

Most Americans had a pretty good idea of what they were fighting for: to defend the country and the people they loved, to destroy the nation's enemies, and to secure American democratic life and the possibilities it afforded for themselves and generations to come. In a May 1942 survey asking people to choose an alternate name for the "Second World War" from a list of ten possibilities, 64 percent selected choices—War of World Freedom (26 percent), War of Freedom (14 percent), War of Liberty (13 percent), Anti-Dictator War (11 percent)—emphasizing freedom and democracy. [19]

More critically, the OPOR associate director Jerome Bruner would write in 1944: "What are we fighting for? People answer readily that we are fighting for freedom, liberty, and democracy. They say it with the sincerity of people who believe it." And yet, he added: "They have lived with the words so long they can't define them any more. They feel them now as they have always felt them before—in the fringe of consciousness. The words are no longer revolutionary. They stand for the things we have had and want to keep." Others put it more personally. As one young bride wrote in a letter to *Good Housekeeping*, not long after her husband's entry into military service in the spring of 1942: "Both Danny and I feel that the democratic way of life is deeply a part of us. We want to defend it with all we have, with our heart and soul. We're young. We've got a future to fight for, we wouldn't want to raise those babies we're going to have in a country that wasn't worth fighting for."[20]

Indeed, the millions of young Americans who went off to fight the Axis knew very well what they were fighting for. For a start, they truly believed that the United States was "the best country in the world." The crash of 1929 and the depression that followed haunted their thoughts, but more compelling than those images were the progressive possibilities that Americans created in the course of pursuing the work of recovery, reconstruction, and reform. And what they encountered overseas—the filth, disease, and backwardness, the tyranny and class-ridden social orders, the living conditions of workers and peasants, and most horrifically the death camps of the German Reich and brutal fanaticism of the Japanese military—would further convince them of how exceptional their country was. Assigned the job of ship's "censor"—which entailed reading the letters written by men on board to make sure they had not divulged "military secrets"—Lieutenant Brown concluded that his comrades' "recollections of what they have had, and their dreams of what they will have again . . . must be listed among the ship's stoutest weapons."[21]

Still, generals and admirals, however much they differed from liberals and progressives, shared their anxiety about Americans' commitments and determination. And to educate the new recruits to what they were up against, the military set up "orientation" programs—for which Frank Capra produced the film series *Why We Fight*, the first part of which, *Prelude to War*, contrasted the regimentation, militarism, and barbarism of the nation's enemies with American democratic life and the New Deal response to the Depression (and won the 1942 Academy Award for Best Documentary).[22]

While the orientation courses inevitably reflected Jim Crow's hold on the military, they also reflected how much had changed in the course of the 1930s—to the apparent chagrin of many a "regular officer." In contrast to the conservative 1927 *Manual of Citizenship Training*, the texts now used, such as *The Democratic Tradition in America*, praised immigrants' contributions to American life, celebrated the nation's diversity, and told of the country's continuing drive to extend and deepen freedom, equality, and democracy. The head of the Army's Morale Services Division even issued a "directive" declaring: "Let our soldiers have a deep and abiding faith in Democracy . . . Our goal is an ever-expanding Democracy—to the end that ALL of our citizens will be assured the abundant life which is expressed and promised in the Four Freedoms."[23]

In that same spirit, the Chaplain Corps stopped preaching an exclusively "Christian tradition" and began to promote a shared "Judeo-Christian heritage." It was a heritage heroically symbolized by the sacrifices of George Lansing Fox (Methodist), Alex Goode (Jewish), Clark Poling (Dutch Reformed), and John Washington (Catholic), four chaplains who, after doing everything they could to save the lives of others, including giving up their own life jackets, went to their deaths "arm in arm, joined in prayer" on board the USAT *Dorchester* when it was torpedoed and sunk off the Greenland coast on the night of February 3, 1943.[24]

Contrary to assertions then and now, however, servicemen's silence regarding "why we fight"—as well as their disdain for patriotic hoopla and idealistic rhetoric—signified neither disinterest in nor a lack of commitment to the nation's cause. Admittedly, U.S. Army Research Branch studies found that GIs were no better at naming the Four Freedoms than their civilian counterparts. But they also found out other things. They learned that the overwhelming majority of the men believed "it was of great importance to them to understand why the war was being fought." And they found out that "Whenever and wherever questions [on ideological orientation] were asked, majorities in the neighborhood of 90 per cent said they felt the United States was fighting for things they personally felt were worth fighting for."[25]

An August 1942 survey of nearly 6,000 white enlisted men found that 65 percent of them actually endorsed the statement "We are in the war to fight until we can guarantee democratic liberties to all peoples of the world." A March 1943 survey asking 7,800 enlisted men—4,800 whites and 3,000 blacks—to respond "yes" or "no" to the statements "The United States is fighting for the protection of the right of free speech for everyone" and "The United States is fighting for a fair chance for everyone to make a decent living" found 89 percent of the whites saying "Yes" to both, and 66 and 70 percent of blacks, respectively, saying the same. Moreover, later studies addressing the views of airborne combat veterans found the majority of men responding to the question "Why did you fight?" in decidedly idealistic terms.[26]

Of course, Americans also fought because they hated their enemies—the "Krauts" and the "Japs." And they fought because they did not want to fail their units and buddies. But they also fought because they were *Americans*, which they believed meant something special, something democratic. They didn't talk about it much. Such talk was taboo. The photographer Margaret Bourke-White wrote on her return from the front lines in Italy that in contrast to their Russian, British, and Chinese allies, GIs don't philosophize, they "organize"— which was to say that they carried the democratic spirit with them. According to the war correspondent Ernie Pyle, the GIs' favorite, they expressed it in their very carriage: "Our boys sing in the streets, unbutton their shirt collars, laugh and shout and forget to salute." One Czech villager summarized it perfectly: "[You Americans] walk like free men."[27]

American soldiers, sailors, and airmen were by no means saints. Like the society from which they came, their ranks contained racists and anti-Semites aplenty. But, ironically enough, the military and the war were "teaching" many of them to question such attitudes. While the armed forces segregated African and Japanese Americans, they brought together every other kind of American. The mix of Eighth Air Force "bomber boys" who flew the B-17 piloted by John Brady and John Hoerr and navigated by Harry Crosby was not unusual: "The engineer, Adolf Blum, was a farmer from upstate New York who spoke with a heavy German accent. The ball turret gunner, Roland Gangwer, was Polish Catholic. One of the waist gunners, Harold Clanton, was part American Indian, the other . . . George Petrohelos, was a Greek from Chicago. The radio operator, Saul Levitt, was a Jew from New York City . . ."[28]

Did such mixing mean anything? Private Stanley Silverman of New York thought so. Wounded in North Africa and awarded a Distinguished Service Cross for "courageous and inspiring actions," Silverman wrote home not of medals, but of something bigger: "We were attacking a German machine gun nest . . . when I was hit with a hand grenade. While I was lying there, unable to move, Sullivan ran through enemy fire and dragged me a quarter of a mile to the medical officer, helped by another buddy, Tony Ferrara, himself suffering badly from shock. How do you like that? A Jew gets hit and an Irishman and Italian save his life. Is there racial prejudice in the Army? Not at the front there isn't!"[29]

A similar leveling was evident during those rare instances when African Americans fought alongside white Americans. It happened in 1943 when the Tuskegee Airmen "Red Tails" of the 332nd Fighter Group flew escort for the "bomber boys" based in Italy; in November 1944 when the 761st Tank Battalion, the "Black Panthers," went into battle in France with the white 26th Infantry Division; and in the winter of 1944–45 when the Army, in desperate need of additional front-line troops, sent 2,500 volunteer black GIs to fight directly alongside white GIs in the Battle of the Bulge—not to mention that officer-candidate schools had been integrated in 1940 and a few of their white graduates actually took it upon themselves to overturn Jim Crow, as Commander Herschel Goldberg of the Navy did when in 1943 he unilaterally ordered the desegregation of the mess hall and barracks at Camp Ducos on New Caledonia.[30]

In late 1944, the *Harper's* editor Frederick Lewis Allen would reflect that Americans had become not simply a "united people," but also one possessed of a "faith which—with the aid of bulldozers—was able to move mountains." And surely the greatest testament to that faith is that those who most suffered the nation's inequalities and injustices went "All Out!" as much as their fellow citizens, if not even more so.[31]

Determined to secure America's promise against both America's foreign enemies and its own racists and reactionaries, minorities served in greater numbers. While American Jews made up only 3 percent of the population, 550,000 joined the army, composing more than 4 percent of Americans in uniform. And Jews were hardly alone in this respect. Latino Americans and Native Americans were overrepresented in the U.S. Army, with 450,000 and 44,500 serving, respectively. And while limited by official quota, a million African Americans served. Even 22,500 Japanese Americans served, despite the fact that many of their own families were interned in camps.[32]

Jewish servicemen had little doubt about what they were doing. In a 1943 survey asking Jewish GIs, "What are you fighting for in this war?" the most frequent replies were: "the Four Freedoms, the Atlantic Charter, the Bill of Rights . . . and making the world safe . . . to raise [our] families." Years later, Robert Rosenthal, who had enlisted in the Air Corps on the morning after Pearl Harbor and went on to fly B-17s in the Eighth Air Force, would recollect: "I'm a Jew, but it wasn't just that. Hitler was a menace to decent people everywhere . . . When I finally arrived [in England], I thought I was at the center of the world, the place where democracies were gathering to defeat the Nazis." Of course, Jews served in the Pacific, too, and no less valiantly.[33]

For many minority GIs the war represented a chance to assert their Americanness by defending the nation and all that it stood for. Fully integrated in the military, "Mexicans" actually became "Mexican Americans" in the course of the struggle. Raul Morin, who fought with the 79th Infantry in Europe, recalled: "Most of us were more than glad to be given the opportunity to serve . . . We knew there was something great about this country worth fighting for. We felt that this was an opportunity to show the rest of the nation that we *too* were also ready, willing, and able to fight for our nation. It did not matter whether we were looked upon as Mexicans, Mexican-American, or belonging to a minority group; the war soon made us all *genuine* Americans . . ."[34]

Similarly, most Nisei, second-generation Japanese Americans, saw military service as both a duty and an opportunity. They never doubted they were anything other than Americans. Rather, as Technical Sergeant Mas Takahashi of the Army put it: "We were fighting to be recognized as Americans." Some, protesting their internment, refused to serve. And yet those who did serve more than proved themselves in battle—whether in the 100th Infantry Battalion, later, in the 442nd Combat Team, into which the 100th had been merged, or in Military Intelligence in the Pacific. The 100th fought at Salerno with such determination and self-sacrifice that it became known as the "Purple-Heart Battalion," and the 442nd ended the war the most decorated unit in the U.S. Army.[35]

Native Americans were drawn to military service, especially in light of the 1934 Indian Reorganization Act granting greater tribal self-determination and the improvements to reservation life known as the "Indian New Deal." Voicing the patriotic sentiments of so many of his people, the Navajo Raymond Nakai, a U.S. Marine "code-talker," stated: "Many people ask why we fight the White man's wars. Our answer is that we are proud to be Americans. We're proud to be American Indians. We always stand ready when our country needs us."[36]

African Americans responded similarly. Sergeant Al Banker of New Orleans said he joined the Marine Corps because "I felt it was the proper thing to do. To be patriotic to my country." But blacks were also fighting to secure "first-class citizenship." Having served in Europe as a sergeant with the all-black 6888th Central Postal Directory Battalion of the Women's Army Corps (WACS), Elaine Bennett explained that she had enlisted "to prove to myself, and maybe to the world, that we [African Americans] would give what we had back to the United States as a confirmation that we were full-fledged citizens." And May Miller told of how her eighteen-year-old son sought to comfort her when his draft letter arrived: "Come on, Ma, don't carry on like that. You're not sick, are you? You want me to fight, don't you—fight for those four freedoms we live for, don't you?"[37]

Whether or not they spoke of the "Double V," blacks knew the struggle was both overseas and stateside. Every day they faced the irony of fighting for democracy while suffering the denial of their own democratic rights, especially down south. Private Charles Williams wrote to the NAACP leader Walter White from Texas, "I was glad to fight for the four freedoms. Now I am confused as to their meaning. I want to soldier. But I want to soldier as a man, not as a nigger." And many would stand up not only to racist civilians and GIs, but also, risking arrest and worse, to local officials and their own officers. In fact, due to persistent black pressure and the need for more fighting men at the front, African-American aspirations would eventually prevail over the racism of the military brass. Black infantrymen, artillerymen, tankers, and pilots would not only be sent into combat, but serve with pride, determination, valor, and hope.[38]

Americans from every walk of life knew well the stakes. They served to bring an end to regimes and ideologies that threatened America and the world. And the majority did it to advance an America dedicated to the Four Freedoms, perhaps even a world so dedicated. That they spoke of these goals in the humblest of terms is no surprise. Embedded in even these phrases, however, was homage to the promise the New Deal had extended to average Americans in the wake of the Great Depression, one now threatened by the Axis powers.

Following a battle with the Japanese on Guadalcanal, the journalist John Hersey asked the marines with whom he had gone into action, "What would you say you were fighting for?" But all he got was silence, as if each were "bothered by a memory." Then, finally, one spoke . . .

He whispered, "Jesus, what I'd give for a piece of blueberry pie."
Another whispered: "Personally I prefer mince."
A third whispered: "Make mine apple with a few raisins . . ."

Yet Hersey understood: "Fighting for pie. Of course that is not exactly what they meant . . . pie was their symbol of home. In other places there are other symbols . . . a good bottle of scotch whiskey . . . a blonde . . . books . . . music . . . movies . . . When they say they are fighting for these things, they mean they are fighting for home—'to get the god-dam thing over and get home.'" And he would write: "Perhaps this sounds selfish. It certainly sounds less dynamic than the Axis slogans. But home seems to most marines a pretty good thing to be fighting for. Home is where the good things are—the generosity, the good pay, the comforts, the democracy, the pie."[39]

Hersey hardly needed to add that these good things had fallen through the floor with the economy in 1929, and the decade in the living memory of these soldiers had been spent under the New Deal that had reattained them.

More than he actually cared to admit, many an American serviceman would find himself thinking, and speaking, of what it was all about. The infantryman John Steber, who had landed at Omaha Beach on D-day, June 6, 1944, recollected to his nephew, the military historian Donald Miller: "When guys are dying around you, you don't think of your country . . . [But] When things quiet down sometimes you'd think: it's those fucking Nazis who started this thing and we've got to take them out before they take over the world." Private Walter Rosenblum, a Signal Corps photographer, wrote of the bravery and self-sacrifice he had witnessed at Normandy. He noted, "The myth of Aryan supremacy is based on the slogan of everyone for himself and devil take the hindmost." What he saw among American troops was, instead, cooperation. Observing them in action, he exclaimed, "How can Hitler win against men such as these!" And the 90th Infantry Division sergeant Harold Radish would recall his utter surprise that, after he and his men were captured in the Battle of the Bulge and stuffed into a German boxcar, his fellow prisoners broke into "God Bless America" when their own planes strafed the train. The historian Stephen Ambrose told of one American POW who defiantly answered his German captor's query "Why are you making war on us?" with "We are fighting to free you from the fantastic idea that you are a master race."[40]

Servicemen would reveal their deepest sentiments in letters home. Rene Gagnon, one of the marines famously photographed raising the flag over Iwo Jima, wrote to his sweetheart in February 1945: "After seeing all this it makes me realize what freedom really means." And Lieutenant Robert Lee Shannon, Jr., of the Navy wrote to his parents from somewhere in the South Pacific in March 1945: "Patriotism? Well, yes, there is patriotism among us, not the synthetic kind that comes forth in the war mongers and profiteers—the kind that is amassed in the throats of people when our national ensign is unfurled, or like as many sheep, cheer at a passing parade—but rather the kind which lies deep and still in the hearts of our defenders."[41]

The President himself knew—presumably all the more confidently so after he learned of a May 1942 Intelligence Survey showing "The Four Freedoms . . . have a powerful and genuine appeal to seven persons in ten"—that while Americans might not recite them correctly, those freedoms mattered to them deeply. In February 1943, just returned from meetings with Churchill in North Africa, where he also met with U.S. servicemen, FDR would tell the White House Correspondents' Association:

> In every battalion, and in every ship's crew, you will find every kind of American citizen representing every occupation, every section, every origin, every religion, and every political viewpoint. Ask them what they are fighting for, and every one of them will say, "I am fighting for my country." Ask them what they really mean by that, and you will get what on the surface may seem to be a wide variety of answers. One will say that he is fighting for the right to say what he pleases, and to read and listen to what he likes. Another will say he is fighting because he never wants to see the Nazi swastika flying over the old First Baptist Church on Elm Street. Another soldier will say that he is fighting for the right to work, and to earn three square meals a day for himself and his folks. And another one will say that he is fighting in this world war so that his children and his grandchildren will not have to go back to Europe, or Africa, or Asia, or the Solomon Islands, to do this ugly job all over again. But all these answers really add up to the same thing; every American is fighting for freedom.[42]

Roosevelt was right. Yet he knew more than he was saying. He knew that even as Americans were fighting for the Four Freedoms overseas, many were also fighting for them at home against American conservatives, reactionaries, and corporate capitalists. Moreover, he knew that not only had most Americans made the Four Freedoms their own, but that many of them were not waiting for military victory to try to advance them—indeed, that their actions were compelling him to do so.[43]

Eager to make "This Time for Keeps," liberals and progressives in and out of the administration had quickly joined FDR in making the Four Freedoms central to their efforts. Writing A Time For Greatness in early 1942, the Pulitzer Prize–winning author Herbert Agar, a World War I veteran who had recently returned to naval service, argued that to secure "Mr. Roosevelt's Four Freedoms" would represent the redemption of the Founders' original intentions: "Freedom of speech and freedom of religion: these are the civil liberties. Freedom from want and freedom from fear: these are security. If we ever succeed in putting the two together we shall be back with the preamble to the Constitution of the United States." And offering "Notes on Democratic Thinking" at the University of Virginia later that year, Attorney General Biddle told a similar "history" of the Four Freedoms: "The two phases of our heritage of freedom have here been brought together: the first and older phase, the protection of individual men and women against tyrants and the tyrant state; the second and newer phase, the protection of individual men and women against what Senator Wagner has called 'social and economic conditions in which human beings cannot be free.'"[44]

Giving his speech "The Price of Free World Victory" in New York City that May, Vice President Henry Wallace rendered an even grander history. Punctuating his narrative with both religious references—"Democracy is the only true political expression of Christianity"—and references to the American, French, and Russian Revolutions, the Vice President wove together FDR's Four Freedoms and Max Lerner's "People's Century" to declare: "Some people have spoken of the 'American Century.' I say that the century on which we are entering—the century which will come out of this war—can be and must be the century of the common man." A former Iowa Republican whom FDR had elevated from Secretary of Agriculture to the Democratic ticket in 1940, Wallace was no radical. However, within his "Century of the Common Man" he provided a progressive alternative to the magazine mogul Henry Luce's more conservative "American Century" and became, despite his Christian rhetoric, a hero to the Left, a status he would steadily enhance by championing the New Deal, labor, and civil rights.[45]

In her own fashion, Mrs. Roosevelt, too, continued to promote the Four Freedoms. Turning up seemingly everywhere to bolster the war effort, she now counseled patience in pursuing the "Four Equalities." And yet she spoke no less firmly of both combating racial and religious discrimination and guaranteeing the rights of all citizens: "[L]iving in a democracy it is entirely reasonable to demand that every citizen of that democracy enjoy the fundamental rights of a citizen."[46]

The Office of Facts and Figures and succeeding Office of War Information also took up the cause of the Four Freedoms. The radio division immediately recruited the writer and producer Norman Corwin to do a new thirteen-week drama series to be broadcast nationally starting in the spring of 1942. Garnering an audience of 20 million, Corwin's *This Is War!* dubbed the Axis enemy "Murder International," but encouraged Americans to think of the struggle as entailing far more than "revenge." The poster division, collaborating with Madison Avenue's new War Advertising Council, began to issue a stream of patriotic images and messages. And the OWI director, Archibald MacLeish, himself commissioned the writing of *The United Nations Fight for the Four Freedoms,* a pamphlet that was to be widely distributed, with the progressives E. B. White, Reinhold Niebuhr, Max Lerner, and Malcolm Cowley contributing Freedom of Speech, Freedom of Religion, Freedom from Want, and Freedom from Fear, respectively.[47]

The cultural home front entailed far more than official initiatives, however. Tens of thousands of artists, writers, actors, and musicians mobilized as well. While many worked in tandem with the government, many more campaigned independently. And everywhere—from radio shows and public art exhibitions that drew vast followings, to the cheap editions of books given to servicemen in the tens of millions; from popular country and swing tunes to symphonic compositions and dance performances; and from Hollywood films to Sunday sermons, college lectures, and even cast-away comments in advertising—evidence abounded that Americans knew they were fighting a progressive war, a war not just against fascism and imperialism, but a war for the Four Freedoms.[48]

"We want to share the promises and fruits of American life."

As Americans and their allies began to turn the tide of war, liberals and leftists spoke all the more determinedly of what defeating the Axis would mean. Most turned to the Four Freedoms either directly or indirectly to do so. At the invitation of the 1943 President's Birthday Ball Committee, the playwright Norman Corwin produced *A Moment of the Nation's Time*, a short but sharp play broadcast on January 30 over all four national radio networks. In the spirit of "they shall not have died in vain," Corwin projected victory as not only witnessing "storm troopers, race-haters, lynchers, ground into the dust," but also securing "The right to food, clothing, shelter, medical care . . ." And that spring the ten-thousand-member-strong Artists for Victory announced a "Four Freedoms Campaign" and graphic-design competition to coincide with the upcoming "Four Freedoms Days" on September 12–19 and culminate in late October with an exhibition of one hundred prints that would run concurrently in twenty-six museums around the country. Addressing "America in the War," entrants were to submit works that portrayed the barbarities of fascism and imperialism, the heroic determination of Americans, and the promise of the Four Freedoms.[1]

Even FDR's former Republican opponent, Wendell Willkie, promoted the Four Freedoms. At the President's invitation, he had flown around the world in 1942 in a converted American bomber, meeting with both U.S. military and diplomatic officials and Allied leaders and citizens. Enthused by what he saw and heard, Willkie wrote *One World,* recounting his journey and advancing his own argument about what Americans needed to do to ensure a better and more just postwar world. While embracing the Four Freedoms, he stepped out ahead of Roosevelt by calling for the United States to seek an end to *all* imperialisms, including its own "race imperialism."

> Our very proclamations of what we are fighting for have rendered our inequities self-evident. When we talk of freedom and opportunity for all nations, the mocking paradoxes in our own society become so clear they can no longer be ignored. If we want to talk about freedom, we must mean freedom for others as well as ourselves, and we must mean freedom inside our frontiers as well as outside.

Willkie urged action now, not later, for, he insisted: "nothing of importance can be won in peace, which has not already been won in the war itself." And to their credit, Americans made *One World* a huge bestseller.[2]

Equally telling of the Four Freedoms' massive popular appeal, the conservative *Saturday Evening Post*—whose corporate president, Walter D. Fuller, was also chairman of the board of the National Association of Manufacturers—ran Norman Rockwell's FDR-inspired paintings in four consecutive issues that February and March, each accompanied by an article on the freedom represented. Rockwell depicted Freedom of Speech as a garage mechanic, Lincolnesque in appearance, addressing an attentive New England town meeting; Freedom of Worship as a multicultural group of people praying together; Freedom from Want as a family gathered for a Thanksgiving

CHAPTER SEVEN

feast; and Freedom from Fear as a couple tucking their children safely to bed. To accompany these democratic images, the *Post* editor Ben Hibbs commissioned the liberal poet and playwright Stephen Vincent Benét to contribute the essay on "Freedom from Fear" and the progressive Filipino immigrant writer Carlos Bulosan to compose the one on "Freedom from Want." Warning against "forces which have been trying to falsify American history," Bulosan recalled American workers' perennial struggles for democratic rights, cited the continuing oppression of workers and minorities, and answered "What do we want?" with "We want complete security and peace. We want to share the promises and fruits of American life. We want to be free from fear and hunger." And he did not end there. "If you want to know what we are," he declared, "—We are Marching!"[3]

The magazine's offices were flooded with requests for copies of Rockwell's paintings. Roosevelt himself praised the pictures and proposed that the essays be translated for international distribution along with the former. The Treasury Department not only made the Four Freedoms the theme of its "Second War Loan Drive." It also cooperated with the *Post* in launching a yearlong "Four Freedoms War Bond Show" that took Rockwell's paintings to big-city department stores around the country. Starting out in Washington, D.C., in April 1943, the show traveled to Philadelphia, New York, Boston, Buffalo, Rochester, Pittsburgh, Cleveland, Chicago, St. Louis, New Orleans, Dallas, Los Angeles, Portland, and Denver, with celebrity-filled gala events staged at each location. Plus, the NBC Symphony Orchestra premiered Robert Russell Bennett's new symphony, *The Four Freedoms*, in a nationwide September broadcast. By tour's end more than 1.2 million people had seen the show—and $133 million in war bonds had been sold.[4]

Additionally, the *Post* decided to run a related series, "What I Am Fighting For," in July 1943. Composed of four GI-authored articles, selected from submissions to an essay contest sponsored by the Service Men's Christian League, the series spoke of family, friends, and "the girl back home," the "American dream," and, naturally, the Four Freedoms. The references to the Freedoms were more than perfunctory. Private

Albert Gerber, a Jewish soldier from St. Louis, eloquently wrote that he was fighting not only for freedom of speech and religion, but also "economic freedom for all." Indeed, he said: "I am fighting for a progressive humane American way of life—not [that of] nostalgic reactionaries who want to go back to the *status quo ante* of 1929. I am fighting so that our river of democracy may roll on and wash away . . . more intolerances, more discriminations, and more inequities and iniquities."[5]

Yet, arguably, the greatest testament to the Four Freedoms' popular appeal was the concerted effort by conservatives, reactionaries, and corporate capitalists to contain and co-opt them. Following the enthusiastic response to the *Post's* Rockwell issues, Hibbs published an editorial, "The Four Freedoms Are an Ideal," which cautioned Americans against reading too much into them. They did not, he insisted, promise to "reward the lazy and incompetent as richly as the able and conscientious," or, as if these were equivalents, "set up a 'welfare state.'"[6]

Self-evidently eager to turn the Freedoms' popularity to its advantage, one reactionary organization, Four Freedoms on the Home Front, Inc., demanded "Freedom from racketeering labor leaders—Freedom from bureaucracy—Freedom of enterprise and individual opportunity—Freedom of State and local rights from Federal Domination" (the last, essentially a call to defend racial segregation).[7]

Most conservatives, however, were more thoughtful in their reactions. Speaking to a convention of several hundred bankers, the NAM board chairman, Walter Fuller, warned in May 1942: "One thing is certain, the people of this country are fighting this war for a better world in which to live. They would like to get it through democracy, liberty, and free enterprise. But they are determined to have this better world of greater security one way or another, and if they don't get it through present principles they will look elsewhere." And, he counseled, "We must either cut the cloth to fit that pattern or the reformers and demagogues will."[8]

Intent upon tailoring Americans' hopes and aspirations to their liking, corporate bosses sought to refashion the Four Freedoms to serve their purposes. Central to their ambitions were the labors of the War Advertising Council, whose "admen" members were going "All Out!" to promote not only the war effort, but also business's role in it. In fact, working closely with the OWI, they would come to dominate the agency and eventually drive out their more liberal colleagues. Leaving the OWI in the spring of 1943, not long after a "dollar-a-year" Coca-Cola executive took charge of the Bureau of Graphics and Printing, the designer Francis Brennan and the artist Ben Shahn captured the transparent effort by corporate America to co-opt the bureau. They created a mock poster that had the Statue of Liberty holding aloft not her torch but four Coca-Cola bottles, with a caption satirizing Coke's own slogan: "The War That Refreshes: The Four Delicious Freedoms!"[9]

Capitalists and their publicists produced many a magazine ad, wall poster, public speech, and radio program equating "the American way" with "free enterprise" and promoting the imperative of securing both home and family and "private enterprise and initiative." In 1943, Republic Steel—making no mention, of course, of the infamous 1937 Memorial Day massacre—ran an ad in which an American soldier says, "I like the way we've always run things back home—you know—the American way of life," which this fictional GI defined as "free enterprise, private enterprise, our commercial competitive system, the American brand of freedom . . . they all help explain the American way of life."[10]

Eager to both restore capital's lost standing and prestige and subdue or temper Americans' democratic impulses and imagination, corporate executives underwrote public relations campaigns that not only advertised the patriotic productivity of their respective companies, but also projected the image of the Arsenal of Democracy directly onto big business by adding a Fifth Freedom to FDR's four. In fact, it became a major talking point. Meeting in Chicago in August 1943, the United States Junior Chamber of Commerce passed a resolution proclaiming a "Fifth Freedom—the Opportunity of Enterprise." In a speech, "The Meaning of Freedom," that September in New York, the Columbia University president, Nicholas Murray Butler, insisted that "Freedom of Individual Enterprise" must be added to the Four Freedoms to make the modern idea of "Freedom" complete. And asserting that the freedoms pronounced by FDR were "meaningless" without it, the Republican congresswoman Edith Nourse Rogers of Massachusetts presented a resolution in Congress to officially add "Freedom of Private Enterprise" to them and asked *The Saturday Evening Post* that it do a cover story on that "freedom."[11]

The more avidly conservatives, reactionaries, and corporate capitalists tried to deny, appropriate, or alter the Four Freedoms, the more passionately did union, consumer, and civil rights activists promote them. In her 1942 book, *The Consumer Goes to War*, Caroline Ware told Americans, "We shall win for democracy in the world only if we win for democracy at home." Insisting that "Tomorrow, we cannot go back," she stated: "We must go on to an economy geared to a high and rising standard for all people and, for all people, a society based on democratic freedoms—freedom from want and fear, freedom for expression and worship." And in a 1943 Labor Day radio broadcast, John Shelley, the head of the AFL's San Francisco Labor Council, decried antiunion conservatives as "filthy creatures . . . who wrap themselves in the flag, scream of patriotism, sneer at every phase of the war effort, and . . . openly declare their advocacy of a world after the war in which there will be no guarantee of the Four Freedoms."[12]

African Americans were as insistent. In *How About It, Dixie*, the poet Langston Hughes voiced black aspirations:

> *The President's Four Freedoms*
> *Appeal to me.*
> *I would like to see those Freedoms*
> *Come to be.*
>
> *If you believe*
> *In the Four Freedoms, too,*
> *Then share 'em with me—*
> *Don't keep 'em all for you . . .*

Freedom's not just
To be won Over There.
It means Freedom at home too—
Now—right here!

And the middle-class sisters of the national black sorority, Alpha Kappa Alpha, declared in November 1942: "Listen, America! American Negroes want to win this war . . . Listen, America! We want the four freedoms right here in America . . ."[13]

More than rhetorical pressure was building for public action in favor of the Four Freedoms. Labor continued to honor its "No Strike Pledge" and union rolls expanded; but rising prices, escalating profits, and intensifying management demands (not to mention injurious and deadly workplace accidents) were exasperating workers. The Toledo UAW leader Richard Gosser expressed labor's anger at his union's August 1942 national convention: "I am for doing everything we possibly can in this nation to win the war and to lick Fascism once and for all, but by God, I am not in favor of letting our employer kick the hell out of us all around the place behind the American flag." And soon the country would not only hear the AFL and CIO condemn the OPA for failing to control inflation, but also see multiplying numbers of wildcat walkouts and a UMW strike for higher wages that forced Roosevelt to order a temporary federal takeover of the coal mines.[14]

Walkouts were usually short-lived and workers quickly made up the losses, but they inevitably incited angry editorials, public ill will, and reactionary legislation to limit labor's industrial and political capacities. Aligned with labor, Max Lerner would charge that the real strikers were "Congress" and "the big corporations." However, opposed to wartime strikes himself, he called on others on the left to smarten up. "The American reactionaries don't give two hoots about the war," he explained, "but they are willing to use it—and are using it—for their own purposes. Under any circumstances we could fight them and beat them, but we cannot fight and beat the war which they are using as their protector." Nevertheless, fed up with rising profits, prices, and demands, workers would walk out all the more in the months ahead.[15]

African Americans, too, did more than talk—and not for nothing did white supremacists anxiously decry "Negro uppitiness" (which they variously blamed on Jews, Communists, and Eleanor Roosevelt). The black journalist Roi Ottley wrote in *New World A-Coming*: "Listen to the way Negroes are talking these days! Gone are the Negroes of the old banjo and singin' roun' the cabin doors. Old man Mose is dead! Instead, black men have become noisy, aggressive, and sometimes de-fiant." And, he could have said, women as well. Championing the role of black women in both her own profession and the broader struggle for equal rights, the nurse Mabel K. Staupers wrote, "Negro women con-tinue to meet the challenge of helping America develop full democracy for all citizens. It is impossible for women to permit their men to return from battlefields and find lack of privilege and opportunity." Indeed, the NAACP and other black organizations were spiritedly assembling and petitioning not just for better jobs and housing but, increasingly, for an end to segregation. Offering a model for a later generation of black student activists, Howard University students staged a sit-in for service in April 1943 at the Washington, D.C., whites-only Little Pal-ace Cafeteria.[16]

At the same time, African-American men and women were eagerly joining unions all across the country, including down south, where "representation elections" afforded many their first real opportunities to vote. Moreover, not only were southern blacks risking life and limb by challenging segregation on public transportation systems, but when whites in Los Angeles, Mobile, Detroit, and other cities rioted against people of color that summer, African Americans fought back—and when they themselves angrily took to the streets of Harlem in August, Mary McLeod Bethune, the foremost black New Dealer, would not apologize for their actions, but observe that they were simply answering FDR's call to fight for "the Four Freedoms."[17]

Blacks did not stand alone. Prominent figures such as Eleanor Roo-sevelt, Wendell Willkie, and the leaders of the CIO, as well as many other white liberals and progressives, were advocating racial equality and integration. And despite the ugliness of the 1943 race riots, there was even reason to imagine that white Americans—at least young white Americans—were coming to see what needed doing. A September 1943 NAACP survey of nearly 13,000 college students nationwide found that 74 percent of them believed that to successfully pursue the "Four Freedoms" globally, the United States had to "take steps to end discrimination against blacks."[18]

Americans were fighting for the Four Freedoms at the military front and on the home front—and many of them were determined to realize those freedoms sooner rather than later. They believed FDR when he said that those freedoms were "no vision of a distant millennium," but "attainable in our own time and generation." And like Wendell Willkie, many of them recognized that "nothing of importance can be won in peace, which has not already been won in the war itself."

Stirred by popular pressure and stunned by the 1942 midterm election results that increased the size and power of the conservative congressional coalition, Roosevelt knew well before the racially explosive summer of 1943 that he had to reassure his fellow citizens of his commitments, while challenging the new Congress. And urged on by the AFL president, William Green, he acted quickly to do both. In mid-November 1942, FDR directed the National Resources Planning Board to publicly release its long-in-the-making proposal for "A New Bill of Rights," a proposal that the President and many a New Dealer such as Robert H. Jackson and Charles Merriam had been hinting at for several years—and the president himself pointed the way forward in his January 1943 State of the Union address.

Reiterating that the Four Freedoms remained the nation's war aims, Roosevelt told Congress and the nation: "When you talk with our young men and women, you will find that [along] with the opportunity for employment they want assurance against the evils of all major economic hazards—assurance that will extend from the cradle to the grave. And this great Government can and must provide this assurance . . . I say this now to this Seventy-Eighth Congress, because it is wholly possible that freedom from want—the right of employment, the right of assurance against life's hazards—will loom very large as a task of America during the coming two years." And that March, he formally sent to Congress the NRPB's *Security, Work, and Relief Policies* (1942) and *National Resources Development—Report for 1943*.[19]

With the latter document prominently citing the Four Freedoms and the "New Bill of Rights," the two reports together called for more than a postwar revival of the New Deal. Proposing that the government guarantee both a full-employment economy and "cradle to grave security," they projected nothing less than the making of a social-democratic United States.[20]

Both *The Wall Street Journal* and *The New York Times* lambasted the proposals. The National Association of Manufacturers not only denounced them as "Socialism." It also issued *JOBS—FREEDOM—OPPORTUNITY*, a report that portrayed New Deal government and organized labor as the most serious threats to postwar freedom and prosperity. The only way to freedom from want and fear, the editors insisted, was the private enterprise way.[21]

However, others warmly applauded the reports. Declaring "We Know What We Want" and seeing the "New Bill of Rights" as the clearest statement of it, the liberal Twentieth Century Fund issued *Wartime Facts and Postwar Problems: A Study and Discussion Manual*, hoping to "fire the popular imagination with the challenge which the peace will bring."[22]

Progressives, too, spoke of the challenges ahead; but they wanted more deliberate action, not more deliberation. Writing in *The Nation*, I. F. Stone perceptively suggested that Roosevelt was sending up "trial balloons" for a possible 1944 reelection campaign. However, Stone further contended that FDR had put into play far more than the possibility of a fourth term. "The President," Stone said, "has launched out on the greatest battle of our time," and the question was not simply whether he would win or lose that battle, but whether the outcome would be a truly democratic one. The answer, Stone insisted, depended not so much on the president as on the men and women of "this generation."[23]

What Roosevelt knew was that Americans stood ready to join in his initiatives. Polls conducted for the White House by Princeton University's Office of Public Opinion Research immediately after he sent the NRPB reports to Congress showed that the vast majority of Americans, Democrats and Republicans, heartily endorsed the prospect of pursuing progressive policies and programs to secure freedom from want and fear at war's end. For starters, the polls registered strong and widespread support for expanding the social security system to assist not just returning veterans, but *all* Americans. Indeed, noting that 94 percent endorsed old-age pensions; 84 percent, job insurance; 83 percent, health insurance; 79 percent, aid for students; and 73 percent, work relief, the OPOR associate director Jerome Bruner would observe: "If a 'plebiscite' on social security were to be conducted tomorrow, America would make the plans of our social-security prophets look niggardly. We want the whole works."[24]

Such polls indicated as well that while most Americans remained suspicious of state "control" of business, nearly 90 percent of them favored joint planning by "government, business, and labor . . . to do away with unemployment after the war"; 73 percent supported launching New Deal–style public-works projects to provide jobs after the war; and the same 73 percent favored a policy in which the federal government would actually "guarantee" a job to those needing one. Plus, 79 percent thought that in order to contain inflation, "price ceilings . . . should be kept on for a while after the war."[25]

Furthermore, despite the disdain Americans said they felt toward the leaders of organized labor (especially the Mineworkers' John L. Lewis), 86 percent actually favored joint "Labor-Management Planning to Prevent Unemployment." And working people definitely wanted to enhance industrial democracy. A February 1943 *Fortune* magazine survey asking a cross-section of factory workers, "Do you think it would be a good idea or a bad idea for workers to have someone they elect represent them on the board of directors or some management council?" found that 75 percent thought it a "Good Idea"—and regarding what questions such representatives should have a "say" in determining, 97 percent checked "Working Conditions"; 95 percent, "Wages"; 81.5 percent, "Promotions"; and 62 percent, "Production plans."[26]

Nevertheless, as much as Roosevelt wanted to act, he hesitated, convinced that the makeup of Congress made it futile to do so at that time—a conviction Congress itself seemed to confirm when it proceeded to defund and kill the NRPB itself. But he did not retreat from the NRPB proposals and the idea of "A New Bill of Rights." Rather, he pushed them indirectly.

The President continued to talk of expanding government's role in assuring economic and social security; however, when he did, he spoke most clearly of the imperative to plan for the needs of the veterans. In a late-July 1943 Fireside Chat, he stated: "While concentrating on military victory, we are not neglecting the planning of things to come, the freedoms which we know will make for decency and greater justice throughout the world. Among many other things we are, today, laying plans for the return to civilian life of our gallant men and women . . ." And he insisted that "The least to which [they] are entitled is . . . mustering-out pay . . . unemployment insurance . . . further education or trade training at the cost of their Government . . . liberalized provision for hospitalization, rehabilitation, medical care for disabled . . . sufficient pensions for disabled." But he also spoke of the need to address the "problem of demobilizing the rest of the millions who have been working and living in a wartime economy," indicating that for this, too, the administration "is drawing up plans." In fact, his "chief of staff" Samuel Rosenman would later write that as much as FDR believed that the "returning soldier and sailor and marine" warranted special attention, he also hoped that granting educational and other assistance to them would serve as an "entering wedge" to more universal postwar initiatives.[27]

While the President hesitated—or feinted—others did not. Mrs. Roosevelt renewed her call to secure the Four Equalities for all Americans. The NRPB member Beardsley Ruml declared that together the Four Freedoms, Atlantic Charter, and new "Nine Rights" provided a "Fighting Creed for America." And some did more than talk.[28]

Aided by the CIO and the AFL, Senator Robert F. Wagner of New York drafted a bill intended to radically expand America's social-insurance system by creating, among other things, a "compulsory national health insurance program." And joined by Senator James Murray of Montana and Representative John Dingell of Michigan, he introduced it to Congress in June 1943. Of course, he knew that "Wagner-Murray-Dingell" would not pass, but he looked forward to the day it might.[29]

And that July the CIO itself mobilized anew. Seeking to push the progressive agenda all the more forcefully, as well as avoid a repeat of the midterm elections, circumvent the clause in the Smith-Connally Act outlawing direct union contributions to political campaigns, and quash the talk in labor circles of forming a third party, the CIO's president, Philip Murray, commissioned Sidney Hillman to organize and build a "political action committee" (CIO-PAC).[30]

Roosevelt did assert himself progressively where he felt he could. Responding to working people's anger about inflation, he and his administration renewed their efforts to address it and once again rallied consumers to join them in doing so. In February 1943, the OWI, not long before Congress defunded its domestic activities, released *Battle Stations for All: The Story of the Fight to Control Living Costs*, a booklet that celebrated labor's organizing advances, called for citizens to fight inflation by "Taking the Profit Out of War," and praised the work of the local "War Price and Rationing Boards ["little OPAs"]." Soon thereafter, the President named Chester Bowles as the new director of the OPA and issued a "Hold the Line Order" on prices. And that fall, with the OPA itself facing a congressional cutback, Bowles not only initiated a "Home Front Pledge" campaign in which 20 million consumers promised to "pay no more than top legal prices" and help "stamp out the activities of all chiselers, profiteers, and black-marketeers." He also recruited Caroline Ware to gather an advisory committee of "labor, consumer, and women's groups" that would soon set itself to mobilizing shoppers to "police" prices at local businesses on behalf of the five thousand "little OPAs" operating around the country.[31]

Roosevelt addressed black concerns anew as well. Responding to MOWM's protests, he made the FEPC an independent agency with enhanced authority and dollars. Plus, irritated by the Navy's slowness in enlisting blacks, he commanded it to speed up its recruitment efforts, which it immediately did.[32]

In the same vein, the War Department not only followed FDR's directive to start sending black units into combat. Acknowledging the problem of "Negro Morale," it also arranged for Frank Capra to produce *The Negro Soldier*. Scripted by the black writer Carlton Moss, the film recounted the long, heroic history of African-American military service, highlighted black GIs' participation in the current war, and stressed interracial unity. Test-shown to separate groups of black and white troops, the film was well received by both and on their popular recommendations it was made "mandatory viewing" for all GIs, shown publicly in three hundred theaters around the country, and soon followed by a second production, *The Negro Sailor*.[33]

Moreover, Roosevelt also actively backed a new Soldier Vote bill introduced in Congress in 1943 by the Democratic senators Theodore Green of Rhode Island and Scott Lucas of Illinois. Projected to benefit men and women of every region and color, Green-Lucas was clearly designed to circumvent the southern elites' cherished "states' rights" and poll taxes. But this time not only Dixiecrats opposed the legislation. So, too, did ardent anti-FDR Republicans. The bill went down in defeat, and that December, Congress once again handed over to the states the responsibility of enabling absentee soldiers, sailors, and marines to vote—instigating Max Lerner to write: "This is . . . the most barefaced betrayal of America by Americans that it has been my duty to comment on . . . I wish the Senators [who defeated the bill] had had the guts to say directly and frankly to our soldiers, 'We don't trust you: you have a right to die for your country, but we fear to let you choose who shall rule your country.'"[34]

None of it escaped the GIs themselves. One white army sergeant serving near the front in Italy spoke for most of his comrades when he told the photographer Margaret Bourke-White: "There shouldn't have to be any legislation made, and argued, so that we can vote—it should be understood and automatic. When men leave their country, give up their jobs, leave their homes, and sometimes even sacrifice their lives to preserve the democratic way of life, why anyone can question this right to vote is beyond me." [35]

Of course, the handling of the soldier-vote question was just one of many things going on back home that aggravated the GIs. Not only Congress angered them. Private Herrett Wilson of Everett, Washington, wrote home to his mother from the Pacific: "I fought and killed so that the enemy might not invade our land and I ask is it all for naught when red, white, and blue fascists drive Nisei about like coyotes and plague the fathers, mothers, and relatives of our colored comrades that fight by our side." But refusing to give up hope, he urged his mom to "raise [her] voice." [36]

The corporate bosses outraged GIs as well. Charles Bolte, who had returned home in 1943 after losing a leg in combat in North Africa, exclaimed that he was "shocked" by how high business profits were and that the magazine ads made him "retch." The infantry rifleman and *Stars and Stripes* cartoonist Bill Mauldin, who created the famous GI characters "Willie and Joe," would recall how "We all used to get sore at some of the ads in the magazines from America. The admen should have been required by law to submit all copy to an overseas veteran before they sent it to the printers." And at least one outraged AFL brother from Arkansas wrote home from overseas that "We service men are out here fighting and dying so we will be free American Citizens . . . and now since so many of us are away from home the big business men have worked their little labor laws . . ." [37]

But it went even beyond all that.

Reporting from London in July 1943, John Steinbeck wrote, "The soldiers fight and work under a load of worry . . . [and] almost universally you find . . . not a fear of the enemy but a fear of what is going to happen after the war." He explained: "They fight under a banner of four unimplemented freedoms—four words, and when anyone in authority tries to give these freedoms implements and methods the soldiers hear that man assaulted and dragged down." More to the point: "They would like freedom from want. That means the little farm in Connecticut is safe from foreclosure. That means the job left . . . is there waiting, and not only waiting but it will continue while the children grow up. That means there will be schools, and either savings to take care of illness in the family or medicine available without savings." But, he continued: "Talking to many soldiers, it is the worry that . . . is most impressive. Is the country to be taken over by special interests . . . ? Is inflation to be permitted because a few people will grow rich through it? Are fortunes being made while these men get $50 a month? Will they go home to a country destroyed by greed?"[38]

"The Four Freedoms define what [the GI] wants," Steinbeck summed up, "but unless some machinery, some foundation, some clear method is shown, he is likely to believe only in that freedom which Anatole France defined—the equal freedom of rich and poor to sleep under bridges." And no doubt with Roosevelt in mind, Steinbeck advised, "Anyone who can reassure these soldiers . . . will put a weapon in their hands of incredible strength."[39]

Liberals in and out of the administration were urging the President to act along those very lines. And FDR himself had every intention of doing so. In fact, after telling journalists in late December 1943 that Dr. Win-the-War was in charge for the duration, he not only detailed "Doctor New Deal's" accomplishments, but stated that "when victory comes, the program of the past, of course has got to be carried on." And just a fortnight later, he would call for far more than simply resurrecting the New Deal.[40]

CHAPTER EIGHT

"And after this war is won we must be prepared to move forward."

On January 11, 1944, Roosevelt delivered his Annual Message to Congress on the State of the Union. In it, he not only reaffirmed his determination to pursue the Four Freedoms for both America and the world. He also articulated the Freedoms anew, especially freedom from want and fear, in the form of an Economic Bill of Rights for all Americans. He knew full well that the current Congress would never endorse it. And yet he had good reason to believe that most of his fellow citizens would. He knew from polling data that a majority of Americans, at home and in uniform, saw the war in terms of the Four Freedoms, and understood the struggles of not just the past three years but the past twelve years in terms of extending and deepening freedom, equality, and democracy in America.

Suffering from the flu and unable to go up to Capitol Hill to speak in person, the President sent the text of his message to Congress at midday and then presented it to the American people in a radio broadcast from the White House that evening. As ill as he was, he spoke vigorously and his remarks were reminiscent of a younger man.[1]

The President began by discussing his recent meetings with Churchill and Stalin at Tehran and the need to translate the wartime alliance into a permanent system of international security. But he soon turned to the subject of the American home front.

After warmly praising the majority of Americans for their labors and sacrifices, Roosevelt tore into the "noisy minority" whose representatives "swarm" around the nation's capital in selfish pursuit of "profits in money or in terms of political or social preferment." Warning of the dangers of "such selfish agitation," he also warned against "Overconfidence and complacency," for, he said, such an "attitude . . . can kill American boys." And yet he did more than admonish. To speed victory, but "maintain a fair and stable economy at home," he recommended five legislative measures to Congress, the first four clearly targeting corporate greed, the fifth evidently directed at labor. Specifically, he called on Congress to: pass a "realistic" revenue act to increase taxes on profits; maintain the law allowing government to renegotiate war contracts to "prevent exorbitant profits and assure fair prices"; approve a law enabling government to more effectively control food prices; renew the Economic Stabilization Act; and enact "a national service law—which, for the duration of the war, will prevent strikes, and . . . make available for war production or for any other essential services every able-bodied adult in this Nation."[2]

Strangely, having rejected a "labor draft" when first discussed in 1942, Roosevelt was now advancing it, apparently in response not only to pressure from the War Department to act against the increasing threat of wildcat walkouts and union-sanctioned strikes, but also out of a deepening personal belief that, in light of the sacrifices GIs were making overseas, it was fair and would help war workers secure postwar benefits along with military veterans.

Critically, while Americans generally supported the idea of such a draft, as they always had, labor leaders did not; indeed, they felt betrayed, seeing it as an assault on workers. And yet Roosevelt had said not only that he believed the "five measures together form a just and equitable whole," but also that "I would not recommend a national service law unless the other laws were passed to keep down the cost of living, to share equitably the burdens of taxation, to hold the stabilization line, and to prevent undue profits." [3]

Given his reasonable expectations that the current Congress was not likely to comply, it would seem the whole exercise was simply that, an exercise. But it was not. Getting at just what the President intended, the editors of *Time* explained it best. Asking why the need for a labor draft now, as opposed to three years earlier, they guessed that the President had "sent his message to Congress and the nation, but another address was written on it in invisible ink: 'To the Soldiers.'" Others should have reached the same conclusion, for FDR immediately went on to chastise Congress for failing to enact legislation guaranteeing "soldiers and sailors and marines . . . the right to vote." [4]

The President then looked ahead: "It is our duty now to begin to lay the plans and determine the strategy for the winning of a lasting peace and the establishment of an American standard of living higher than ever before known." And in favor of that he proposed the recognition and adoption of a Second Bill of Rights. [5]

Recalling the arguments of his 1932 Commonwealth Club speech, Roosevelt said: "This Republic had its beginning, and grew to its present strength, under the protection of certain inalienable political rights . . . They were our rights to life and liberty. As our Nation has grown in size and stature, however—as our industrial economy expanded—these political rights proved inadequate to assure us equality in the pursuit of happiness." But he continued: "We have come to a clear realization of the fact that true individual freedom cannot exist without economic security and independence. 'Necessitous men are not free men.'" And evoking Jefferson, the Founders, and Lincoln, he contended that "In our day these economic truths have become accepted as self-evident," and "We have accepted, so to speak, a second Bill of Rights under which a new basis of security and prosperity can be established for all regardless of station, race, or creed." This Second Bill of Rights included:

> The right to a useful and remunerative job in the industries or shops or farms or mines of the Nation;

The right to earn enough to provide adequate food and clothing and recreation;

The right of every farmer to raise and sell his products at a return which will give him and his family a decent living;

The right of every businessman, large and small, to trade in an atmosphere of freedom from unfair competition and domination by monopolies at home or abroad;

The right of every family to a decent home;

The right to adequate medical care and the opportunity to achieve and enjoy good health;

The right to adequate protection from the economic fears of old age, sickness, accident, and unemployment;

The right to a good education.

In sum, he stated: "All of these rights spell security. And after this war is won we must be prepared to move forward, in the implementation of these rights, to new goals of human happiness and well-being."[6]

An audacious declaration, but Roosevelt did not leave it there. Distinguishing "clear-thinking businessmen" from the rest, he alerted his fellow citizens to "the grave dangers of rightist reaction." Then, putting Congress itself on the spot, he said: "I ask Congress to explore the means for implementing this economic bill of rights—for it is definitely the responsibility of Congress to do so." And finally, linking the question of addressing the needs of the veterans to that of "implementing" the new bill of rights in a universal program of economic and social security, he declared: "Our fighting men abroad—and their families at home—expect such a program and have the right to insist upon it."[7]

Congress was not moved, at least not in the direction in which the President had pointed. It not only passed a Revenue Act, which he would dub in his veto message a "tax relief bill providing relief not for the needy but for the greedy." It overrode his veto. Moreover, Congress once again rejected the Green-Lucas soldier-vote bill and instead approved a "states-rights" bill that became law without the president's signature.[8]

The alliance of narrow interests—Republican conservatives, southern segregationists, and corporate elites—continued to exercise a unique capacity to bend, if not deny, the national will. In fact, Congress might also have turned its back on any major initiative for veterans had not, ironically enough, the ultraconservative American Legion made that cause its own.

Determined to secure a veterans bill that would enable returning GIs to reclaim their former lives, but eager not to get one that might reinvigorate the New Deal, Legion leaders latched on to the Roosevelt administration's diverse plans and drafted their own omnibus bill, one even more generous in its provisions for unemployment, educational assistance, and "farm, home, and business loans." And to get Congress to pass it, they mobilized their "12,000 posts and 9,500 auxiliary units" in a massive national grassroots lobbying campaign.[9]

Unable to resist the pressure building "from below," congressional conservatives worked hard to at least limit the bill's size and to make sure it would not enhance the authorities or responsibilities of any "New Deal" agencies. Still—testifying to how popular democratic pressures for a fair measure of economic security and opportunity proved hard to contain—what Congress went on to enact would be nothing less than history-making.

Signed into law by FDR in June 1944, the Servicemen's Readjustment Act or "G.I. Bill of Rights" would in the next decade provide 12.4 million veterans with one or more sorts of benefits: 8.3 million collected "readjustment allowances"; 7.8 million received education grants; and 4 million secured "VA-guaranteed loans to finance a home, farm, or business." It was historic, however, not only because of who and what it covered. One of the most progressive, indeed, transparently social-democratic achievements in American history—a measure beloved, trumpeted, and subsequently lauded by Left and Right—the G.I. Bill was a high-water mark in fulfilling the nation's purpose and realizing the Four Freedoms. The most democratic war this nation has ever fought produced one of the most democratic initiatives ever—an initiative that would enable a generation to radically transform themselves and their country for the better.[10]

In his 1944 State of the Union message, Roosevelt had sounded something like the political warrior he had been in the 1930s. And yet this time he did not come out fighting, apparently physically incapable of doing so. Diagnosed with congestive heart failure that March (a fact kept secret from the American people), he left Washington for an urgently needed monthlong rest. But even after that he guarded his energies for the battles that lay immediately ahead.[11]

Meanwhile, inspired and encouraged all the more by FDR's words, liberals and leftists renewed their quest for the Four Freedoms. And the CIO-PAC led the way. Headed by Sidney Hillman, the "PAC" mobilized the political resources of the labor congress and its allies around a broad progressive agenda that it laid out in *The People's Program for 1944*. While the "People's Program" did not call for expanding industrial democracy in the workplace along the lines of either Philip Murray's or Walter Reuther's war-industry plans, it clearly proclaimed the CIO's unwavering support not only for the war effort and the Roosevelt administration, but also for the "full realization of the Four Freedoms" both overseas and at home—the latter by creating a "Full Employment" economy, adopting the "New Bill of Rights," and guaranteeing the equal rights of women and minorities and overseas GIs.[12]

Hillman himself worked strenuously to build the PAC. In addition to creating departments for public relations, art work, and a speakers' bureau, and for black, women's, and youth affairs, he traveled the country setting up fourteen regional offices, launching voter-registration drives, and organizing conferences, meetings, and rallies. Moreover, he not only arranged an alliance with the progressive National Farmers Union, but also put together an "auxiliary" National Citizens Political Action Committee that enlisted the energies of a vast host of "celebrity" liberals and progressives such as the former U.S. senator George Norris, *The Nation* editor Freda Kirchwey, *The New Republic* editor Bruce Bliven, *PM* columnist Max Lerner, the actor-producer Orson Welles, the black New Dealer Mary McLeod Bethune, the performing artist Paul Robeson, and the theologian Reinhold Niebuhr. Plus, Hillman published a stream of well-written and smartly illustrated pamphlets, guides, and posters (several of the last created by the artist and OWI-veteran Ben Shahn).[13]

Filled with references to the Declaration of Independence, the Constitution and Bill of Rights, *and* the Four Freedoms and Economic Bill of Rights, PAC literature highlighted the nation's postwar prospects and possibilities and professed an "Americanism" that—while acknowledging the country's record of denying equal rights, especially to blacks—was both welcoming and compelling. Replete with photographs capturing the country's rural and industrial landscapes and working people's economic and political energies, the PAC pamphlet *This Is Your America* celebrated the nation's diversity. In answer to the question "How, then, can you tell an American?" it replied: "He or she is an American who lives in the United States or any of its possessions, and who believes in our way of life, our Democratic Way"—that is, "He believes that all men are created equal . . . He believes in freedom of speech, freedom of the press, freedom from fear and freedom from want—for *all* our people . . . He believes in freedom of opportunity for all men and women . . . He believes in a government of the people, by the people, and most important of all, for the people." Furthermore, it emphasized that Americans have duties as well. These included defending the rights of all, turning out to vote, and striving *"to create a more perfect union."* And in that spirit, true Americans were called on "to destroy prejudice against the foreign-born and the hatred of Negroes and other peoples . . . protect the rights of labor . . . And [create] a lasting peace in which all our people will have jobs at fair wages."[14]

While some AFL local councils worked directly with the PAC, the national AFL did not. However, it actively backed FDR's reelection and its own *Post-War Program* closely paralleled the CIO's *People's Program*. Reiterating the Federation's commitment to "the struggle of workers for economic and social democracy" and the "Four Freedoms," the AFL program called not only for "equal opportunity" and "civil liberties" for all, but also for "1) the establishment of full employment, 2) the expansion of social security, and 3) the creation of a nationwide housing redevelopment program."[15]

Working people themselves acted ever more forcefully, staging a record number of walkouts in 1944—though, notably, time lost that year was "the lowest proportionally since the 1920s." As one worker explained: "Corporations were showing no sense of patriotism or loyalty . . . All the sacrifices were on the part of the workers. When real and pressing grievances arose and there was no solution and management hid behind the no-strike pledge, the people felt that they were justified . . . in forcing a settlement."[16]

Moreover, encouraged in their actions by groups ranging from the left-wing League of Women Shoppers to those such as the "General Federation of Women's Clubs, League of Women Voters, American Association of University Women, Parent-Teachers Association . . . and American Legion Auxiliary," hundreds of thousands of homemakers were now voluntarily serving as OPA's "eyes and ears" in helping to enforce price controls.[17]

Roosevelt acted, too, and in a telling moment showed his solidarity with labor by ordering armed U.S. soldiers to take over the Montgomery Ward Corporation that spring. The reactionary chairman, Sewell Avery, who refused to recognize his workers' union and repeatedly ignored National War Labor Board settlements, was forcibly removed from his office and the secretary of war was tasked with seizing company plants and facilities in six states. When Sewell sued the government in federal court, he lost.[18]

Continuing to promote the Four Freedoms and now, too, FDR's proposed Economic Bill of Rights, liberals and progressives planned specific initiatives to realize them. At New York's "I Am An American Day" festivities in Central Park that May, Senator Wagner told a "record city crowd" of 1.4 million that the nation's postwar objectives must include a new "world concert of nations," the "expansion of social security," the "promotion of a higher standard of health," the building of "decent housing," the provision of "opportunities in education," "equal opportunity for all . . . regardless of race, creed, or color," and the "preservation and extension of the great freedoms to think, to speak, to write and to worship without molestation." And in a four-part National Council of Catholic Men radio series on the Four Freedoms that August, Reverend Brendan Larnen stated that in order to avoid what happened in the wake of the First World War "we must guarantee those freedoms," and that in view of what Americans were accomplishing in the war effort "Freedom from want is perhaps the easiest to achieve." He also called for public action to assure that "every man who is willing to earn his economic security be allowed to do so" *and* that "vested interests and economic royalists" not be permitted to "exploit and victimize us."[19]

Prominent African Americans called for initiatives as well. A January 1944 conference of black leaders that included A. Philip Randolph, Walter White, and Mary McLeod Bethune issued a "Declaration by Negro Voters" that, along with reiterating their support for the war effort and insisting that "Victory must crush Hitlerism both at home and abroad," demanded "Full Citizenship" for "the Negro people." Furthermore, it declared that "the party or candidate who refuses to help control prices, or fails to support the extension of social security, or refuses to support a progressive program for post war employment, or opposes an enlarged and unsegregated program of government-financed housing, or seeks to destroy organized labor, is as much an enemy of the Negro as is he who would prevent the Negro from voting."[20]

Bolstering African-American campaigns for equality and integration, the Swedish sociologist Gunnar Myrdal published *An American Dilemma: The Negro Problem and Modern Democracy* that same winter. A highly regarded 1,500-page report on race relations commissioned by the Carnegie Corporation before the war and carried out by a biracial research team under Myrdal's direction, the work not only added scholarly heft to black arguments and demands, but also challenged Americans to live up to their own ideals. Appreciating their widely and deeply shared belief in the "American Creed of liberty, equality, justice, and fair opportunity for everybody," Myrdal called on Americans to make their nation "the America" they publicly prized, both for their sake and the world's: "America feels itself to be humanity in miniature. When in this crucial time the international leadership passes to America, the great reason for hope is that this country has a national experience of uniting racial and cultural diversities—and a national theory, if not a consistent practice, of freedom and equality for all." The "Negro problem," he concluded, "is not only America's greatest failure but also America's incomparably great opportunity for the future."[21]

No doubt rattling white southern sensibilities even more, the Supreme Court decided in 1944 in *Smith v. Allwright* that "all-white primaries" were unconstitutional. And that same year middle-class blacks in South Carolina, joined by some progressive whites, bravely challenged the state's white power structure by not only organizing the South Carolina Progressive Democratic Party, but also running their own gubernatorial candidate, Osceola McKaine, a black World War I veteran who regularly referred to World War II in his speeches as "the Four Freedoms war." Plus, if all that were not enough to unsettle Dixie, Roosevelt himself appointed a new Secretary of the Navy, James Forrestal, who proceeded to order the full integration of the WAVES (Women Accepted for Volunteer Emergency Service) and the crews of twenty-five navy ships.[22]

Roosevelt did disappoint many on the left that summer when he allowed Democratic Party leaders to talk him into replacing his increasingly progressive Vice President, Henry Wallace, on the presidential ticket with Senator Harry S. Truman of Missouri. But FDR was not moving to the right. Truman was a loyal New Deal Democrat who—despite his political origins in Kansas City's "Pendergast political machine"—had garnered a reputation as a solid figure for his chairing of the "Truman Committee," the Senate committee that investigated defense contracts. Moreover, Roosevelt made sure that the party's platform reflected the 1944 Annual Message, and in fact went beyond it.[23]

The Democratic Party platform of 1944 declared, with only a bit of exaggeration, "We believe that mankind believes in the Four Freedoms." And the ensuing campaign would reveal just how compelling the promise of the Four Freedoms and Economic Bill of Rights had become. With little to offer but fear, conservatives went after the President and his supporters with false accusations and vile rumors. Targeting Sidney Hillman in particular, and lacing their remarks with anti-Semitism, Republicans, reactionary southern Democrats, and other right-wingers began to conjure up a new "Red Scare" by charging that the CIO-PAC was dominated by Communists who were out to create a "Soviet America." Moreover, the Right not only fed public anxieties about FDR's health, but also spread anew the nasty fiction that the President had known Japan was going to attack Pearl Harbor but kept quiet to allow it to force the United States into the war.[24]

For all its fearmongering, the Republican Party platform actually testified to the popular appeal of FDR's vision for America by formally embracing central elements of the New Deal—even as it promised to shrink the bureaucracy and reduce taxes. While Republicans accorded state and local governments a greater role in administering them, they called for expanding Social Security, protecting labor's right to bargain collectively, providing federal aid for medical care and housing, and underwriting a new round of public-works projects. In fact, the Republican presidential nominee, Governor Thomas E. Dewey of New York, not only announced he was in favor of making full employment a "first objective of national policy" but also nearly embraced a national health care system: "We must help to develop a means of assurance of medical service for those of our citizens who need it and cannot otherwise obtain it."[25]

Despite declining health, FDR came out fighting that fall. In speeches, radio talks, and press conferences, he not only responded directly to the red-baiters, whom he rightly portrayed as bigots. He also called for reconversion assistance for "war workers"; insisted that the "right to vote must be open to our citizens irrespective of race, color or creed—without tax or artificial restriction of any kind"; recommended that the FEPC become a permanent government agency; and proposed a TVA-style program of public works for the Missouri Valley. Addressing 125,000 supporters at Soldiers' Field in Chicago on October 28, he declared: "the American people are resolved that when our men and women return home from this war, they shall come back to the best possible place on the face of the earth—they shall come back to a place where all persons, regardless of race, and color, or creed or place of birth can live in peace and honor and human dignity—free to speak, free to pray as they wish—free from want—and free from fear." And after repeating the Economic Bill of Rights exactly as he had presented it in January, he said:

> Some people . . . have sneered at these ideals, as well as at . . . the ideals of the Four Freedoms. They have said that they were the dreams of starry-eyed New Dealers—that it is silly to talk of them because we cannot attain these ideals tomorrow or the next day. The American people have greater faith than that. I know that they agree with these objectives—that they demand them—that they are determined to get them—and that they are going to get them.[26]

From Chicago, Roosevelt headed east to Boston. And there, on November 4 at Fenway Park, he spoke proudly of American diversity, as he had before in this city sorely marked by racism and anti-Semitism: "Today, in this war, our fine boys are fighting magnificently all over the world and among those boys are the Murphys and the Kellys, the Smiths and the Joneses, the Cohens, the Carusos, the Kowalskis, the Schultzes, the Olsens, the Swobodas, and—right in with all the rest of them—the Cabots and the Lowells," adding that "All of these people, and others like them, are the life-blood of America. They are the hope of the world. It is our duty to them to make sure that, big as this country is, there is no room in it for racial or religious intolerance—and that there is no room for snobbery."[27]

Three days later Roosevelt won reelection with 25,611,939 votes to Dewey's 22,013,371. His 53.5 percent of the total vote represented his lowest margin of victory in four presidential contests. And yet it was a solid win. He not only picked up 432 electoral votes to Dewey's 99, but the Democratic Party, though it lost a seat in the Senate, gained twenty in the House. Moreover, several million GIs had applied for state absentee ballots and 3.2 million of them actually voted—nearly 60 percent of them for FDR.[28]

On April 12, 1945, Roosevelt, just three months into his new term and only sixty-three years old, passed away in Warm Springs, Georgia. Asked to provide a short eulogy for nationwide broadcast, the Pulitzer Prize–winning playwright Robert Sherwood, who had joined FDR's White House team in 1940 and directed the Overseas Division of the OWI in 1942–44, wrote: "To those of us who knew and loved the President . . . the greatest memory we hold today is the memory of his indomitable good humor—his indomitable courage—his love for our country, his faith in our country . . ." It was that love and that faith, Sherwood stated, that not only enabled Roosevelt to confront the crises of economic depression and war without fear or hesitation, but also made him "one with every man who has fought for our country." Indeed, Sherwood said: "There wasn't a moment . . . when he wasn't spiritually on the front line with the men who were fighting for freedom." And finally, after urging Americans to honor their fallen President by "pledging renewed and increased devotion to the country and cause which he served so valiantly and for which he gave his life," Sherwood declared: "We do not surrender to Death, as we would not surrender to the Nazis or Japanese. We continue to stand up and fight for our country and our cause. We continue to fight for Freedom of speech. Freedom of religion. Freedom from want. Freedom from fear."[29]

FDR's death shocked Americans. One Detroit woman exclaimed: "It doesn't seem possible. It seems to me that he will be back on the radio tomorrow, reassuring us all that it was just a mistake." And Private First Class Lester Rebuck, a medic with the 104th Infantry Division, told a journalist in Paris: "It was just like somebody socked me in the stomach when I wasn't looking. I just couldn't get it through my head he was really dead."[30]

The nation grieved. But the people Roosevelt had led for twelve years were not about to fall to pieces. His presidential legacy was not simply a personal one. It was also a democratic one. Sounding every bit the American that FDR himself had so admired, Private Rebuck quickly went on to say: "For my money, that guy was one of the greatest guys that ever lived. You can put him next to Lincoln or Washington or anybody." Noting the diversity of the mourners who lined the funeral procession's route through Washington, *The Nation* columnist I. F. Stone reflected: "Somehow we pulled through before, and somehow we'll pull through again. In part it was luck. In part it was Mr. Roosevelt's leadership. In part it was the quality of the country and its people. I don't know about the rest of the four freedoms, but one thing Mr. Roosevelt gave the United States in one crisis after another . . . was freedom from fear." And the GI editors of *Yank* wrote, "*If Franklin Roosevelt's hopes and dreams are deep enough in the hearts and minds of the people, the people will make them come true.*"[31]

Just weeks after FDR's passing, Hitler committed suicide and Nazi Germany surrendered. The struggle continued in Asia and the Pacific. But on May 8, Americans and their allies celebrated V-E Day. That same night, CBS broadcast *On a Note of Triumph,* a play Norman Corwin had prepared specifically for that long-awaited and hard-fought-for moment. Its opening lines clearly voiced the popular exultation:

> *So they've given up.*
> *They're finally done in, and the rat is dead in an alley back of the*
>   *Wilhelmstrasse.*
> *Take a bow, G.I.,*
> *Take a bow, little guy.*
> *The superman of tomorrow lies dead at the feet of you common men*
>   *of this afternoon.*
> *This is It, kid, this is The Day, all the way from Newburyport to*
>   *Vladivostok.*
> *You had what it took and you gave it, and each of you has a hunk of*
>   *rainbow 'round your helmet.*
> *Seems like free men have done it again.*[32]

Many more Americans were still to die in liberating the Philippines and in taking Okinawa, and it looked like the struggle might go on for many months to come. But suddenly, on August 14, after the United States dropped atomic bombs on Hiroshima and Nagasaki, Imperial Japan, too, finally gave up. And on September 2, 1945, the war was officially over.

Soon—though not soon enough for all concerned—the troops started returning to America, and they were welcomed home as heroes. But they themselves knew otherwise.

Every son of a World War II combat veteran remembers the silence they met when, years later, they asked their fathers about "the war." We all got the same response: "The real heroes never came home."[33]

Americans had sailed on every kind of warship from destroyers and aircraft carriers to submarines and minesweepers; they had flown bombers, fighters, and gliders; and they had driven tanks, trucks, and jeeps. They had built roads, bridges, buildings, and docks, hauled men and goods, and landed on and battled their way on foot, and many times on their bellies, through every imaginable—for many, previously unimaginable—landscape and climate. And they had tended the wounded and buried the dead. Not all saw combat, but many did, and the sacrifices were great—more than 400,000 never made it home and of those who did 800,000 had been wounded or injured. Many millions more had labored in factories, fields, shipyards, offices, and every mode of transport to produce and deliver the weapons and supplies to make victory possible. Here, too, the costs were tremendous—300,000 lost their lives on the job and 1,000,000 suffered some permanent disability.

Yes, the world needed radical reconstructing. Yes, the powers and profits of capital had grown. Yes, racism and segregation persisted. And yes, there were those both in and out of Congress who were eager not just to "file away the Four Freedoms with the Ten Commandments," but also to erase any and all references to the idea of an Economic Bill of Rights and to halt, if not reverse, the democratic advances of the past twelve years.[34]

Nevertheless, Americans had transcended the Great Depression, destroyed their enemies, and liberated millions. Moreover, they had done it all, contrary to the dire predictions of conservatives and isolationists, without turning their own democracy into a dictatorship. Indeed, against the ambitions and efforts of so many of the former, Americans had not only sustained the nation's democratic life, but also continued to make the United States freer, more equal, and more democratic in the process. Regulating capital and the economy, they had made the commonwealth richer, and progressively transformed the "We" in "We the People." Working people were better off, better organized, and all the more conscious of what they could accomplish. Blacks and Latinos, too, were better off, better organized, and more determined to lay claim to their rights as citizens. And women had stepped into every realm of public life and proved themselves indispensable to both winning the war and improving the state of the nation.

Our fathers and mothers and their generation have come down to us over time as the Greatest Generation and surely their achievement was as great as any generation of Americans. Nonetheless, the superlative justly attaches to them not because of the clarity of the evil they confronted, but because of the purpose with which they fought, bled, and died. An overwhelming percentage of adult Americans were swept up not just in four years of war, but in twelve years of struggle across fronts both foreign and domestic. Measuring their accomplishments in beachheads and battles won has become the easier work of later generations. However, the generation that actually engaged those struggles so successfully kept a different yardstick.

The Americans of the New Deal and Second World War had fought, labored, and sacrificed in the name of democracy and the Four Freedoms. Those who died in the struggle could not speak. But their fellow citizens—especially the soldiers, sailors, marines, and airmen who had fought alongside them—surely heard them. Given just one night to prepare a program for nationwide broadcast on the evening of the Japanese surrender, Corwin composed a "message of victory" titled simply "14 August." And he closed it with these words: "Remember them when July comes round . . . Remember them in the fall of the year . . . Remember them in the sleeting months . . .

> They're dead as clay for the rights of men,
> For people the likes of you,
> And they ask that we do not fail them again
> Tomorrow, tomorrow."[35]

CHAPTER NINE

"Why should we have to fall back?"

Having witnessed the liberation of the Dachau concentration camp and the fall of Nazi Germany, William Harlan Hale, a veteran Army intelligence officer and peacetime journalist, went looking in America's past for "facts and feelings" that he and his generation might take with them into the "new age." Reflecting on that search in *The March of Freedom*, he wrote: "All along our course I thought I could see the same clash between those who had faith in the mass of men and those who feared them; between those who sought to extend opportunity and those who wanted to restrict privilege."[1]

Hale's search discovered "no law of inevitable progress" or even any "guarantee that the mass of the people would automatically retain the gains they had won." But he said history clearly showed *"There is no limit to what the American people can do . . . if they get together through the instrument of self-government and plan it."* And asking, "Why should we have to fall back?" he called on his fellow citizens to renew the march of freedom by once again harnessing the powers of democratic government—to curb the power of capital, create economic growth and development, end poverty, and "enable people to advance themselves."[2]

Hale spoke for the majority of Americans. Prevailing over the forces that had threatened to destroy them, they had learned the hard way that neither laissez-faire economics nor isolationism had secured them and the nation they loved. They had no intention of falling back. Most wanted to go forward. And in critical ways they would.

Empowered by the massive public investments of the New Deal, the war effort, and the new GI Bill; by the increased purchasing power and enhanced well-being of working people afforded by twelve years of progressive democratic government and popular struggles; and by the profits, savings, and technical advances and "know how" accumulated in the fight against fascism and imperialism—not to mention a generation's eagerness to make up for lost time—Americans were to initiate a process of economic growth and development that would not only see the gross national product increase 250 percent by 1960, but engender a global economic boom that was to continue for more than a quarter of a century. And as a result, while inequality and poverty persisted, almost all Americans would enjoy higher living standards.

At the same time, Americans not only followed through on FDR's plan of turning the wartime "United Nations" into a permanent United Nations organization, the charter of which committed member nations to strive for peace and the Four Freedoms. They also took the lead in establishing the "Atlantic Alliance" and defending the liberal-democratic West against the Soviet-dominated Communist East in a global "Cold War" that would go on for forty years.[3]

And even as Americans began to do all of that, many of them also set out to "renew the march of freedom." Propelled by the promise of the Four Freedoms, a fresh surge of democratic aspiration and energy swept the country. Liberals and progressives advocated reviving the New Deal. Labor leaders called for fortifying "political democracy" with "economic democracy" and millions of workers challenged their bosses in a flood of strike actions. African Americans and Mexican Americans also mobilized to lay claim to their rights as citizens. As the historian Jack Metzgar, the son of a Pennsylvania steelworker and union shop steward, put it: "People came roaring out of our victory over Fascism with a sense that they would never allow things to be as they had been."[4]

But not everyone did so.

Americans had confronted the crises that had placed the nation and all that it stood for in mortal jeopardy by doing what the greatest of American generations before them had done in the face of existential crises—fighting like hell against their enemies and making America freer, more equal, and more democratic in the process. Indeed, they had transformed the nation and themselves more than anyone could ever have imagined them doing. And having vanquished depression and fascism, many Americans were not only eager to enjoy the postwar opportunities, but were prepared to conclude that the promise of the Four Freedoms had been essentially achieved in the course of the past twelve years or, at least, that attaining it no longer required social struggles to do so. More insidiously, even among those committed to advancing the Freedoms there were those who did not want to do so for *all* Americans.

Moreover, that powerful minority of conservatives, reactionaries, and capitalists that had opposed the enhancement of American democratic life in the 1930s and war years remained as determined as ever to try to put a stop to it all and, if possible, to restore the pre–New Deal political and economic order. They knew what they wanted and they would act aggressively to realize it. They could not take the country back to the 1920s. Those Americans who had just sacrificed so much would never let them. But within just a few years they would succeed in containing the democratic surge. And though the struggles for the Four Freedoms were far from finished, exploitable ambivalences had crept in—and conservative and corporate interests would become ever more skilled at exploiting them.

FDR was gone, but just weeks after Japan's surrender, President Harry Truman sent Congress a twenty-one-point "special message" that reaffirmed America's commitment to the Four Freedoms. Putting "freedom from want and fear" at the forefront of the nation's domestic agenda, he laid out initiatives to not only pursue the reconversion effort, such as maintaining price controls, raising the minimum wage, and providing unemployment compensation to uncovered categories of workers, but also build upon the achievements of the Roosevelt years, such as enacting the "Full Employment" bill already before Congress, making the wartime Fair Employment Practice Committee permanent, and launching major new public-works projects. And to make sure everyone got "the message," he included FDR's "Economic Bill of Rights" in it in full and two months later sent Congress yet another message outlining plans to assure health care coverage to all Americans.[5]

Liberals and progressives in and out of the administration spoke of turning Roosevelt's visionary pronouncements into policy. In *For This We Fought*, the Twentieth Century Fund economist Stuart Chase enumerated Americans' shared hopes for freedom, security, and opportunity, recommended public actions to realize them, and challenged labor to lead a movement to assure it all happened. In *Sixty Million Jobs*, the former Vice President and now Secretary of Commerce, Henry Wallace, argued not only for government planning and public works, but also for civil rights and racial equality. And in *Tomorrow Without Fear*, the former Office of Price Administration director Chester Bowles called for government to help create "A Better Division of a Bigger Economic Pie."[6]

Citing the promise of the Four Freedoms, labor leaders sought even more. The CIO and United Steelworkers president, Philip Murray, urged Congress to pass the pending "Full Employment" bill and renewed his prewar call for "industrial councils." And the United Auto Workers' GM Section head, Walter Reuther, who was soon to become UAW president and eventually president of the CIO, proposed "Peace Production Boards" with full labor participation, pushed for legislation to make jobs, education, housing, and health care available to all Americans, and campaigned to continue to raise workers' purchasing power.[7]

Joined by returning veterans, workers themselves went into action. One-third of them—15 million in all—belonged to unions; their solidarity was strong; and they knew what they wanted: job security, higher wages, better working conditions, and more respect and say in the workplace. Fed up with capital's wartime profits and pressures, and squeezed by companies reducing work hours and employees as they retooled for peacetime production, 5 million workers—oil workers, autoworkers, steelworkers, rubber workers, packinghouse workers, electrical-appliance workers, textile workers, longshoremen, teamsters, coal miners, and others—staged the largest strike wave in U.S. history in the fall and winter of 1945–46. Most Americans opposed walkouts, but they told pollsters that they backed labor's demands. Workers not out themselves showed their support in sympathy strikes and secondary boycotts. And several cities, including Houston, Rochester, and Pittsburgh, witnessed actions on the scale of general strikes. The nation's leading conservative, Senator Robert Taft of Ohio, the son of the late President and Chief Justice William Howard Taft, would remark that in most cases "the men are more radical than their leaders."[8]

Unionists knew they needed more friends in Congress and that to gain them they had to not only get out the labor vote but also expand it, especially below the Mason-Dixon Line. Acknowledging what animated their base, the CIO Political Action Committee issued "The People's Program for 1946." Quoting both the "Four Freedoms" and the "New Bill of Rights," the Program condemned the mutual ambitions of "greedy captains of industry and finance" and "reactionary Democrats and Republicans" and appealed to Americans to vote for candidates who supported progressive initiatives such as restoring price controls to fight inflation, passing bills to fund home construction and national health care, and enacting civil rights laws to protect minorities. Concurrently, the PAC commenced a southern voter-registration drive and the CIO itself initiated "Operation Dixie," a major southern organizing campaign to which it committed a $1 million budget and two hundred organizers—which instigated the AFL to follow suit with its own organizing campaign.[9]

Likewise, all across the South civil rights groups such as the National Association for the Advancement of Colored People and the Southern Conference for Human Welfare—along with the CIO-PAC—launched energetic voter-registration drives. Returning black GIs served as "the shock troops of the modern civil rights movement." In Mississippi, they helped to organize the Progressive Voters' League and succeeded in securing an investigation of U.S. Senator Theodore Bilbo for inciting violence against black voters—and then filled the hearing room to register their democratic anger and determination. In the Peach State, they created the Georgia Veterans League and took part in a voter-registration drive in which they told prospective registrants: "I spent over two years . . . in the armed services. I had hopes that my service would provide you with freedom from want and fear. Above all else I wanted to maintain YOUR freedom of speech." And in Alabama, one hundred of them marched to the courthouse in Birmingham in drill formation to register to vote. Despite fierce, often violent, resistance, the number of those who were registered increased from 250,000 to 1,000,000 between 1944 and 1950.[10]

Meanwhile, up north and out west, the NAACP, the Congress of Racial Equality, and the Urban League—reinforced by homecoming black GIs and a host of newly organized black veterans groups—pressed for an antilynching act, a permanent Fair Employment Practice Committee, and state laws to ban discrimination in housing and employment. The NAACP, the largest of the civil rights groups, continued to operate locally through its chapters and nationally by way of lobbying and lawsuits. And allied with liberal white groups it would win some critical and promising victories both at the state level and in the federal courts, including decisions banning segregation in interstate transport and restrictive housing covenants. They also succeeded in requiring some states to honor further the "equal" in "separate but equal" in their provision of professional education and training.[11]

Mexican Americans, too, were asserting their rights as citizens. The League of United Latin American Citizens remained their most significant civil rights group, but Latino aspirations and activism were expressed in various ways. Bringing together a coalition that included Jewish, Japanese, African, and Filipino Americans, Mexican Americans in Los Angeles organized the Community Service Organization (CSO) to work not only on community-development projects, but also at getting liberals and progressives elected to office—and soon CSO chapters were sprouting up in cities around California. At the same time, thousands of agricultural workers were joining the National Farm

Labor Union (NFLU), an affiliate of the AFL's Southern Tenant Farmers' Union, and striking for recognition by California's cotton and fruit growers. As NFLU supporters put it, these workers were fighting for the "Four Freedoms" and against the "Four Fears—fear of competition for the job; fear of inadequate wages; fear of unemployment; and fear of destitution." And in Texas, seven hundred Mexican-American veterans in the Corpus Christi area founded the American GI Forum and built it into the largest Latino veterans group in the Southwest. Committed to combating racism, promoting civic engagement, and securing "the blessings of democracy," the Texas GI Forum fought discrimination at the Veterans Administration, worked to end the segregation of Mexican-American children in the state's public schools, and campaigned against the poll tax.[12]

White veterans reflected white America. Overwhelmingly, they revered FDR, appreciated the New Deal, and supported the rights of labor. Still, they were no more or less political than white nonveterans, and, as odd as it may seem, many of those who returned from service to take up industrial jobs saw no contradiction in joining unions and the traditionally antilabor American Legion, whose membership between 1941 and 1946 tripled to more than 3 million. For most of the men, joining the local "post" represented a simple way to get involved in their community and a place to have a beer with men who understood what they had been through—not to mention the Legion had been crucial to securing the GI Bill.[13]

Notably, when the Army surveyed GIs in 1945 about the kind of veterans' group they might join, 20 percent replied it would probably be one that promoted "good government, national prosperity, democracy, [and] social programs." And failing to find such, a determined cohort of them created the American Veterans Committee (AVC), whose motto was "citizens first, veterans second."[14]

The AVC grew rapidly, gaining 100,000 members by 1947, among them prominent figures such as FDR's son Franklin Delano Roosevelt, Jr., the Pulitzer Prize–winning cartoonist Bill Mauldin, the actors Melvyn Douglas and Ronald Reagan, and the much-decorated war hero Audie Murphy. Moreover, the AVC practiced what it preached. While the national office lobbied Congress to enact progressive legislation and programs, local chapters worked with local union and civil rights groups in backing workers' struggles and fighting racism. And in contrast to the American Legion and Veterans of Foreign Wars, the AVC not only welcomed women veterans as equal members. It also required all of its chapters to be racially integrated, even those down south, where it actively campaigned for black voting rights. As the AVC chairman Charles Bolte put it: "We Fight for What We Fought For."[15]

They confronted, however, a congressional coalition of Republicans and southern Democrats not only already accomplished at killing New Deal agencies and blocking progressive bills, but also intent on both ending the wartime "Third New Deal" and scaling back the power of government and labor alike. The "Dixiecrats" were as committed as ever to defending their white supremacist regimes. And corporate bosses and former "dollar-a-year men" were eager both to exercise their "right to manage" and to advance their favorite freedom, the artfully termed Fifth Freedom, Free Enterprise. Possessed of their respective but not so discrete ambitions for postwar America, conservatives, reactionaries, and capitalists alike were ready to make the most of the nation's "reconversion" difficulties, persistent social antagonisms, and growing Cold War confrontation with the Soviet Union to counter the democratic surge.

Making matters worse, Harry Truman was no FDR and, his initial rhetoric aside, didn't appear to want to be. The new President replaced New Dealers with "conservatives, cronies, and hacks" and seemed to go out of his way to alienate Left, labor, and civil rights activists. Instead of moving to place himself, as Max Lerner had said of Roosevelt, "at the head of the urban and agrarian masses," Truman ignored the CIO's calls to enhance industrial democracy, failed to back the labor and the civil rights campaigns down south with federal resources, and not only wavered on issues of importance to working people and minorities such as maintaining the OPA and price controls and making the FEPC permanent, but all too often ended up deferring to the conservative-controlled Congress and corporate interests. And while he said he favored wage increases, he responded to labor's industrial actions by seeking congressional authority to constrain and discipline them—which in May 1946 included threatening to conscript striking railway workers if they did not return to their jobs. Only when 10 million politically disgruntled workers gave Congress to the GOP by failing to turn out to vote in the 1946 midterm elections, and it looked like northern blacks might well return to the party of Lincoln, would Truman start acting like a progressive.[16]

Moreover, no longer rallied by FDR against the crises of the Depression and the war and the forces of reaction, the movements and currents that drove the democratic surge would not stand united against the manifold assaults from the Right and conservative rich. Liberals and progressives alike wanted to revive the New Deal and renew the march of freedom, but they differed critically over how to handle the Soviets and America's own Communists and quickly split into, respectively, the anti-Communist Americans for Democratic Action (ADA/ formerly the Union for Democratic Action) and the open-to-all-on-the-left Progressive Citizens of America (soon to become the ill-fated Progressive Party). Labor not only witnessed renewed civil war between the AFL and the CIO, but also battles within the CIO that would lead to a purge of its Communist-led unions. The labor movement would continue to grow, but cease to be the militant progressive force it had been. And from the NAACP to the SCHW, the civil rights movement experienced similar difficulties, divisions, and purges over the question of how to handle Communists and radicals in their ranks.[17]

Worst of all, as much as the war effort had reduced ethnic and religious antagonisms, and the Holocaust had delegitimized racialist ideologies, color continued to divide Americans and severely impede their democratic struggles. Though the CIO's Operation Dixie recruited 218,000 new members, it would ultimately fail for a variety of reasons, not least among them racism, which southern bosses played on over and over again to counter labor organizers' appeals to class "solidarity." In fact, hoping to deter "race-baiting," the CIO's Southern Organizing Committee opted—despite labor's wartime successes in organizing southern black workers—to distance Operation Dixie from the CIO-PAC's voter-registration drive and to all but ignore those industries in which African Americans predominated. And while the AFL officially opposed racial segregation and discrimination, many of its constituent unions continued to practice it in their own affairs.[18]

Within just a few years the democratic surge would crash and break on the rocks of reaction and division. Americans would continue to pursue the promise of the Four Freedoms, but how they did so would change. As early as July 1948, Max Lerner would write: "The creative capacity itself seems to have gone out of American political life . . . What strikes me hardest about all this is the terrible waste of history it involves . . . The worst part of it is that most liberals seem to feel hopeless unless a new Great Depression comes. Can it be true that the greatness of the American people can be evoked only in adversity, and that liberalism is a plant that flowers only among the ruins?"[19]

Fully expecting the postwar resurgence of democratic aspirations and energies, conservatives, reactionaries, and capitalists mobilized to contain, redirect, and suppress it. Still dominated by the conservative coalition, Congress not only pulled the plug on the OPA and the FEPC. It also blocked anything that smacked of social democracy and higher taxes such as national health care and new TVA-style projects. The Full Employment bill was turned into a "maximum employment" act and federal "job creation" was limited to taxing and spending policies. Congress would entertain dozens of bills to corral labor. Plus, right-wingers did not hesitate to use the Cold War to bolster their efforts.[20]

America did confront a new adversary in the Soviet Union, and Americans were broadly united in the felt need to contain communism. Given Soviet actions in Eastern Europe and East Asia, this was more than understandable, but it had broader consequences. Whereas a hot war had spurred a determination to seek freedom from fear, the cold one seemed only to breed it.

Truman responded aggressively to Soviet machinations—too aggressively for some such as Henry Wallace, who would be fired from the cabinet and go on to run for President in 1948 as the nominee of the new Progressive Party. In 1947, Truman not only secured congressional approval for the Marshall Plan, a massive aid program to assist in Europe's reconstruction. He also proclaimed the "Truman Doctrine," which registered the nation's determination to "contain" communism globally; signed into law the National Security Act, establishing a unified Department of Defense and a new Central Intelligence Agency (CIA); and sent vital assistance to right-wing forces in Greece and Turkey to keep those countries from "going Communist."[21]

Conservatives, however, wanted to contain not just Soviet communism. They wanted to contain American democracy as well. In 1946, Republicans—most notably, the Navy veteran and future President Richard Nixon, then a candidate for Congress from California—jumped on revelations of Soviet espionage to accuse their Democratic opponents of being "Communist sympathizers" or worse (a tactic Nixon repeated in his 1950 campaign for the U.S. Senate). Whether or not the "red-baiting" was decisive in the GOP's victories, it led Truman to preemptively order a "loyalty review" of all federal employees. Far from deterring such attacks, the review—which itself undermined Americans' civil liberties by way of the broad authority it granted the Attorney General—gave conservatives even greater license to launch House Un-American Activities Committee investigations into the Communist presence in America from D.C. to Hollywood.[22]

Such "investigations" had little to do with exposing subversion. Congressional red-hunters were far more interested in smearing as "reds" New Dealers and just about everyone else on the left via "guilt by association." Max Lerner wrote of the 1947 hearings on the film industry: "The target is not Communism . . . which has no substantial roots in the American mind. The real objective is the muzzling of the movies." And such inquisitions, along with the red-baiting, red-hunting, blacklisting, firings, prosecutions, legislative acts, *and* equating of dissent with subversion that we would forever call "McCarthyism"—after the opportunistic and mendacious Wisconsin Senator Joseph McCarthy—would not only cost people their livelihoods and careers, but constrain political debate and imagination for years to come.[23]

Meanwhile, Dixie's rulers seemed bent on proving true what FDR had said in 1938—that they were no better than fascists. Southern senators continued to filibuster civil rights bills. The powerful and propertied "down home" continued to wield racism, anti-Semitism, anti-Catholicism, and anti-Communism against liberal and progressive calls for change. And their local minions continued to not only terrorize labor and civil rights organizers, but also assault and even kill blacks to keep things as they were—often with police complicity and, usually, the fearful silence of the majority of local citizens. In the only "official" lynching in Florida in 1945, a young black father and sharecropper, Jesse Payne, was taken from his jail cell in Madison County— where he was awaiting trial on doubtful charges—and was tortured and murdered with the apparent cooperation of the local sheriff. Unnoted in the news stories and later historical accounts was the bitter irony that the people of Madison County had not long before erected a Four Freedoms monument in memory of one of their native sons killed in combat.[24]

As John Egerton put it, the South witnessed "An epidemic of random murder and mayhem"—an epidemic against which even black GIs had no immunity. In February 1946, police in Batesburg, South Carolina, arrested Sergeant Isaac Woodard on highly questionable charges of disorderly conduct. Newly discharged from the Army and en route home by bus after fifteen months' service in the South Pacific, Woodard had quarreled with the white driver. No doubt to reacquaint Woodard with southern life, the police proceeded to beat and eventually blind him.[25]

The reactionary South found common company with corporate executives, who, flush with profits from the war, were eager to reassert their "right to manage." They fought price controls with everything from lobbying and public relations campaigns to withholding goods from the market, as the meatpacking industry did in 1946. They resisted workers' wage demands as long as they could, knowing that when price controls were lifted they could, if necessary, grant wage increases and pass the costs on to consumers. And through business organizations such as the National Association of Manufacturers, the U.S.

Chamber of Commerce, and the smaller but more elite and moderate Committee for Economic Development (CED), they pressed Congress to free them from regulations, taxes, and the power of labor. Nor did they stop there. They also sought to stifle all the popular talk of industrial and social democracy.[26]

Truman's national–health care proposal they portrayed as "communist inspired"—a claim that garnered critical backing from the ever-conservative American Medical Association (AMA), which spent $5 million opposing the President's plan. The corporate Right and its allies were not even above hijacking FDR's vision. The AMA president Donovan Ward went so far as to tell legislators: "I am calling on you as a believer in the principles of democracy and free enterprise and the much publicized 'Four Freedoms' to stand firmly against any legislation which has a tendency to subjugate American medicine." It was indicative of much to come. The more time passed, the more readily, and seemingly easily, would conservatives blur the memory and meaning of FDR's war-defining inspiration.[27]

Many a capitalist wished for an immediate return to the 1920s. But most recognized the impossibility of doing so. As the GM board chairman Alfred Sloan put it: "It took fourteen years to rid this country of prohibition. It is going to take a good while to rid the country of the New Deal, but sooner or later the ax falls and we get a change." Even the ever-belligerent NAM shifted from trying to destroy unions outright to the more realistic goal of constricting their power and growth. And in the wake of the 1946 midterm elections that goal came into reach.[28]

Firmly in command of Congress after the midterm elections, the Republicans responded to corporate desires—NAM spent $3 million in lobbying efforts—and proceeded to pass the Labor-Management Relations Act of 1947. Unions called it a "slave labor law." Better known as the Taft-Hartley Act, it outlawed sympathy strikes and secondary boycotts; prohibited foremen's unions; permitted states to enact "right-to-work" laws banning the closed shop; required leaders of unions seeking National Labor Relations Board (NLRB) services to sign affidavits stating they were not Communists; and made the NLRB less of an "advocate of unionism" and more of an industrial relations "conciliator." And to further hamstring the NLRB, Congress cut its budget and staff. All of which not only weakened the 1935 National Labor Relations Act ("Wagner Act") and made labor organizing, solidarity, and action all the more difficult, but served to keep the South relatively union-free. In consequence, the South became increasingly attractive to capital investment by northern companies seeking to escape organized workers.[29]

Corporate bosses aspired to do more than win recurrent political and industrial battles, however. They yearned to reshape public debate so as to obviate such conflicts. Most immediately, they wanted to conduct Americans' democratic aspirations and energies in a less progressive direction. Toward that end, business groups from NAM and the U.S. Chamber of Commerce to the essentially CED-aligned and "public-service"-oriented Advertising Council (formerly the War Advertising Council) initiated a new round of "PR" campaigns warning of the dangers of a too-powerful state and promoting Free Enterprise as the "American way" to prosperity. While other campaigns would be bigger and costlier, the most spectacular was surely the Freedom Train, a public-history exhibition of many of America's most treasured documents and artifacts that traveled town to city by rail.[30]

The idea for the Freedom Train originated in the Justice Department. Attorney General Tom Clark described it "as a means of aiding the country in its internal war against subversive elements and as an effort to improve citizenship by reawakening in our people their profound faith in the American historical heritage." However, both to avoid criticism of the cost and to calm Republican fears that the project might serve to boost the Democrats, the Truman administration handed it off to the American Heritage Foundation, a syndicate of leading business executives who proceeded to not only raise the necessary funds, but also gather the "appropriate" documents and objects from the National Archives.[31]

Setting out from Philadelphia in September 1947 on a sixteen-month journey that would take it to 322 cities, the Freedom Train received 3.5 million visitors and up to 50 million people would participate in Train-related events. To its credit, the American Heritage Foundation not only stressed racial and religious pluralism in its publications, but also stipulated, in response to black pressure, that if southern towns wished to receive the Freedom Train they had to suspend their segregationist laws for its visitations, which Birmingham, Alabama, and Memphis, Tennessee, refused to do.[32]

Nonetheless, the Freedom Train exhibit remained true to its directors' aim to "re-sell Americanism to Americans." While including a first edition of Paine's *Common Sense*, Jefferson's draft of the Declaration of Independence, the Bill of Rights, the Emancipation Proclamation, and the Nineteenth Amendment (the Women's Suffrage Amendment), conspicuously missing were documents celebrating the democratic initiatives and struggles of the Roosevelt years. You would have searched in vain for the Social Security and Wagner Acts, the executive order creating the FEPC, *and* FDR's addresses enunciating the Four Freedoms and Economic Bill of Rights. The directors even split up Norman Rockwell's Four Freedoms paintings. The official Freedom Train booklet, *Good Citizen: The Rights and Duties of an American*, contained images of Rockwell's *Freedom of Speech* and *Freedom of Worship*, but tellingly not *Freedom from Want* and *Freedom from Fear*.[33]

The Freedom Train proffered a history that essentially called on "good citizens" to defend and sustain, but not extend and deepen, American freedom, equality, and democracy. The goal was to contain democratic aspirations by suggesting America's promise was already achieved. The Professional Club of Miami, a progressive black group, rightly criticized it for offering an "uncritical and unquestioning acceptance of America as it is . . . [Which] repudiates the once popular concept of progress and regards America as a finished product, perfect and complete."[34]

Americans nevertheless responded enthusiastically to the Freedom Train. Paid for by corporate interests, it was designed to inspire national pride at the dawn of the Cold War rather than call forth progressive principles and new commitments. In fact, it rendered an image of the country that was already becoming the one more and more Americans, particularly white and rising middle-class Americans, wanted to embrace. Not every American, however, was willing to follow that script. Local organizers in Kansas City, Missouri, used the Train's visit to proclaim "Agriculture, Industry, and Labor Day." And their counterparts in Miami, Florida, put together a "Four Freedoms Day" in which even the women of the American Legion Auxiliary participated.[35]

The Right and conservative rich would have done well to listen to the notes of dissent. As the elections of 1948 were to show, the 1946 vote that put so many Republicans in office represented more of a protest against Truman and his party than an endorsement of what the Grand Old Party and its allies wanted to do to America.[36]

With Democrats scheming to replace him at the head of their ticket—and the Left and labor considering the formation of third parties—Truman set out to recover his "base." He not only began to project plans for a "Fair Deal." He also vetoed both Congress's latest tax bills, saying that they benefited the rich not working people, *and* the Taft-Hartley Act, promising, when Congress overrode his veto, to seek its undoing.

Even more impressively, Truman became an advocate of equal rights for African Americans. In December 1946, he responded to the mounting racial violence down south by creating the President's Committee on Civil Rights (PCCR) and requesting of its members that they not only study the question, but also recommend serious action to address it. In June 1947, he became the first president ever to speak to the NAACP convention and, doing so at the Lincoln Memorial, he not only highlighted FDR's Four Freedoms, but also told the assembled delegates that when he referred to the "rights of Americans" he meant "all Americans." And in October he released the PCCR's final report, *To Secure These Rights*, which—citing the Declaration of Independence, the Bill of Rights, and the Four Freedoms—not only forcefully condemned segregation, but also set the agenda for the postwar civil rights movement by advancing a host of legislative and other initiatives to guarantee "safety and security . . . citizenship and its privileges . . . freedom of conscience and expression . . . and equality of opportunity" to all Americans.[37]

Truman did not stop there. In February 1948, he sent Congress a "Special Message on Civil Rights" proposing a permanent FEPC, an antilynching law, and a federal guarantee of the right to vote. Then, in July, he called Congress into special session to address the civil rights question. And when Congress convened but did nothing, he acted. Responding to continuing black pressure and a threat by A. Philip Randolph that he would urge young men to resist the draft if the U.S. military was not desegregated, Truman issued two executive orders. The first established new nondiscriminatory rules for federal employment and the second commanded the integration of the armed forces. And that same summer, liberal Democrats, led by the mayor of Minneapolis, Hubert Humphrey, succeeded in putting a serious civil rights plank into their party's campaign platform—which drove many a southern delegate into a new States' Rights Party.[38]

The GOP renominated Governor Thomas E. Dewey of New York as its 1948 presidential candidate, and it was widely assumed that he would readily defeat Truman, if only because the Democratic Party lost its left and right wings that year to the new Progressive and States' Rights parties, respectively. But in the spirit of FDR, Truman fought back, aggressively campaigning on a pro–New Deal, pro-labor, pro–civil-rights platform. Traveling the country by train, he delivered hundreds of speeches in which he vigorously attacked the GOP-controlled Eightieth Congress as the "do-nothing Congress," bluntly charged that big business and its Republican servants were perverting American politics, and spoke strongly and often of America's historic purpose and promise. At Gilmore Stadium in Los Angeles, he said:

> The Democratic ideal of America is summed up in the Four Freedoms: Freedom from Want; Freedom from Fear; Freedom of Worship; and Freedom of Speech. The Republican ideal, as I have seen it in action, is summed up in one phrase, "Big business first." Today, I regret to say certain great business interests are trying to corrupt the American idealism. With the Republican Party as their instrument, they are waging a war against the aspirations of our people.[39]

Truman won reelection and the Democrats regained control of Congress. But victory did not see the enactment of his Fair Deal. The President forwarded domestic policy proposals to Congress and the Justice Department joined the NAACP in challenging segregation in the courts, but the unrepentant cohorts of the conservative coalition continued to block progressive legislation. The minimum wage was raised, Social Security was enlarged to cover 8 million more workers, and a major housing bill was passed. However, Congress killed national health care; Dixiecrats filibustered civil rights bills to death; and the Taft-Hartley Act lived on. And with the Soviets acquiring the atomic bomb, China falling to the "reds," war breaking out in Korea, new revelations of Soviet espionage, and Senator Joe McCarthy taking up the anti-Communist crusade and issuing outrageous accusations, Truman gave most of his attention to foreign affairs and national security. He dramatically increased the defense budget, ordered the "Berlin Airlift" to break a Soviet blockade of the city, established the North Atlantic Treaty Organization (NATO), sent U.S. troops to Korea, and authorized the Justice Department to prosecute the leaders of the Communist Party for "advocating the overthrow of the government."[40]

Despite what the majority of Americans said they wanted in casting their ballots, few domestic advances were made. But that mattered little to the likes of "Mr. Republican," Senator Taft, who called the Fair Deal a species of "socialism" and said his fellow citizens "did not understand the issues" when they voted.[41]

Truman had won reelection by rallying Americans to defend the promise of the Four Freedoms. But he did nothing to mobilize Americans to fight for the initiatives he proposed. And most Americans did not push for more aggressive action. Many, particularly white Americans, were enjoying a fast-growing economy and increasing prospects of prosperity. Many other Americans were worried about a new world war breaking out and constrained by red-baiting and race-baiting. The focus of the war years waned, though hardly for all, and never completely.

Truman's victory did instigate some folks to take more aggressive action. Corporate executives, seeing they could not suppress Americans' democratic aspirations and energies, set themselves all the more to containing or channeling them. Apparently taking to heart the NAM leader Walter Fuller's advice of 1942—"One thing is certain, the people of this country are fighting this war for a better world in which to live . . . We must either cut the cloth to fit that pattern or the reformers and demagogues will"—they stopped denying the promise of the Four Freedoms and increasingly sought to refashion the idea to their purposes.[42]

Just one week after the 1948 elections, the Advertising Council launched a massive new "PR" blitz to "educate" Americans to the wonders of the "American Economic System." Broadcast in every medium, and to venues from corporate cafeterias to school classrooms, the new campaign reflected a new approach. As much as it promoted "free enterprise," it acknowledged the right of workers to "organize and to bargain collectively" and the need for government "to undertake socially desirable projects when private interests prove inadequate to conduct them." These acknowledgments enabled the Advertising Council to garner endorsements for the campaign from prominent liberals and labor leaders, including ADA co-founder Reinhold Niebuhr, AFL president William Green, and CIO president Philip Murray.[43]

Moreover, without ever mentioning the Four Freedoms, the Advertising Council sought to incorporate them in its pro-business narrative. Its official booklet *The Miracle of America* declared: "Men follow two great impulses—to be politically free and to be economically *secure*. In America we have won political freedom and we are winning economic security. Dictators promise security if the people will give up freedom. But experience shows that freedom and economic security *must* grow together. The history of the United States proves it." And while the campaign highlighted the unmatched productivity of the American Economic System, it did not present that system as perfect. Noting that it had flaws that needed fixing, the campaign explained, tellingly, how everyone could address them—though, of course, the "how" had nothing to do with harnessing the powers of democratic government or curbing the power of capital:

If we all work together to increase our productivity, then we can spread its benefits through increased wages, lower prices, shorter hours, more jobs and better collective bargaining, as well as assure adequate return to investors and owners. Only in this way can we hope to level off the ups and downs of prices and jobs, lessen the chances of recurring depressions, reduce industrial disputes and enjoy the good things for all which our economic system *can* give us.[44]

Corporate executives clearly knew they needed more than good PR, however. Americans remained committed to the concrete goals behind the Four Freedoms, but the postwar, post-FDR world left many uncertain as to how to attain them. Knowing that, some capitalists began to advance a "private" way to "freedom from want and fear."

In 1948, General Motors took the lead in trying to "cut the cloth to fit that pattern" by offering the UAW a two-year contract with "quarterly cost-of-living adjustments" pegged to the consumer price index and an "annual improvement factor" based on GM productivity—the cost of which they now knew they could pass on to the consumer in the form of higher prices. UAW president Walter Reuther himself had already said, "There is no evidence to encourage the belief that we may look to Congress for relief. In the immediate future, security will be won for our people only to the extent that the union succeeds in obtaining such security through collective bargaining." But Reuther and his union colleagues were still hesitant to accept the offer, for they recognized that it represented a critical diversion from the public and universal path they had been pushing for, as well as a recipe for inflation. And yet, seeing the public and universal path repeatedly blocked, and showing no sign of opening up, they took the offer.[45]

With the conservative coalition retaining command of Congress that November, unions had little choice but to follow the collective-bargaining path to win both higher wages and better benefits. They had to threaten and regularly strike to secure their goals. But the way ahead became all the more firmly set in 1950 when the UAW and GM signed the so-called Treaty of Detroit, a five-year contract guaranteeing "pensions, health insurance, the union shop, and a 20 percent increase in the standard of living of those auto workers who labored under its provisions." Labor continued to promote the cause of national health care, but the "Treaty" ended the progressive postwar drive for a more democratic economy and the "social citizenship" projected in the Economic Bill of Rights and paved the way to the uniquely American, "divided" or "public-private" welfare state.[46]

Not only labor leaders were heading in new directions. So, too, were many a liberal and Left intellectual. But whereas labor seemed compelled to do so, Left intellectuals seemed self-propelled. Some were crossing over to the Right. Others were moving to the center, among them prominent figures in the founding of Americans for Democratic Action, such as Reinhold Niebuhr, the historian Arthur M. Schlesinger, Jr., and the economist John Kenneth Galbraith.[47]

In books titled *The Irony of American History*, *The Vital Center: The Politics of Freedom*, and *American Capitalism: The Concept of Countervailing Power*, Niebuhr, Schlesinger, and Galbraith, respectively, sought both to distance liberalism and themselves from their progressive, if not radical, pasts, and to develop it as a movement or "fighting faith" militantly opposed to the extremes of right and left alike. The horrors of fascism, Nazism, and communism had led them and their colleagues to question the prospect of giving too much power and authority to "the state." And the somewhat mistaken assumption that those "totalitarian" regimes had been raised into power by "mass movements" of the working classes had made them distrustful, if not downright fearful, of the democratic impulses of the "common man."[48]

These "new liberals" still wanted to regulate capitalism and expand the "welfare state," but they no longer called for "the people" to harness the powers of democratic government to curb the power of capital, redistribute wealth and income, and progressively transform America. Conceiving of organized labor as a "countervailing power" to capital, they now argued that government needed to serve as the "umpire" among competing classes and groups and, given the social reforms of the New Deal, they recommended public policies and programs to stimulate economic growth so as to provide "more" for everyone: higher profits for business, higher wages for workers, and greater opportunities for the poor. The head of the UAW's Washington office, Donald Montgomery, would tell Walter Reuther that while he did not oppose working with them, it was important to realize that these very liberals "don't trust the people and therefore interpret democracy in terms of doing good for people rather than having the people do it." Indeed, as much as these "vital centrists" would champion the memory and legacy of the Roosevelt years, they were already forgetting a good deal about both the President and the people who made it all possible.[49]

By the early 1950s, liberals were tamed, progressives and radicals were marginalized, and calls to renew the march of freedom were dismissed as "un-American." The CIO had expelled its Communist-led unions, terminated Operation Dixie, and opened reunification talks with the AFL. The NAACP had ejected its Communist members and shifted its attentions back from economic rights to a more narrowly conceived "civil rights." And the progressive Southern Conference for Human Welfare, which had won the heartfelt endorsement of Eleanor Roosevelt, had folded up altogether. Even the once so promising American Veterans Committee was struggling to survive after suffering red-baiting from the right and Communist factionalism on the left. Speaking volumes, *Life's Picture History of World War II*, published in 1950, mentioned the Four Freedoms only in passing—referring to them as simply "the commonplaces of Anglo-American propaganda."[50]

In 1952, the Republicans nominated the war hero General Dwight D. Eisenhower ("Ike") as their presidential candidate and won both the White House and Congress with a platform that essentially accused the Democrats of treason. Declaring that the Roosevelt and Truman administrations had "so undermined the foundations of our Republic, as to threaten its existence," it stated: "We charge that [the Democrats] have arrogantly deprived our citizens of precious liberties . . . that they work unceasingly to achieve their goal of national socialism . . . that they [are] fostering class strife . . . that they have shielded traitors to the Nation." Even more telling, the Democrats drafted a platform that no longer cited FDR's peroration and proceeded to nominate, with the blessing of liberals, Illinois Governor Adlai Stevenson, a candidate who rejected the idea of national health insurance, questioned legislating civil rights at the federal level, seemed unsure about repealing Taft-Hartley, and proceeded to name a southern segregationist, Senator John Sparkman of Alabama, as his running mate.[51]

The political scientist Clinton Rossiter would bluntly write, "We Americans are now passing though a period of political and cultural conservatism quite without precedent in all our history." Rather ironically, the defeated Stevenson would only later opine to fellow party members: "Where are [Franklin Roosevelt's Four Freedoms] today? Who speaks for them now? Those gallant hopes of yesterday have given way to the confusion of today. The Four Freedoms have been replaced by the Four Fears—fear of depression; fear of communism; fear of ourselves; fear, if you please, of freedom itself."[52]

Stevenson was right to ask, but raising the question after defeat, and only to party members, demonstrated how much he failed to grasp the larger implications. Liberal intellectuals and Democratic politicians may have become forgetful, fearful, and even relatively conservative, but most Americans had not. The generation that had won the war, a generation with roots into the New Deal and Great Depression, a generation that was great before being anointed Great, had not. They had given up neither their hard-won achievements nor the promise that encouraged them. Postwar prosperity, McCarthyism, and the politics of race had blunted the felt urgency of their commitments, but critically absent was any politician or party rallying them to the principles they had fought and won a global war for. A generation continued to feel America's democratic imperative and impulse. And the powers that be knew it. Their task would be to control and redefine not just the Four Freedoms, but the very animating impulse of the men and women who had given their all in service to the historic progressive vision of America's potential.

CHAPTER TEN

"What has it been asked to do that it has not done?"

Dwight Eisenhower never cited the Four Freedoms as President. But he never lost sight of them. Knowing what they had meant to his troops, Ike surely figured that just because Democratic politicians were giving up FDR's words didn't mean Americans had given up the promise they pronounced. He said to his press secretary in 1954: "This party of ours . . . will not appeal to the American people unless the American people believe that we have a liberal program." And fed up with rich far-right Republicans trying to tell him what he should do, he wrote to his brother Edgar: "Should any political party attempt to abolish social security, unemployment insurance, and eliminate labor laws and farm programs, you would not hear of that party again in our political history."[1]

To the dismay of the Right, the struggles of the late 1940s engendered not a conservative political consensus, but a liberal one—subject to Cold War and corporate imperatives and led by a Republican, but liberal nonetheless.

Eisenhower was a conservative. He didn't like the New Deal, labor unions, or civil rights activism. He filled his cabinet with corporate executives and lawyers, refused to challenge Senator McCarthy, and—

though he ended the Korean War in a stalemate—pursued the Cold War aggressively, which included not only bolstering or propping up anti-Communist dictators from Central America to Southeast Asia, but also secretly using the CIA to overthrow reformist leaders in Iran and Guatemala.[2]

But Eisenhower wanted a stable, prosperous, and strife-free America and he knew what that demanded. Calling himself a "Modern Republican," he kept tax rates on corporations and the rich high, approved the largest public-works project in American history, the Interstate Highway System, signed bills making Social Security nearly universal and raising the minimum wage by 33 percent, established the Department of Health, Education and Welfare, and even warned against the power of the "military-industrial complex" in his Farewell Address. Furthermore, he appointed a Chief Justice, Earl Warren, who would lead the Supreme Court in 1954 to unanimously declare in *Brown v. Board of Education* that racial segregation in the nation's public schools was unconstitutional—a historic decision that in 1957 would compel Eisenhower to federalize the Arkansas National Guard and send army troops into Little Rock to uphold the Constitution when Governor Orval Faubus tried to use the Guard to prevent the court-ordered desegregation of the city's Central High School.[3]

Ike had won in 1952 because he was a war hero. And though voters returned Congress to Democratic control in 1954, he defeated Adlai Stevenson again in 1956 because for most Americans things were going well and promised to get even better.

Millions of veterans had used the GI Bill to get a college education or become skilled in a trade and to buy homes in one of the thousands of burgeoning new suburban developments. Stella Suberman, the wife of a veteran Air Corps bombardier and "GI Bill Boy," would write, "America had put its faith in its veterans and its veterans did not intend to let America down." And they didn't. They created unprecedented economic growth and widely shared prosperity—indeed, more and more of them were on their way to securing "middle class living standards."[4]

Americans were moving not just city to suburb, but also west. And

while southern blacks were still heading north, industry—though profits were already soaring—was heading south to nonunion labor and
lower wages and taxes. At the same time, the postwar "baby boom" was
sending the U.S. population up from 140 million at war's end to 180
million in 1960, and both the new medium of television and a growing
network of highways were connecting Americans in new ways.[5]

Many a writer has presented the 1950s as a fearful time. However,
while A-bombs and red scares took their tolls on public life and imagination, polls showed Americans actually fretted little about Communists either overseas or at home. And as the journalist and Office of
War Information veteran James Reston would point out in 1960: "In
the 15 years of the atomic age, [Americans] increased the population
of the nation by more than 40,000,000, which is not the action of a
frightened people."[6]

In fact, America witnessed a new sort of democratic surge. The men
and women who beat fascism and imperialism did not erect war memorials. Taking their cue from the New Deal and the war effort, they built
communities. As *Time* reported in 1953: "there is a tremendous amount
of building going on: new store buildings, clubhouses and public institutions, and dozens and dozens of modern schools." But they were not just
putting up buildings. They were joining groups like the American Legion, the Elks, the Lions, the Rotary Club, the League of Women Voters, and the PTA, and becoming congregants of their respective faiths'
churches and synagogues—and where such did not yet exist, they were
creating them. A "civic generation," they also turned out to vote in
greater numbers than their parents did or children would.[7]

Moreover, Ike was right. Americans remained liberal in spirit. Polls
indicated a growing majority believed that the federal government
ought not only "to see to it that everybody who wants to work can find
a job," but also "help people get doctors and hospital care at low cost."
And while "right-to-work" laws effectively blocked labor organizing in
Dixie and some states out west, unions grew elsewhere. By 1955, 35
percent of all workers, 18.5 million in all, had joined one, and all knew
it was "the union" that brought them their rising incomes. When a
walkout was called, solidarity prevailed—and despite a high level of

strike activity, polls showed that 75 percent of Americans approved of unions.[8]

Still other polls revealed real progress in racial attitudes. Whereas in 1942 a majority of whites said that blacks were not as smart as whites, that they did not want black and white children in the same schools, and that having black neighbors would bother them, an ever-growing majority—outside of the South—now said otherwise on every question. Admittedly, attitude change was hardly enough. While America's new suburban neighborhoods came to resemble the bomber crews of the war for their ethnic mix, they also did so because blacks were usually excluded. And yet black Americans were making significant strides in public life not just from big-league sports to popular music, but politically as well. In addition to winning the *Brown* decision, the NAACP and its allies secured "fair employment" laws in twenty-nine northern and western states.[9]

The South, however, remained another country. Encouraged by *Brown*, local civil rights groups, often led by black World War II veterans, fought on against Jim Crow. But Dixie's rulers issued a "Southern Manifesto" calling for "massive resistance"; middle-class whites formed Citizens' Councils just steps up from the KKK; and it seemed pretty clear that the Eisenhower administration did not intend to actually push school desegregation. As the Mississippi NAACP activist and war veteran Aaron Henry recalled, "It was plain that we could expect no help from local, state or federal authorities." And still, he said: "[We] were in the fight . . . all the way. We had to hang on."[10]

Thus the struggle continued and even won a promising victory in Montgomery, Alabama, when the black community, led by the young Reverend Martin Luther King, Jr., protested the arrest of Mrs. Rosa Parks in December 1955 for refusing to give up her bus seat to a white man by staging an arduous and ultimately successful yearlong bus boycott to secure the integration of the system.[11]

But the liberal spirit was not mobilized into a popular politics. There was no call to action. The Democrats failed to emulate FDR and liberal intellectuals continued to see labor as a "countervailing power" at best and the working class as a potentially dangerous force.

Some even argued that the nation had transcended the contradictions and conflicts of the past by developing a "people's capitalism" with a "mixed economy" and "welfare state," a new politics of "pluralism," and a "middle-class society." And hoping that such developments would eventually weaken Dixie's fierce opposition to racial equality, many retreated to a politics of "gradualism" on civil rights. *Time* said of American intellectuals: "the man of protest has . . . given way to the man of affirmation."[12]

Organized labor did little better. The 1955 merger of the AFL and CIO may have enhanced its lobbying power, but it did not reinvigorate unionism as a social movement. Walter Reuther and A. Philip Randolph continued to call for progressive action and organizing the unorganized and the million-strong New York City labor movement was actually turning Gotham into a social-democratic city. But they were in the minority. The AFL-CIO remained committed to repealing Taft-Hartley, securing national health care, and promoting racial equality. However, headed by George Meany, an AFL bureaucrat who reportedly took pride in never having walked a picket line (not to mention having arranged for the federation to collaborate with the CIA against radical unionism overseas), it not only abandoned the CIO vision of industrial democracy, it also failed to require unions with race-exclusive policies to do away with them. Praising "private-enterprise" for what it was affording workers, Meany wrote: "We do not seek to recast American society . . . We seek an ever rising standard of living."[13]

Meanwhile, discounting a generation's phenomenal civic activism, and exaggerating the spread of "affluence," a chorus of elitist social critics decried the "masses" for their "privatism," "materialism," and "conformism." Even the radical sociologist C. Wright Mills referred to working people as "cheerful robots." But as James Reston would rightly counter: "this generation . . . may be more concerned about its private interests than about the public interest, but if a man is offered a choice between a Cadillac and a swift kick in the pants, we should not be surprised if he doesn't bend over." Indeed, Reston asked, "What has it been asked to do that it has not done?"[14]

The liberal consensus did not roll on simply by inertia, however. On the right, the National Association of Manufacturers and U.S. Chamber of Commerce still campaigned against the New Deal, labor unions, and "freedom from want and fear," and conservative activists readily found rich folk prepared to underwrite new endeavors such as the American Enterprise Institute "think tank," the *National Review* magazine, and the even more reactionary and ever-paranoid John Birch Society. But those who actually led the nation wanted to sustain the "postwar settlement," not wreck it.[15]

Like Eisenhower, the country's foremost politicians and corporate executives—who, along with its military chiefs, C. Wright Mills dubbed the "power elite"—knew they still had to attend to Americans' democratic impulses. So they, too, waged expensive new "PR" campaigns, the most notable conducted by the Advertising Council. And as the Council's booklet *People's Capitalism* stated, their goal was "to create a *consensus* that *could* become the possession of the average man." However, in contrast to the Right, they did not bewail the state of American freedom. They celebrated it.[16]

The clearest statement of their vision appeared in *What Is America?* Based on the deliberations of a panel of "distinguished" business, academic, and labor figures—all white men—the book advanced a narrative in which Americans had triumphed over inequality, racism, concentrations of power, and crises due to their shared values of faith, freedom, individualism, hard work, brotherhood, dissent, and civic association.[17]

Much was exaggerated, glossed over, or denied in the telling. Corporations were praised for their contributions to "our economic performance." Unions were valued, but labor's historic struggles received no attention. And America was celebrated as a "classless society." Jim Crow racism was reduced to a matter of discrimination that blacks could escape by simply moving away from it. McCarthyism was ignored. And though the Great Depression and selected New Deal programs were noted, neither the New Deal nor FDR was ever named. Moreover, while the story clearly incorporated the Four Freedoms, they, too, were never named. Most critically, however, Americans were portrayed as forever preferring to pursue their needs and aspirations individually or through business enterprise and "voluntary organizations"—not by mobilizing and harnessing the powers of democratic government.[18]

As the Ad Council's continuing "roundtables" attest, the distinguished men were not unmindful of the nation's problems—including the fact that more than 20 percent of all Americans still lived in poverty. But they insisted they could solve them by simply expanding the U.S. economy still further. And most Americans seemed to agree.[19]

The progressive Max Lerner, too, spoke of the United States in superlatives. But he urged his fellow citizens to remember *"We have not come to the end of history."* And even as he did so, events and developments were causing tensions to flare, democratic impulses to quicken, and the governing elites to think again.[20]

The Cold War was not just going all the more global with the decolonization of Asia and Africa, but also coming closer to home by way of the Cuban Revolution, and even taking off into space with the Soviets launching *Sputnik*, the first orbiting satellite, in 1957. Still more troubling, the severest recession since the war struck that same year. Unemployment once again became a public issue; "ghetto life" got tougher as black joblessness soared to 16 percent (compared with a bad enough 5.8 percent for whites); and urban race relations grew tenser as competition for jobs increased—especially as businesses were seeking to "automate" production and starting to export jobs overseas. All of which, along with the Little Rock school desegregation battle, afforded rich material for Soviet propaganda directed at the nonwhite "Third World."[21]

Taking advantage of the rising unemployment and falling industrial-union rolls, the Right and capital moved quickly against labor. Senate conservatives opened investigations into "labor racketeering" that exposed rampant corruption in the Teamsters and several other unions and led to passage of the Landrum-Griffin Act, subjecting unions to still greater government scrutiny. GOP legislators in six midwestern and western states placed "right-to-work" referenda on their states'

1958 ballots. And executives sought to roll back workers' gains of the previous ten years.[22]

The AFL-CIO, however, fought back. Rallying voters, it not only defeated the antiunion ballot initiatives in five of the six states, but also helped to give the Democrats huge wins in the 1958 midterm elections and to sizably increase the number of liberals in Congress (though still not enough to overcome the conservative coalition).[23]

Labor also battled capital directly and, while defeats were suffered, victories were won, including one in the steel industry in 1959 that saw 500,000 workers go out on strike, the largest union action ever in U.S. history. And public employees—whose postwar ranks included growing numbers of women and minorities—were organizing their own unions, demanding collective-bargaining rights, and winning breakthrough victories in New York City in 1958 and Wisconsin in 1959.[24]

Civil rights activism continued as well. Following the Montgomery victory in 1957, King and the Reverend Ralph Abernathy, a World War II veteran, launched the Southern Christian Leadership Conference (SCLC). And organized black pressure and the competition for northern black votes led a coalition of congressional Republicans and northern Democrats to push through a civil rights bill that, though watered down in the Senate, did give the federal government some muscle to enforce voting rights.[25]

Determined to sustain the postwar settlement, the governing elites responded. The Rockefeller Brothers Fund, the magazine mogul Henry Luce, and the Eisenhower administration organized high-profile panels to, respectively, consider the nation's "Prospects," reformulate the "National Purpose," and propose "Goals for Americans." Like the Ad Council's roundtables, these, too, expressed tremendous pride in the nation's accomplishments and great expectations of its future. However, attending more critically to its challenges and problems, they called for not only private and corporate but also *public* initiatives to address them. And yet they still insisted that the pursuit of the Cold War and the inclusion of the excluded in America's promise required greater economic growth and development—not democratic mobilization or redistribution.[26]

But "the wind is beginning to change," the historian Arthur Schlesinger, Jr., observed and, writing more impatiently, the former OWI director Archibald MacLeish argued that America's purpose remained what it always was—"to set men free"—and the task was not to articulate it anew "but to *exercise* it." Which is just what black collegians and their supporters were doing that very spring when, following the lead of four North Carolina A&T students in Greensboro, 50,000 of them staged lunch counter sit-ins across the South and the nation demanding not just service, but an end to segregation. Apparently anxious about what it all portended, the right-wing editors of *The Freeman* published a direct attack on the Four Freedoms in their April 1960 issue.[27]

Effectively setting the new decade's public agenda, both major parties issued campaign platforms that summer more liberal than their previous ones. Priding itself the party of Lincoln, the GOP included a strong civil rights plank in its own. And recommitting themselves to not only Jefferson's "Rights of Man" but also "the Economic Bill of Rights which Franklin Roosevelt wrote into our national conscience," the Democrats declared they would act to create full employment; strengthen workers' rights and protect consumers; improve the nation's environment, public infrastructure, and cities; ensure decent housing, education, and health care; reform immigration; assure women's equality; safeguard civil liberties; and—referring to the recent "peaceful demonstrations for first-class citizenship"—guarantee civil rights and actually end segregation.[28]

Admittedly, the parties' nominees, World War II veterans all, were not as liberal as the platforms on which they ran. The Democratic presidential nominee, Senator John F. Kennedy (JFK) of Massachusetts, a son of the wealthy former America Firster and FDR antagonist Joseph P. Kennedy, voted with liberals in Congress, but he had not opposed McCarthy, was no champion of labor or civil rights, and, to signal southerners that he would not try to impose integration or abolish Taft-Hartley, had selected as his running mate Senator Lyndon Baines Johnson (LBJ) of Texas, a once-avid New Dealer who, while never an ardent segregationist, had turned into a big-business-friendly politician. And the GOP nominee, Vice President Richard Nixon, who was to lose in 1960 but come back to win in 1968, was an infamous red-baiter; though, oddly, his running mate, the former Massachusetts Senator Henry Cabot Lodge, Jr., had belonged to the progressive American Veterans Committee in the late 1940s. Nevertheless, not only did each man necessarily embrace his respective party's platform, but all who would actually become President in the 1960s—Kennedy, Johnson, even Nixon—would be led by his fellow citizens to move in a more liberal direction while in the White House.[29]

The generation that had carried out the New Deal and the war effort was coming to see that history was not over and that renewed democratic public action was called for. Entering middle age and the middle class, most, absent a major crisis, were not likely to take to the streets to demand it. But many were already demonstrating a readiness to defend their achievements and their ability to pursue America's promise. And there were others—believing in that promise no less, but still excluded from too much of it—who were ready to march.

Joined by sympathetic whites, southern blacks in particular would courageously, nonviolently, and ever more determinedly demand their rights as citizens. Some would be killed and many bloodied. And yet they would move the nation to finally bring an end to Jim Crow's rule, while demonstrating that the making of American democracy was not over, encouraging others to act as well.[30]

Moreover, Americans of every color and creed had instilled a belief in America's purpose and promise in their children. And many of those children would not only serve in the military or the new Peace Corps or VISTA, but also—inspired by both the civil rights movement and the struggles and achievements of their parents' generation, as well as voices from it—rally around groups such as the Student Nonviolent Coordinating Committee (SNCC), Students for a Democratic Society (SDS), and Berkeley's Free Speech Movement and help push their parents to even more affirmatively answer the question posed by *Yank's* editors in 1945: *"If Franklin Roosevelt's hopes and dreams are deep enough in the hearts and minds of the people, the people will make them come true."*[31]

As ever, the ranks of the once-young men and women of the 1930s and 1940s included conservatives and reactionaries high and low who would oppose and even resist the renewed "march of freedom." Sadly, they were also to witness assassinations, riots, and movements that scorned their accomplishments. Even more tragically, they would allow the United States to descend into a war that would sorely divide the nation, limit democratic possibilities, and—after taking 58,000 American lives—end in defeat. And yet, in the course of the "long decade of the 1960s," they would not only continue to expand the economy, but also once again harness the powers of democratic government to extend and deepen American freedom, equality, and democracy.

They would start in 1960 by electing JFK, a Democrat publicly committed to his party's progressive platform agenda and the first Roman Catholic ever to serve as President. Moreover, it was most of all men and women of their own generation who, having set that agenda, organized the campaigns to pursue it and enacted so much of it.

Kennedy's victory seemed to assure democratic action. As a candidate, JFK spoke more of "New Frontiers" than of the New Deal. But he celebrated the Four Freedoms, promised to act rapidly to fulfill his platform commitments, if necessary by way of executive orders, and appointed to his cabinet several former AVC members, including Orville Freeman at Agriculture, Stewart Udall at Interior, and Arthur Goldberg at Labor. In fact, hearing his inaugural address, one might have been reminded of FDR. Proclaiming "Let the word go forth from this time and place, to friend and foe alike, that the torch has been passed to a new generation of Americans," the new President said: "Now the trumpet summons us again—not as a call to bear arms . . . but a call to bear the burden of a long twilight struggle . . . a struggle against the common enemies of man: tyranny, poverty, disease and war itself."[32]

And yet, after telling Americans to "ask not what your country can do for you—ask what you can do for your country," Kennedy didn't ask very much of them. Worried about antagonizing business and a still conservative Congress—and apparently more determined to fight the

Cold War from Cuba to Southeast Asia than to renew the New Deal—
he failed to move quickly on his campaign promises. He also opted for
an economic growth strategy that entailed seeking major tax cuts favoring corporations and the rich rather than greater spending on public works and job creation.[33]

Liberals and progressives, however, went to work. While AFL-CIO
leaders lobbied the White House to act on the Democratic agenda, a
cohort of prominent unionists, including Walter Reuther, set up Four
Freedoms, Inc., to push for federal initiatives for the elderly and develop their own plans to build senior citizen housing. And the labor
federation joined a coalition of ethnic and religious groups in calling
for changes to America's racist immigration law.[34]

Still others sought to renew "the movement" in the labor movement itself. Fed up with the AFL-CIO's failure to ban race-exclusive
unions, A. Philip Randolph led a new Negro American Labor Council to promote unionism in the black community and try to get all-
white unions to recruit blacks. Concurrently, in 1962, César Chávez,
a World War II navy veteran, organized thousands of California Mexican-American agricultural laborers into a new United Farm Workers
(UFW) by addressing both pay and civil rights issues (though the UFW
co-founder Dolores Huerta contended their success owed in good part
to "the New Deal tradition among older Americans"); Leon Davis, a
Polish-born Jew whose labor career began in 1932, and Moe Foner,
a longtime progressive unionist and World War II army veteran, led
New York's multiracial Hospital and Healthcare Workers Local 1199
in a strike against the city's private hospitals that pioneered the recognition of hospital employees' rights; their fellow New Yorker Al Shanker led the city's teachers' union to win a precedent-setting contract;
and Reuther and the UAW not only actively backed the civil rights
movement, but also helped underwrite the early organizing efforts of
both the new UFW and the "New Left" SDS that emerged out of the
"old left" Student League for Industrial Democracy (SLID) and whose
"founding" took place at the UAW's Port Huron, Michigan, Franklin
Delano Roosevelt Labor Center.[35]

Energized by the black collegians who sat in at lunch counters and formed the SNCC in 1960, and led by veterans of the fight for the "Double Victory," civil rights activists went to work as well. Roy Wilkins, editor of the NAACP's *The Crisis* in the 1930s and 1940s, now headed the NAACP itself. Whitney Young, Jr., a World War II combat veteran, directed the National Urban League (NUL). James Farmer, Jr., a 1942 co-founder of the Congress of Racial Equality, now led it. The youngest of the cohort, Martin Luther King, Jr., who had learned about not only the Social Gospel but also FDR's "Freedom from want and fear" from his father, Reverend King, Sr., and the Morehouse College president Benjamin Mays during the war, still led the SCLC. And Ella Baker, whose progressive organizing career began with the WPA's Worker Education Project in the 1930s, now mentored SNCC's young activists. The NAACP and NUL intensified their political and business lobbying efforts and CORE, the SCLC, and SNCC staged Freedom Rides, demonstrations and marches, and voter-registration drives in which Americans young and old, black and white, male and female, put their lives on the line across the South to reveal to all how brutally oppressive segregation remained.[36]

At the same time, liberal and progressive women were placing the question of gender equality all the more directly on the political table. In January 1961, the Oregon Democrat Edith Green, who first worked as a lobbyist for the Oregon Education Association in the 1940s, introduced a House bill to guarantee "equal pay for equal work." That same year, the director of the Labor Department's Women's Bureau, Esther Peterson, who became a union and consumer activist in the 1930s, persuaded JFK to set up the President's Commission on the Status of Women with Eleanor Roosevelt as its chair. And the writer Betty Friedan, who started out as a left-wing labor journalist in the 1940s, would challenge women to reflect on their lives and status in her 1963 bestseller, *The Feminine Mystique,* and launch a new wave of feminist activism.[37]

Others, too, were raising their voices. In 1962, the biologist Rachel Carson, a veteran of the Roosevelt-era U.S. Fish and Wildlife Service, published *Silent Spring.* Warning of how chemical pesticides were endangering American lives, she incited a vicious barrage of attacks against her by the chemical industry but succeeded in revolutionizing public understanding of humanity's impact on nature and turning the conservationist movement into the "environmental movement." No less urgently, the ecologist Barry Commoner, a World War II navy veteran, mobilized scientists and public opinion against nuclear weapons tests. And the socialist Michael Harrington published *The Other America*, a small work that helped to make poverty a major national issue.[38]

Lobbied, pressed, and gaining little ground in Congress or the South, Kennedy began to act in 1962. He nominated the Labor Secretary, Arthur Goldberg, to the Supreme Court, an appointment that solidified the "Warren Court's" liberal majority and led to landmark decisions on separation of church and state (*Engel v. Vitale*, 1962), "one person, one vote" (*Reynolds v. Sims*, 1964), and the rights of the accused (*Miranda v. Arizona*, 1966); issued executive orders granting 2 million federal employees collective-bargaining rights and integrating federal public housing; and called for enactment of a Consumer Bill of Rights: "the right to safety, the right to be informed, the right to choose, the right to be heard." And in 1963, buoyed politically by his apparent success in handling the "October Missile Crisis," he not only directed federal agencies to start drawing up plans for an antipoverty program, proposed changes to America's immigration law, signed the Equal Pay Act, appointed a scientific advisory committee to investigate the use of chemical pesticides, and signed the Nuclear Test Ban Treaty. He also responded firmly to the intensifying racial violence down south—the worst of it that spring in Birmingham, Alabama, where white supremacists had set off bombs in the black community and police officers attacked a children's march with fire hoses and dogs, film of which Americans saw on the television news that evening.[39]

On June 11, Kennedy announced to the nation that he was going to ask Congress "to act, to make a commitment it has not fully made in this century to the proposition that race has no place in American life or law"—the need for which was made all the more evident when the Mississippi NAACP leader Medgar Evers, a World War II combat veteran, was assassinated outside his home in Jackson that same night.[40]

One week later, the President sent Congress a bill to outlaw segregation and discrimination in public facilities and accommodations. The bill disappointed many for it contained no significant voting rights provisions or any serious initiatives to address black joblessness and poverty. But it was radical in its implications, and everyone expected strong opposition and a southern filibuster—which made civil rights activists wonder just how hard Kennedy would actually fight for it.

Determined to once again make a Democratic President do the right thing, and this time Congress, too, A. Philip Randolph, aided by the veteran organizer Bayard Rustin and Walter Reuther and the UAW, mobilized a grand coalition of rights, religious, and labor groups and that August staged the historic 250,000-strong March on Washington for Jobs and Freedom on the National Mall—at which King delivered his famous "I Have a Dream" speech.[41]

Kennedy was assassinated in Dallas on November 22, 1963. But the democratic swell did not subside and, stunningly, Lyndon Johnson set out not simply to realize JFK's nascent initiatives, but also, as he put it, to "finish Franklin Roosevelt's revolution."[42]

Insisting he was always more liberal than Kennedy, Johnson explained his renewed progressivism by saying the presidency had "freed" him to once again act so. An ambitious man of humble beginnings who had moved expediently to the right in the late 1940s, LBJ had become a rich wheeler-dealer politician, indeed "Master of the Senate" in the 1950s. And yet this grandson of a Populist carried with him both a deep desire to help the poor, derived in part from experiences teaching Mexican-American students in rural Texas in the late 1920s, and a good idea of how he might do it based on his work as director of the WPA's National Youth Administration in Texas and as a congressman before and after his wartime service in the navy.[43]

Entering the White House, Johnson wrapped himself in Roosevelt's cloak. And he clearly had the promise of the Four Freedoms in mind when in the course of 1964 he declared "unconditional war on poverty"; proposed the Economic Opportunity Act with its Head Start, Neighborhood Youth Corps, and Job Corps programs; worked to secure a historic Civil Rights Act; told students at the University of Michigan that they were "appointed by history" to build a "Great Society"; and campaigned against the 1964 Republican presidential nominee, the conservative Arizona Senator Barry Goldwater. He spoke of it even at state dinners. In a toast to the visiting President of Italy, he said: "Mr. President, if we are to inspire others with our hopes, we must make doubly sure that in our own countries there is actually freedom from want and fear."[44]

Labor and rights leaders now joined Johnson in trying to get Congress to pass the civil rights and antipoverty bills. The AFL-CIO's George Meany not only agreed to LBJ's request that they hold off on seeking repeal of the Taft-Hartley Act's section 14(b), permitting state right-to-work laws, and concentrate first on winning enactment of those bills. He also committed the federation to lobbying aggressively for them. And while King, inspired by the GI Bill of Rights, now called for a Bill of Rights for the Disadvantaged, he and most other black leaders accepted an appeal by Johnson to temporarily cease mass demonstrations.[45]

But democratic activism from below did not cease. Looking to engage poor blacks directly in the struggle for their rights, the SNCC's Robert Moses launched Mississippi "Freedom Summer," a voter-education and -registration drive that—despite the brutal murder by Klansmen of three young activists, two white and one black—saw nine hundred, mostly white, northern college students join the project. And that fall thousands of University of California, Berkeley, students, led by Freedom Summer veteran Mario Savio, rose up in a "Free Speech Movement," demanding freedom of speech and expression on campus.[46]

Conservatives and reactionaries reacted as they had since the 1920s to evidence of organized and organizing progressivism—they branded it as "un-American." In a nationally televised speech that October endorsing Barry Goldwater for president, the actor turned right-wing political voice Ronald Reagan portrayed the New Deal legacy and projected Great Society initiatives as the "abandonment" of "the American Revolution" and as movements toward "totalitarianism."[47]

The overwhelming majority of Americans, however, knew better and they made clear what they wanted at the polls in November. They gave Johnson the greatest presidential election triumph since FDR's of 1936 and sent enough liberals to Congress to finally overcome the conservative coalition, shut down the southern filibuster, and move on the Democratic agenda. Johnson and his running mate, Senator Hubert Humphrey of Minnesota, not only garnered 61 percent of the vote and every state but Goldwater's Arizona and five in the Deep South, their party also gained firmer control of the House (295–140) and Senate (68–32). And liberals and progressives now prevailed in both, among them many World War II veterans such as the senators Philip Hart (Michigan), Joseph Clark (Pennsylvania), Edmund Muskie (Maine), Paul Douglas (Illinois), Gaylord Nelson (Wisconsin), Claiborne Pell (Rhode Island), and the Republican Jacob Javits (New York)—the last four of whom were former AVC members.[48]

So empowered, Johnson called in his January 1965 State of the Union message for "eliminating every remaining obstacle to the right and the opportunity to vote"; a "program in education to ensure every child the fullest development"; new laws to protect the environment and new initiatives in urban and regional development; repeal of Taft-Hartley's section 14(b) and extension of the minimum wage to "2 million unprotected workers"; health care coverage for the elderly; an immigration law "based on the work a man can do and not where he was born or how he spells his name"; and a National Foundation for the Arts. Almost all of which and more the new Eighty-ninth Congress would give him in the Voting Rights Act, the Elementary and Secondary Education Act, a new Social Security Act creating Medicare and Medicaid, the Water Quality and Clean Air acts, the Immigration Act, and acts establishing the Department of Housing and Urban Development and National Endowments for the Arts and Humanities.[49]

The democratic swell now turned into a new democratic surge. The AFL-CIO played a crucial role in securing Medicare and Medicaid and, looking forward to building labor and a more liberal south, began to push anew for the repeal of Section 14(b). And led by its newly elected president, Jerry Wurf, a staunch progressive who first began organizing workers during the war, the American Federation of State, County, and Municipal Employees (AFSCME) launched campaigns that, alongside those of the American Federation of Teachers and National Education Association, would unionize, and secure the bargaining rights of, 4 million public employees in thirty-six states by 1975.[50]

King took the civil rights struggle back to Alabama in early 1965 to fight for voting rights—a heroic fight that led Johnson to proclaim, "We shall overcome," in a speech before the full Congress. Inspired by the War on Poverty's New Deal–like code of "maximum feasible participation," poor people gathered around the country to formulate plans to improve their communities. And yet for some the democratic surge acted as a painful reminder of promises so long deferred. Now, more than twenty years after their articulation, in some pockets of the country the wellspring of hope had gone dry. Blacks in the Watts ghetto of Los Angeles erupted in six days of rioting that August that left thirty-four dead and a thousand injured. But ever determined, A. Philip Randolph—whom Johnson had named as Honorary Chair of an upcoming 1966 White House conference, "To Fulfill These Rights"—responded to both the new possibilities and the new dangers by proposing a ten-year, $185 billion "Freedom Budget" that, endorsed by 150 prominent academic, labor, and foundation leaders, promised to create full employment, wipe out slums, and "Achieve 'Freedom from Want' for all Americans" by 1975.[51]

Meanwhile, paralleling efforts by congressional liberals to translate JFK's call for a Consumer Bill of Rights into law, the attorney Ralph Nader published *Unsafe at Any Speed: The Designed-In Dangers of the American Automobile*, an indictment of the car industry's pursuit of profits over safety that fueled the rise of a new consumer movement. Tony Mazzocchi, a Battle of the Bulge artillery veteran, took up the post of political director of the Oil, Chemical, and Atomic Workers and, informed by the work of Carson and Commoner, moved his union up to the front of the environmental struggle and fight for workplace health and safety. And heartened by the Civil Rights Act outlawing racial, religious, and gender discrimination, Betty Friedan and other feminists founded the National Organization for Women (NOW) in 1966 to achieve women's "full participation in the mainstream of American society."[52]

The Right, of course, fought back. Mentored by *National Review* editor William F. Buckley, Jr., conservative students organized Young Americans for Freedom in 1960. And while most corporate leaders still subscribed to the liberal consensus, and even backed LBJ's reforms, rich conservatives had backed far-right Republicans in winning brief control of the GOP and nominating Goldwater in 1964. But as Ike could have told them, a generation had not forgotten the promise they had articulated and fought for.[53]

On February 23, 1966, Johnson received the National Freedom Award in a ceremony at New York's Waldorf-Astoria Hotel. Accepting the honor, he spoke not of himself, but of Roosevelt and the Four Freedoms. And proudly noting not only the progress his generation had made in realizing FDR's vision, but also its continuing commitment to advance it further both at home and overseas, he said: "Thus we address the spirit of Franklin Roosevelt, 25 years after his message to America and the world, with confidence and with an unflagging determination."[54]

Securing rights, fighting poverty, enhancing the environment, and advancing education and the arts, Johnson had good reason to evoke Roosevelt's spirit. And yet in critical ways he still stood closer to JFK than to FDR. As his further remarks in accepting the Freedom Award attest, he remained more committed to following the corporate and Cold War imperatives of the postwar settlement than to redeeming the progressive politics of the Age of Roosevelt. While he credited both the "free enterprise system" and "enlightened public policy" for the nation's steady advance toward "liberation from want," he made no reference to democratic mobilization and redistribution. And though in his January 1966 State of the Union message he had lamented how the Vietnam War was already limiting the War on Poverty, he proceeded that evening at the Waldorf—as four thousand antiwar protesters marched outside—to speak at length of his plans to intensify the fight in Southeast Asia.[55]

Johnson was seeking to complete Roosevelt's revolution, and on race he was pushing well beyond it. But whereas FDR had mobilized Americans to redeem the nation's promise by both enlisting their labors in the New Deal and empowering them to organize and fight the forces that opposed their pursuit of that promise, LBJ did neither. Ignoring how industry was moving out of the north to the right-to-work and low-tax South and to foreign countries, he rejected the idea of public-works and job-creation initiatives and instead insisted on programs of education and training that were supposed to prepare the poor to take advantage of the opportunities afforded by America's fast-growing economy. He also refused to rally his fellow citizens against corporate power and practices. Asserting, "I never wanted to demagogue against business," Johnson would signal in many ways that he thought FDR had seriously erred in calling business leaders economic royalists. To labor's dismay, LBJ effectively left Dixie in the hands of the Right and capital by failing to exercise his presidential power and influence to counter corporate lobbying and kill a GOP-led Senate filibuster blocking a vote in 1965 to repeal Taft-Hartley's section 14(b).[56]

Moreover, LBJ not only accepted the governing elites' assumption that achieving the nation's "goals" required simply more economic growth, not redistribution—at least not from capital and the rich to working people and the poor. He also championed Kennedy's strategy of cutting taxes on corporations and the wealthy—even as he was planning to spend vast sums fighting both the War on Poverty and the War in Vietnam.[57]

But most tragically, whereas Roosevelt had recognized that to truly secure America's promise he had to break isolationism's hold on American thinking, LBJ did not see that to do so in the 1960s demanded loosening the Cold War's grip. Having learned, like most of his generation, that tyranny and aggression must not be ignored, he, too, readily followed Ike and JFK in seeing all Third World struggles merely in terms of Soviet expansionism. And fearing the political consequences of "losing" Vietnam, he acted to prevent the defeat of the authoritarian and corrupt U.S.-created South Vietnamese state by the Communist

North and revolutionary Viet Cong. Under Johnson, America's involvement in the war steadily expanded—to the point of sending more
than 500,000 troops to the country by 1968.

Johnson would go on to secure further initiatives like the Model
Cities program, the 1968 Fair Housing Act, and an increase in the
minimum wage—and to his credit the poverty rate would drop from
22 to 13 percent by decade's end. But he placed the War in Vietnam
above the War on Poverty.

Americans did mobilize, but not as LBJ might have envisioned.
With hopes and expectations raised, but opportunities limited and oppression unrelenting, blacks rioted in ghettos across the nation in the
summers of 1966, 1967, and 1968. And no longer urged by their President to build a Great Society, but called by their draft boards to fight a
war that seemed to contradict America's purpose of "setting men free,"
college students turned out in growing numbers to march in opposition
to it. The democratic surge continued, but increasingly moved in di-
vergent, if not counter, currents.

The war not only financially constrained the fight against freedom
from want and fear. It also split the nation and sundered the forces
of the Left. While Meany and the AFL-CIO, despite the Taft-Hartley debacle, stayed loyal to Johnson, unions divided and Reuther, exasperated by Meany's conservatism on a host of issues, actually led the
UAW out of the labor federation. The civil rights movement divided,
too. While the NAACP and NUL continued to work for racial integration, CORE, SNCC, and the new Black Panther Party militantly called
for "Black Power." And the mushrooming antiwar student movement,
with SDS in the vanguard, not only became all the more radical, all
the more hostile to Johnson and liberals generally, and all the more vocally "anti-American," it also spawned a "counter-culture" of "hippies"
and "Yippies" that spurned the achievements and ideals of the generation that had made America a "middle-class" nation. All of which an-
tagonized middle-aged white working-class people, so many of whom

were now bearing a greater tax burden and suffering the loss of industrial jobs and a real decline in their wages. As they sent their sons into the military while college men received deferments, they felt a sense of abandonment by an administration committed to fighting racism, poverty, and communism, but not corporate power and inequality.[58]

Nevertheless, the majority of Americans were neither turning right nor giving up the idea of harnessing the powers of democratic government to enhance American life. While urban riots and Black Power rhetoric angered them, most Americans continued to support the cause of equal rights and the fight against poverty. While bureaucrats and taxes irritated them, they still favored the idea of national health care. And while antiwar demonstrators aggravated them, they were coming to see the war as having been a costly mistake. In fact, in a certain way they were moving left. Not only were workers now staging strikes over both wages and shop-floor control on a scale not seen since the postwar 1940s, their fellow citizens were growing all the more suspicious of big corporations and backing demands for more strenuous federal regulation of business activities.[59]

But continuing losses in Vietnam, turmoil at home, and a serious challenge for the Democratic nomination by the antiwar Senator Eugene McCarthy of Minnesota, who had worked for military intelligence during World War II, were draining LBJ of energy and support. And on March 31, 1968, he announced he would not run for reelection.

The violence that had come to haunt his presidency did not cease, however. Less than a week later, King was assassinated in Memphis and riots broke out in dozens of cities, including the nation's capital. Two months after that, JFK's brother, Senator Robert F. Kennedy of New York, who had just won the California Democratic primary, was killed in Los Angeles. And that summer, rioting erupted once again, not only in ghettos around the country but also outside the Democratic National Convention in Chicago when police attacked crowds of young antiwar demonstrators. Angry battles broke out on the convention floor itself that would sorely hamper the chances of the Democratic presidential nominee, Vice President Hubert Humphrey, winning in November. Expressing his generation's frustration and bewilderment, one World War II veteran and lifelong Democrat asked his son, "What is wrong with your generation?"[60]

Running again for president in 1968, Richard Nixon attacked both liberal Democrats and urban rioters and student protesters. However, he did not talk of reversing LBJ's Great Society or, as Goldwater had, FDR's New Deal. He knew better than to do so. Like Eisenhower, he was a conservative, but also like Ike, he knew that Americans, especially his own generation, remained committed to the promise of the Four Freedoms. He spoke directly to it. Interviewed for television by the British newsman David Frost, he said: "You remember Franklin Roosevelt's four freedoms? . . . Freedom from fear and freedom from want. That was enough in the Thirties because to achieve that goal would have been magnificent. Now, most Americans have achieved it, and they find it isn't enough. Now we must move to Freedoms *to*."[61]

But Nixon also knew that Americans were worried about the state of the nation and the future of America—and he spoke to that as well. Accepting the GOP nomination, he said, "We see Americans dying on distant battlefields abroad" and "We see Americans hating each other; fighting each other; killing each other at home." And he asked: "Did American boys die in Normandy, and Korea, and in Valley Forge for this?" Then, directing his words, a few borrowed directly from FDR, to "the forgotten Americans—the non-shouters; the non-demonstrators . . . [who] work in American factories . . . run American businesses . . . serve in government . . . provide most of the soldiers who died to keep us free"—the men and women he would later call "the Silent Majority"—he reassured them that "America is a great nation" and promised "a new policy for peace abroad [and] a new policy for peace and progress and justice at home." Projecting "a day when we will again have freedom from fear in America and freedom from fear in the world," he called a percentage of the country to a percentage of FDR's famed promise.[62]

Nixon didn't give any details of his plans. He didn't have to. Americans were looking for a way out—a way out of riots, protests, and a war they never wanted—and he seemed to offer it. That November, the Democrats held on to the House and Senate, but he won the presidency.

President Nixon preached "law and order"—a veiled way of speaking to white racial fears—and held liberals accountable for the lawlessness and violence of the day. However, he was not looking to undo what remained of the liberal consensus, but rather, to win over anxious white working-class voters and make the GOP the majority party of that consensus. And knowing from private White House polls what most Americans wanted, he realized he had to do more than just talk about the Four Freedoms.[63]

Thus, Nixon cooperated with Congress not only to increase spending on the poor, but also—despite the opposition of business leaders, so many of whom had supported his candidacy—to raise taxes on corporations and the rich; create the Environmental Protection Agency (EPA), Occupational Safety and Health Administration (OSHA), and Consumer Products Safety Commission; and institute temporary wage-and-price controls to contain inflation and unemployment. In fact, he also proposed both a guaranteed-minimum-family-income program to replace welfare and a national health insurance program, though neither would be passed, for conservatives opposed them on principle and liberals for being too stingy.[64]

Moreover, while Nixon began to significantly revise the terms of the Cold War by opening up relations with China in 1971 (a feat, arguably, only an old red-baiter could pull off), his new policy for Vietnam entailed both intensifying the bombing of the North and pushing into Cambodia to try to cut off Vietcong supply lines in hopes of forcing the North to negotiate an acceptable peace. The latter incited massive antiwar demonstrations at home in the spring of 1970 and led to a nearly complete shutdown of America's colleges after National Guardsmen killed four student protesters at Ohio's Kent State University. Most Americans, however, did not protest. As much as they wanted out of the war, they longed for a "peace with honor." It was not to be. The war that had cost Johnson his agenda ended in defeat. The peace treaty signed in 1973 was mere prelude. South Vietnam would fall to the Communists in 1975.

In 1972, Nixon defeated the liberal and antiwar Senator George McGovern of South Dakota in a landslide, winning 60.7 percent of the popular vote and every state but Massachusetts and the District of Columbia. McGovern, a World War II bomber pilot and former history professor, had led the Democrats to carry out reforms in the wake of 1968 that, while strengthening minority and women's representation in the party, had reduced the power of labor. Meany and other AFL-CIO leaders walked out of the 1972 party convention, refusing to endorse him, and thereby enabled Nixon to portray his opponent as the dangerously radical "antiwar" candidate.[65]

Still, with Democrats holding on to Congress, and liberals gaining a few seats, Nixon's victory actually registered no critical shift by Americans to the right. It did, however, show that a Republican could win states all across the conservative South, and offered sad testimony to liberal and progressive leaders' declining ability to inspire and move their fellow citizens.

Nixon was to resign the presidency in August 1974 after congressional investigations revealed an ugly record of lies, cover-ups, and illegalities by him and his staff. A bungled 1972 break-in by GOP operatives at Democratic National Committee offices at Washington's Watergate complex proved to be the tip of an iceberg. And with the Republicans in disrepute, the former Georgia governor Jimmy Carter, a veteran postwar naval officer, peanut farmer, and "Born-Again Christian," would win the White House in 1976 by defeating Nixon's successor, Gerald Ford. Carter's victory, however, would not lead to a renewal of the fight for the Four Freedoms, but to its suppression.

A series of major crises struck the nation in the early 1970s—not only the traumas of military defeat and presidential resignation, but also a 1973 Arab oil embargo and energy crisis, intensifying industrial competition from Germany and Japan, and an eighteen-month-long recession that, starting in November 1973, would devastate American manufacturing, drive the unemployment rate up to 9.2 percent (a number not seen since 1941), drain municipal coffers (most unsettlingly, those of New York City), and begin to turn the industrial Northeast and Midwest into the "Rust Belt." Intellectuals right and left wrote of it all as if the nation had simply run out of steam—some, as if it augured the "twilight" of capitalism and the West.[66]

In response, Americans grew ever more critical of corporate power and practices and ever more interested in social-democratic policies and programs. Yet even as, in *Time* magazine's words, "Blue collar workers are gaining a renewed sense of identity, of collective power and class that used to be called solidarity," the Democratic Party failed to engage them politically.[67]

Watergate would bolster the Democratic Party. But Democrats would not mobilize a broad, popular, and progressive democratic politics. Older leaders bore the scars of the late sixties and seemed incapable of inspiring. And younger party politicians and activists, whether they were advocating the "New Politics" of fiscal conservatism and "neoliberalism" or the "movement" and "identity" politics of race and gender, were eschewing the New Deal political tradition in favor of remaking the party as a coalition of middle- and upper-middle-class professionals, women, and people of color. Elected to the Senate from Colorado in 1974, Gary Hart, a rising star of the neoliberals, actually campaigned with a stump speech titled "The End of the New Deal" and spoke dismissively of labor.[68]

Labor was opening up all the more to women and minorities. Nonetheless, with the AFL-CIO still headed by George Meany, who remained perversely averse to organizing—"Why should we worry about organizing groups of people who do not want to be organized?"—unions continued to endure not only political and industrial defeats, but also, especially in manufacturing, dramatically declining membership rolls.[69]

While the Left and labor did not mobilize, business did. Corporate leaders were besieged from below—as Chase Manhattan Bank's David Rockefeller observed: "It is scarcely an exaggeration to say that right now American business is facing its most public disfavor since the 1930s. We are assailed for demeaning the worker, deceiving the consumer, destroying the environment, and disillusioning the younger generation." They felt betrayed by President Nixon and squeezed by

global competition. The response: take up the struggle against the Four Freedoms anew. Some to simply halt the democratic surge; others to reverse the recent liberal and progressive advances; still others to undo the labors of a generation and truly bring an end to the Age of Roosevelt—but all to restore the power, prestige, and profits of capital.[70]

In a confidential 1971 memorandum to the Chamber of Commerce, the corporate attorney Lewis Powell, whom Nixon was soon to name to the Supreme Court, laid out the strategy business was to follow—a strategy recalling those of the Liberty League in the 1930s and NAM and the Chamber following World War II. Specifically, Powell called for organizing executives, mobilizing stockholders, and recruiting cadres of scholars to spread capital's message in print, public lectures, and the media, monitoring academe and cultivating alliances with graduate schools of business, promoting corporate priorities in lobbying, public relations, and advertising campaigns, and counterattacking labor, environmental, and consumer rights activists in the courts.[71]

Business executives rallied to reshape public debate, opinion, and policy. They not only revitalized the Chamber, NAM, and their respective industrial associations; used the local chapters of those organizations to launch grassroots campaigns; and formed new "peak" organizations, the most impressive of which was the Business Roundtable, whose membership was limited to the CEOs of the nation's top corporations, all personally committed to lobbying efforts. They also set up new political action committees (PACs) and increased their contributions to candidates of both parties—all of whom grew ever more dependent on such money. Plus, they enhanced the endowments of think tanks such as the American Enterprise Institute and newly established Heritage Foundation; sponsored right-wing "public intellectuals" to advance pro-business ideas and arguments; and underwrote a vast array of campaigns to promote "free enterprise" and assail the unions, regulations, and taxes that they insisted were deterring business investment, innovation, and economic growth and development.[72]

Their campaigns spoke of freedom, but they made no secret of their antidemocratic ambitions, not even the so-called liberals among them. The Trilateral Commission, organized by David Rockefeller as

an association of prominent corporate, political, and even labor figures from Western Europe, Japan, and the United States, issued a 1975
report, *The Crisis of Democracy*, in which Democracy was found wanting. The co-author Samuel P. Huntington, a Harvard government
professor, wrote that the "democratic surge" of America's minorities,
public-employee unions, women, students, public-interest groups, and
"value-oriented intellectuals" had produced a "democratic distemper,"
a "problem of governability," indeed, an "excess of democracy."[73]

Furthermore, not only did corporations continue to transfer industry and jobs south and, increasingly, overseas to Third World countries
where unions were banned or state-controlled, they also endeavored to
"decertify" existing unions—and where workers tried to organize them,
managers illegally fired the "troublemakers" and defended themselves
with teams of union-busting lawyers. By the mid-1970s, complaints
to the National Labor Relations Board skyrocketed, union membership fell to just 25 percent of the labor force, private and public sectors
combined, and the great wave of public-employee organizing began to
ebb.[74]

Meanwhile, rich far-right folk such as Adolph Coors, the Koch
family, and the Bradley and John M. Olin foundations funded efforts to
mobilize Christian evangelicals around "culture war" questions such as
abortion and school prayer, and white working people generally around
issues of law and order and taxes—the last of which was especially ap-
pealing. As wages fell with middle-class standards of living, voting for
someone who promised to lower your taxes seemed an immediate redress. And in the late 1970s the nation was to witness a spate of "tax
revolts."[75]

By decade's end, capital and the Right would prevail. They would
not do so simply by their own devices, however. Americans would continue to believe in the promise of the Four Freedoms, but as jobs were
lost, as workers' incomes stagnated or declined, and as the nation's
troubles piled up, more and more of them wondered if the Democrats
still did. And they were right to do so.[76]

Celebrating the U.S. Bicentennial in 1976, the city of Evansville, Indiana, erected a Four Freedoms Monument composed of four tall columns, each intended to represent one of Franklin Roosevelt's Four Freedoms. However, city leaders somehow saw fit to rename one of those freedoms. Apparently too closely tied to the New Deal and progressive struggles, Freedom from Want was replaced with "Freedom from Oppression." Worse was to come. Not only would the new Democratic President, Jimmy Carter, never mention the Four Freedoms when speaking to his fellow citizens, he would pave the way to the White House for a conservative who was set upon radically rewriting them.[77]

To secure the 1976 Democratic nomination and victory in November, Jimmy Carter had run to his left—far enough left to encourage many an eager liberal, labor, and rights activist to believe a Carter presidency might enable them to revive the democratic surge of the 1960s. But such was not to happen. Carter did embrace his party's new progressive platform. And notably, he not only spoke in his nomination acceptance speech of both the party's tradition of liberal leadership from FDR to LBJ and its record of "progressive" legislation. He also pointed a finger at the "political and economic elite" who have "shaped decisions and never had to account for mistakes or to suffer from injustice." However, as he was soon to show, campaign rhetoric aside, he was no liberal or progressive in the Roosevelt tradition.[78]

Democrats came together behind Carter in hopes of making the tax structure more progressive, creating a more effective consumer protection agency, establishing a national health care system, enacting a real full-employment bill, and strengthening labor's ability to organize and defend itself against union-busting efforts. But one by one, the legislative initiatives to realize these goals would be killed off. Repeatedly, corporate executives would mobilize to block them. Repeatedly, Carter would give way or fail to fight. And repeatedly, congressional Democrats would fall apart in the face of corporate pressures and inducements. UAW president Douglas Fraser, a World War II army veteran whose union activism began in the 1930s, expressed the thoughts of most on the left when he quit the President's Labor-Management Ad-

visory Group following the filibustered defeat of the labor-law reform
bill in July 1978. Essentially delivering the eulogy for the liberal consensus, Fraser explained in his resignation letter why he could no longer cooperate with the corporate elite: "I believe leaders of the business
community . . . have chosen to wage a one-sided class war today in this
country—a war against working people, the unemployed, the poor, the
minorities, the very young and the very old, and even many in the middle class of our society."[79]

Carter and the Democratic-controlled Congress didn't just give
way to the corporate elite's ambitions. Deregulating much of the transportation industry and initiating the deregulation of finance and banking, they actually inaugurated what the political writer Michael Lind
has termed the "Great Dismantling of the New Deal."[80]

Even as crises were deepening or erupting anew, even as inequality was widening, and even as communities were rallying to try to save
their plants and jobs, Carter was turning his back on the memory and
legacy of FDR and the men and women of the 1930s and 1940s. In his
January 1978 State of the Union message, he spoke of the crises confronted by Lincoln and Roosevelt, and the challenges faced by Truman, and noted how at such times it was "the task of leaders to call
forth the vast and restless energies of our people to build the future."
But Carter did no such thing. Making no reference whatsoever to the
corporate elite's efforts to subdue democracy and break labor or even
to how capital was shuttering factories and exporting jobs overseas, he
told Americans: "We need patience and good will . . . Government
cannot solve our problems, it can't set our goals, it cannot define our
vision. Government cannot eliminate poverty or provide a bountiful
economy or reduce inflation or save our cities or cure illiteracy or provide energy. And government cannot mandate goodness."[81]

Nine months later, as "stagflation"—high unemployment and high
inflation—shook working people's lives all the more, Carter made his
neoliberal fundamentalism all the clearer. Speaking to the nation on
the need to fight inflation and cut the government deficit (as opposed,
essentially, to fighting unemployment), he stated, "We must face a
time of national austerity." He called for limiting prices and wages,

and proclaimed the need to liberate capital by reducing government regulation—a line he continued to push in his January 1979 State of the Union address: "Let's reduce government interference and give it a chance to work . . . We cannot afford to live beyond our means . . . The duty of our generation . . . is to renew our Nation's faith . . . against the threats of selfishness, cynicism, and apathy."[82]

Far from nothing to fear but fear itself, Carter told Americans to fear each other. In July 1979, in an address that would forever be known as "The Malaise Speech," he acknowledged that Americans were looking for "more effective leadership and action." But instead of affording it, he lectured them on what he asserted was a more critical threat than energy shortages and inflation: "I want to talk to you right now about a fundamental threat to American democracy . . . a crisis of confidence . . . threatening to destroy the social and political fabric of America." In lieu of a call to action, rather than call forth Americans' historic commitment to a freer, more equal, more democratic nation, Carter asked, "Whenever you have a chance, say something good about our country." His call to action was as vacuous as it was ineffectual: "With God's help and for the sake of our Nation, it is time for us to join hands in America. Let us commit ourselves together to a rebirth of the American spirit. Working together with our common faith we cannot fail." Americans did not. Carter undoubtedly did.[83]

Forsaking what made those whom we have come to call the Greatest Generation and its greatest leader truly great, Carter not only failed to renew the nation's spirit and redeem America's promise, he also went on to lose the presidency to a figure of that generation—a figure who had never forgotten the fight for the Four Freedoms and, knowing what was at stake in the struggle, was determined to bury the progressive memory and legacy of it.

On June 6, 1984, President Ronald Reagan went to Normandy, France, to speak at events commemorating the fortieth anniversary of D-day. Addressing statesmen, dignitaries, and veterans of those landings and their families, he spoke eloquently and movingly, especially at Pointe du Hoc, where GIs of the 2nd Ranger Battalion had fought their way up a 100-foot cliff while deadly German fire hailed down upon them. He talked there of the struggle and of those who pursued it—and he spoke directly to those men: "You were young the day you took these cliffs. Yet, you risked everything here. Why? . . . We look at you, and somehow we know the answer. It was faith and belief [and] loyalty and love . . . You all knew that some things are worth dying for. One's country is worth dying for, and democracy is worth dying for . . . All of you loved liberty."[84]

A beautiful act of remembrance, Reagan's visit to Normandy was at the same time a carefully staged political event. With his 1984 reelection campaign upcoming, Reagan and his advisors saw the trip, as the historian Douglas Brinkley has told it, as an opportunity to promote a "New Patriotism"—a new "political consensus . . . based on an unflinching devotion to all things American." Reagan went some way in doing that and won reelection. He also expressed the long-felt yet understated admiration and affection for the generation that the men of Normandy represented and essentially "triggered the so-called Greatest Generation phenomenon."[85]

But there was even more to it. Whenever Reagan spoke of that generation, his own generation, he was not so much trying to remind Americans of its great democratic struggles and achievements as to keep them from remembering too much of them.

He won the White House in 1980 because of Carter's failures in addressing fuel shortages, stagflation, an armed takeover of the U.S. Embassy in Iran, and a Soviet invasion of Afghanistan. All of which, coming in the wake of the upheavals of the late 1960s, the Nixon-Watergate scandal, defeat in Vietnam, and a devastating mid-1970s recession, had incited talk of national "exhaustion" and "decline" and led Carter, even before the embassy takeover, to call on Americans to lower their expectations.[86]

Inviting Americans to join him in a "crusade" to restore the nation's strength, pride, and values, Reagan pulled together a "New Right" Republican electoral alliance of corporate elites, Christian evangelicals, and a host of conservative special-interest groups and picked up the votes of millions of disenchanted Democrats—millions more simply did not vote—with a platform of lowering taxes, limiting government, deregulating business, reducing the power of unions, cutting welfare spending, and expanding the military.

Reagan intended, however, a far grander restoration. He wanted to do what the Right and conservative rich had been trying to do for de-cades—bring an end to what he called "the long, liberal experiment that began in the 1930's."[87]

A New Deal Democrat and World War II veteran who so admired FDR that he memorized key lines of his speeches, Reagan had moved right in reaction to the Cold War—so far right he took to not only praising "free enterprise" but also decrying New Deal "liberalism," "big government," and the "welfare state" as threats to American liberty and, even, defending "states' rights." But he realized most Americans had not.[88]

Indeed, Reagan recognized how they continued to not only revere Roosevelt, embrace the achievements of his presidency, and believe in the promise that FDR and so many of them had articulated and fought for, but also draw strength and encouragement from them. He saw it in the struggles and initiatives of the 1960s to secure equal rights for minorities and women, combat poverty, organize new unions, and reg-ulate business to protect consumers, workers, and the environment. Moreover, while he had won the governorship of California in 1966 by damning student protesters, urban rioters, and the liberals who he con-tended abetted them, unsuccessful bids for the White House in 1968 and 1976 had taught him it was dangerous to attack Roosevelt and his legacy.[89]

By 1980, Reagan knew that whatever else he did he had to refash-ion American memory and imagination—especially regarding the generation he was to celebrate at Normandy. He still charged that liberalism endangered liberty but, harkening back nostalgically to an America that valued "family, work, neighborhood, and religion," and making no reference to what his generation had progressively accom-plished, he now targeted strictly "the Sixties." He not only denied the advances made. He also insisted that the politics and programs of those years had brought on the nation's problems and, as he used to say of the New Deal, betrayed America's promise. No less audaciously, he hijacked the story of American democracy and harnessed to his cause figures venerated by the Left and working people. In his presidential nomination acceptance speech, he declared what pundits were to call the "Reagan Revolution" by quoting none other than Thomas Paine, Abraham Lincoln, and Franklin Roosevelt to proclaim: "We have it in our power to begin the world over again"; a "new birth of freedom"; and "this generation today has a rendezvous with destiny."[90]

Reagan sustained that rhetoric as President even as he pursued policies that undermined the democratic labors of a generation and made the rich richer and working people poorer. He even occasionally referred to "the Four Freedoms." And yet he never stated what they were—which reflected neither ignorance nor innocence but, as he was soon to reveal, a desire to reconstitute them. Speaking at a 1987 Independence Day celebration at the Jefferson Memorial sponsored by the U.S. Chamber of Commerce, Reagan announced plans to seek enactment of an "Economic Bill of Rights that guarantees four fundamental freedoms: The freedom to work. The freedom to enjoy the fruits of one's labor. The freedom to own and control one's property. The freedom to participate in a free market."[91]

Reagan sought to erase or override the progressive memory and legacy of Roosevelt and the generation of the 1930s and 1940s right up to his last days in office. In his January 1989 Farewell Address, Reagan noted the "resurgence of national pride" that he believed his presidency had inspired. But warning that "it won't last unless it's grounded in thoughtfulness and knowledge," he recalled his visit to Normandy and urged "more attention to American history." Most of all, he said— clearly determined to not just echo the Right's wartime call for a Fifth Freedom, but also expunge "Freedom from want" and "Freedom from fear" altogether—Americans needed to remember that "America is freedom—freedom of speech, freedom of religion, freedom of enterprise."[92]

Reagan not only gave voice to American admiration and affection for those who fought the Second World War. He also gave them shape and direction. Those who were to celebrate the Greatest Generation made no mention of the Four Freedoms.

Even more critically, he initiated a conservative and corporate ascendancy that has succeeded in undoing so much of what that generation fought for and achieved.

But, of course, Reagan could not have done all of that—hell, he could not even have become President—if those whom he opposed had not already forgotten or forsaken what made the Greatest Generation and its greatest leader truly great: That they saved the United States from economic destruction and political tyranny and turned it into the strongest and most prosperous nation in history by making America freer, more equal, and more democratic than ever before. That they were, measured by their achievements, the most progressive generation in American history.

CHAPTER ELEVEN

"It is time for the country to become fairly radical for a generation."

We have not forgotten the promise of the Four Freedoms— the promise of "Freedom of speech and expression, Freedom of worship, Freedom from want, Freedom from fear." Indeed, despite all the efforts by conservatives and the corporate elite to deny, erase, or rewrite that promise—the promise that Franklin Roosevelt and our parents and grandparents proclaimed, fought for, and made the promise of America—we not only still remember it. We yearn to realize it all the more.

We yearn to be like our parents and grandparents. We yearn to renew America's purpose and promise and reinvigorate America's strength and prosperity. And yet we have seemingly forgotten how we might do so. We sense that we, too, "have not yet fully explored the democratic way of life," but seem to have forgotten that "Democracy is never given. It must be taken." Even as we continue to erect monuments to honor our parents' and grandparents' courage and sacrifices, even as we deliver tributes and memorials declaring our eternal gratitude for all that they accomplished and afforded us, we fail to remember what really made those whom we call the Greatest Generation and its greatest leader great.

So, we need to remember. Now, especially, before all those men and women have passed away, and before we allow all that their generation achieved to pass away with them, we need to remember how a President and people—in the face of powerful conservative and corporate opposition, and despite their own faults and failings—saved the United States from economic destruction and political tyranny and turned it into the strongest and most prosperous nation in history by mobilizing, harnessing the powers of democratic government, and making America freer, more equal, and more democratic than ever before.

In 2008—having endured more than thirty years of concerted class war from above that has laid siege to the democratic achievements of a generation, returned America to the inequality of the late Gilded Age of the 1920s, and led to an economic crisis that threatened nothing less than a new Great Depression—we voted to redeem and reaffirm the promise of the Four Freedoms. We not only elected the first black President in American history, Barack Obama, a young Democratic senator from Illinois who preached the "Audacity of Hope," who ran on a platform that included subjecting corporate power and practices to greater democratic scrutiny and regulation, protecting and enhancing workers' rights, and enacting a national health care program, and who spiritedly told his fellow citizens, "Yes, we can!" We also elected an overwhelmingly Democratic Congress to enact that agenda and help prove him right. And we did it so decisively that politicians and pundits envisioned the President-elect and his party bucking history and gaining even more congressional seats in the midterm elections of 2010—just as Roosevelt and the Democrats had strengthened their hold on Congress in the 1934 midterm elections.[1]

It was not to happen.

It definitely did seem as if we were on the verge of a new Age of Roosevelt—that we would launch a "new New Deal" to tackle the nation's unfolding economic crisis, widening inequalities, and continuing

industrial and infrastructural decay—that we would undertake reforms
and initiatives that would propel democratic politics and possibilities
for years to come—that we would once again progressively advance the
Four Freedoms. Even before the 2008 campaign, Speaker of the House
Nancy Pelosi affirmatively answered the question of whether Democrats had any ideas for the nation with just three words: "Franklin Delano Roosevelt." Presidential candidate Obama himself not only spoke
admiringly of FDR, but also, often and proudly, of his "Greatest Generation" grandparents who had donned uniform and overalls to serve the
nation in World War II. And following the November elections, magazines both political and popular were running cover stories projecting
the newly elected President Obama as nothing less than the Second
Coming of Roosevelt.[2]

A sense of that arrival was evident in the discomfiture of pundits
and critics. Seemingly anxious about what it all portended, *Newsweek*
editor Jon Meacham essentially advised the Democratic candidate on
the eve of his presidential election victory that he ought not to push
his agenda too far or too fast, for "America remains a center-right nation." Even more anxiously, right-wing scribes reiterated their absurd
claim that "the New Deal made the Depression worse" and intensified their attacks on the promise that FDR pronounced in 1941. The
snide dismissal of the Greatest Generation's achievements was transparent in the archconservative South Carolina Senator Jim DeMint's
declaration: "Socialists are now marching under the banner of a new
secular-progressive style of freedom: the freedom from responsibility,
the freedom to behave destructively without moral judgment, the freedom from risk and failure, the freedom from want, the freedom from religion, and the freedom to have material equality with those who work
and accomplish more."[3]

But most important—just as the Right feared—the majority of
Americans wanted democratic action and many of us were ready to
go into action. You could feel it in labor councils, community centers,
and college classrooms across the country and you could actually see it
that January at the Presidential Inauguration when 2 million Ameri-

cans in all their diversity turned out to witness history and listen for their marching orders.

For all that, however, no new New Deal, no new progressive politics, no new democratic surge ensued. Yes, there were significant accomplishments. President-elect Obama firmly endorsed and made possible massive bailouts of not only the supposedly "too-big-to-fail" banks, which stabilized the collapsing financial system, but also the stalled automobile industry, which kept General Motors and Chrysler from going out of business and laying off their workers. Once in office, he and the Democratic-controlled Congress quickly enacted an $800 billion stimulus package, the American Recovery and Reinvestment Act of 2009, which funded an array of "shovel-ready" public-works projects around the country, rescued many a state and local government budget, and saved possibly 2 million jobs. And in the ensuing months, he went on to seek and ultimately secure passage of the 2010 Patient Protection and Affordable Care Act (aka "Obamacare"), health care reform that dramatically expands health care coverage to millions of previously uncovered Americans.[4]

Nevertheless, instead of a new Age of Roosevelt, the country witnessed the startling rise of the "Tea Party," a right-wing populist movement of mostly white, middle-class, "mad as hell" middle-aged men and women handsomely underwritten by billionaire reactionaries such as the brothers David and Charles Koch and heavily promoted by the FOX News cable network and a cohort of conservative talk-television and talk-radio figures. These Tea Partiers and their benefactors and publicists virulently opposed Obama's health care plans, forcefully pressed for lower taxes and less government, and ardently promoted "pro-life and traditional family values." And the strength that their movement gathered not only propelled the Republican Party even further to the right, but also to an astounding comeback in the 2010 midterm elections—a comeback that saw the GOP win control of the House, pick up six seats in the Senate, and secure six new governorships and seven hundred seats in state legislatures. All of which enabled an "I told you so" chorus of politicians and pundits to start chanting, "America is a center-right nation"—"Obama went too far, too fast," and, indeed, "he asked too much of Americans."[5]

Obama did not ask too much of Americans. He asked too little.

It was not just, as many an exasperated leftist argued, that Obama was always too quick to compromise—as he did in the fight for national health care by both secretly negotiating with the insurance and pharmaceutical industries and dropping the plan to create a "public option" in deference to conservatives of both parties, and as he did again in the contest over the question of the federal deficit by appointing a high-profile National Commission on Fiscal Responsibility co-chaired by the "deficit hawks" Erskine Bowles and Alan Simpson. Nor was it simply, as more moderate liberal critics sadly lamented, that the "silver-tongued" Obama had failed to "master the persuasive powers" of the presidency, speak like a populist, and offer "broad and convincing arguments." Rather, it was that he never engaged his fellow citizens' energies in the process of redeeming the nation from the political and economic devastation wrought by more than three decades of conservative and corporate ascendance.[6]

Even as the "Great Recession" was doing its worst, even as millions of Americans continued to lose jobs and homes, even as poverty increased and inequality widened, Obama failed to respond in the fashion he had promised. Even as the Right and conservative rich were mobilizing to halt the renewal of the fight for the Four Freedoms, the president issued no call to action—no call to mobilize and demand a truly universal national health care system—no call to mobilize and push Congress to rescind the Bush administration's massive tax cuts of the early 2000s that were making the rich all the richer and the nation all the poorer—no call to rally in favor of greater federal spending on public needs, public works, and job creation. For all of his expressed admiration and appreciation of FDR and the Greatest Generation, Obama forgot, or, like too many another recent Democratic president, simply turned his back on what made them great.

Despite his campaign promises—and as ready as Americans were to act—he did nothing to engage them in the labors and the struggles of recovery, reconstruction, and reform, nothing to empower them to organize workplaces and communities to challenge the "economic royalists" of our day, nothing to call them forth to fill the public squares and spaces and press Congress and himself to act before the Tea Partiers did. Even after the electoral debacle of November 2010, he not only still refused to call for popular democratic action, he also failed to honor his campaign promise to march, or at least stand, in solidarity with workers to protect their rights—most blatantly so in the spring of 2011 when tens of thousands of Wisconsin workers and their fellow citizens turned out over and over again at the state capitol building in Madison to protest and try to block the stripping of public employees' collective-bargaining rights by the newly elected Republican governor, Scott Walker, and the GOP-controlled legislature.[7]

At the same time, Obama compromised all the more with the now-strengthened Republicans by making "deficit reduction" a foremost priority of his presidency, and turned the social-democratic legacy of FDR and the Greatest Generation into a bargaining chip in his dealings with the GOP's congressional leadership. In a major address on the federal deficit question at George Washington University in April 2011, he stated that "any serious plan to tackle the deficit will require us to put everything on the table." Three months later, in his national Weekly Address of July 2, 2011, he repeated the conservative mantra "Government has to start living within its means, just like families do" and then echoed the neoliberals of the 1970s: "We have to cut the spending we can't afford so we can put the economy on sounder footing, and give our businesses the confidence they need to grow and create jobs." And that same week he urged congressional Democrats who were resisting such deal-making "to accept major changes to Social Security and Medicare in exchange for Republican support for tax revenue."[8]

Still, the majority of Americans did not turn to the right. We may have been disappointed, but we had no intention of handing the country over to conservatives and reactionaries. While the Occupy Wall Street movement that erupted and spread across the country in 2011 never reached the scale of the Tea Party, it expressed the views of far more Americans when it challenged the power and wealth of the "One Percent." And in 2012, we not only reelected the President, but also increased the number of Democrats in both houses of congress. In fact, while the GOP retained control of the House of Representatives due to redistricting, half a million more Americans cast their votes in congressional races for Democrats than for Republicans.[9]

One cannot help but recall Max Lerner's lament of 1948: "What we did once we can resume. The tragedy lies in the waste of our experience, in the waiting while all the old blunders are committed over again."[10]

But we do not have time to lament.

We need to remember—and we need to act.

We can neither reelect Roosevelt nor prevent the passing of a generation. But we can still attend to their words and actions. We can recall FDR's argument: "These economic royalists complain that we seek to overthrow the institutions of America. What they really complain of is that we seek to take away their power. Our allegiance to American institutions requires the overthrow of this kind of power." We can embrace his challenge: "A true patriotism urges us to build an even more substantial America where the good things of life may be shared by more of us, where the social injustices will not be encouraged to flourish." And just as our parents and grandparents did—to the point of pushing FDR himself further than he would otherwise have gone—we can recognize that "Democracy is not a static thing. It is an everlasting march," and "it is time for the country to become fairly radical for a generation."[11]

Moreover, we can do far more to honor our parents and grandparents than once again proclaim our eternal gratitude. We can restore to them their democratic lives and achievements and recognize them for who they were—the most progressive generation in American history.

Even more than that we can honor them by remembering who we

are. And in so doing we will see that to truly honor them we must not simply defend and secure their memory and legacy, but also redeem the promise of the Four Freedoms and make the United States stronger and more prosperous by mobilizing, harnessing the powers of democratic government, and making America freer, more equal, and more democratic than ever before.

ry Society, Ken Germanson, David Newby, Stephen Meyer, Joanne and
us Ricca, Steve Cupery, Bob Agen, James Reiland, Candice Owley, Will
ones, Judy Gatlin, Paul Cigler, Laurie Wermter, and Carmen Clark; *and* my
eloved companions of the Christmas/Chanukah "kids table" in D.C., Dan
Arnaudo, Paul Arnaudo, Catie Bauman, Fiona Kaye, and Michael Bauman.

For their progressive commitments and energies, I give special thanks
and salutes to the men and women of Florida Veterans for Common Sense
who have so warmly included Lorna and me, a nonveteran, in their ranks.
Especially I give hugs to Gene Jones, Dennis Plews, Eddie Robinette, Geoff
Morris, and, most of all, our dearest of friends Mike and Cynthia Burns.

For allowing me to develop and broadcast my ideas and arguments at
The Guardian, Campaign for America's Future, History News Network, The
Daily Beast, New Deal 2.0 (now Next New Deal), The Huffington Post, *Dis-
sent,* and Salon, I thank Michael Tomasky, Robert Borosage, Isaiah Poole,
Rick Shenkman, Lucas Wittman, Lynn Parramore, Bryce Covert, Tim Price,
Michael Kazin, Nick Serpe, and Julian Brookes. And I want to register a spe-
cial note of appreciation for the students left, right, and center at the Yale
Political Union who invited me to New Haven to speak and debate with
them in 2009.

I must also acknowledge a University of Wisconsin–Green Bay Sabbat-
ical Award in 2007–2008, which enabled me to make significant progress
on the research and writing of this book. And as ever, I owe a huge debt
to the University of Wisconsin–Green Bay and Brown County librarians
who were so ready and enthusiastic to help me get what needed getting for
my research—Jeffrey Brunner, Anne Kasuboski, Joan Robb, and Mary Jane
Herber.

My father always said, "Make sure your friends are smarter than you"—
and I have closely followed his advice. My friend and editor Thomas LeBien
at Simon & Schuster is brilliant, talented, and invaluable. And while he may
think I was kidding when I said, "You write the book and I will edit you," I
usually was not.

And most especially, for their love, affection, and confidence in my labors, I thank my "Greatest Generation" mom, Frances Kaye, my sister and
brother-in-law, Phyllis and Bill Bauman, my daughters, Rhiannon and
Fiona, Rhiannon's husband, Dave, and the woman who truly keeps me
going, Lorna.

ACKNOWLEDGMEN

Freedom, Equality, and Democracy. But let us not forget Solida
that spirit I have many people to thank for helping me in the wr
work.

For their knowledge of past and present, their love of history
and their readiness to share them, I celebrate Allida Black, And
Dave Jowett, Jerry Rodesch, Sid Bremer, Craig Lockard, Jeremi
chael Kazin, Eric Foner, the late Jim Lorence, David Voelker, Vince
Stephen Perkins, Derek Jeffreys, Brad Creed, Ken Burchell, Robe
Elizabeth Borgwardt, Peter Dreier, Christopher De Rosa, Roger 1
Kriste Lindenmeyer, Cass Sunstein, Mark Shulman, Nikki Mandell
ces Fox Piven, John Nichols, Gary Gerstle, Joshua Freeman, Joe McC
Eileen Boris, Nelson Lichtenstein, Frank Wetta, Mark Novelli, Ron
Elliott Gorn, John Wertheimer, Patricia Sullivan, Alison Standinger
Jonathan Holloway.

For appointing me a historical advisor to the Franklin Roosevelt 1
Freedoms Park Project (Roosevelt Island, New York City) and compell
me to think about FDR and the Four Freedoms in a most public way, I tha
Ambassador William vanden Heuvel, his colleagues Gina Pollara, Sally N
nard, Kathy Sloane, and Robert Clark, and my super "FDR & ER" bud
Allida Black.

For their support and encouragement along the way, I thank Nor-
man Lear, Bill Moyers, Chris Terrien, Scott Hildebrand, Andrew Austin,
Tim Dale, Brent Weycker, Pat Jowett, Steve Hein, Bruce Shepard, Lesley
Groetsch, Doug Hartman, Zachary Sutter, Brit Hvide, Sean Sime, Tim
Nixon, and especially Sarah Russo; my comrades of the Wisconsin Labor His-

NOTES

Note: *PPAFDR* = Public Papers and Addresses of Franklin Delano Roosevelt

Introduction

1. Roosevelt, "Inaugural Address," March 4, 1933, in *PPAFDR—Volume Two: The Year of Crisis, 1933,* p. 11, and " 'We are Fighting to Save a Great and Precious Form of Government for Ourselves and the World'— Acceptance of the Renomination for the Presidency," June 27, 1936, in *PPAFDR—Volume Five: The People Approve, 1936,* p. 235.
2. Roosevelt, "The Annual Message to Congress," January 6, 1941, in *PPAFDR—1940 Volume: War and Aid to Democracies,* p. 663.
3. Roosevelt first introduced the idea of America as the "Arsenal of Democracy" in a Fireside Chat radio broadcast on December 29, 1940 ("There Can Be No Appeasement with Ruthlessness . . . We Must Be the Great Arsenal of Democracy," *PPAFDR—1940 Volume,* pp. 633–44).
4. Roosevelt, "The Annual Message to Congress," pp. 664–72 (italics added).
5. Stephen E. Ambrose, *Citizen Soldiers: The U.S. Army from the Normandy Beaches to the Bulge to the Surrender of Germany, June 7, 1944–May 7, 1945* (New York: Simon & Schuster, 1997); Tom Brokaw, *The Greatest Generation* (New York: Random House, 1998); James Bradley with Ron Powers, *Flags of Our Fathers* (New York: Bantam Books, 2000); Steven Spielberg, Director, *Saving Private Ryan* (1998); and Ken Burns and Lynn Novick, Directors, *The War* (2007), plus Geoffrey C. Ward and Ken Burns, *The War* (New York: Alfred A. Knopf, 2007). On the FDR Memorial, see Lawrence Halprin, *The Franklin Delano Roosevelt Memorial* (San Francisco: Chronicle Books, 1997); David Dillon, *The FDR Memo-*

rial (Washington: Spacemaker Press, 1998); and Robert Dallek, "The Franklin Delano Roosevelt Memorial, Washington, D.C.," in William E. Leuchtenburg, ed., *American Places: Encounters with History* (New York: Oxford University Press, 2000), pp. 67–77. And on the World War II Memorial, see Nicolaus Mills, *Their Last Battle: The Fight for the National World War II Memorial* (New York: Basic Books, 2004), and Douglas Brinkley, ed., *The World War II Memorial: A Grateful Nation Remembers* (Washington: Smithsonian Books, 2004).

6. A primary example of the Right's assaults on FDR is Amity Shlaes, *The Forgotten Man: A New History of the Great Depression* (New York: HarperCollins, 2007). And on Republicans' continuing efforts to identify themselves with the Greatest Generation, see Harvey J. Kaye, "Will the Florida GOP Dishonor the Greatest Generation?" Huffington Post, April 5, 2011, http://www.huffingtonpost.com/harvey-j-kaye/florida-gop-veterans_b_844369.html.

7. Emily S. Rosenberg, *A Date Which Will Live: Pearl Harbor in American Memory* (Durham, NC: Duke University Press, 2003), p. 113ff. In fact, while the critics granted that the tribunes themselves were not necessarily pursuing a conservative agenda, they failed to appreciate the tribunes' own liberal views. Ambrose, who passed away in 2002, never hid the fact that he had strongly opposed the Vietnam War. Brokaw highlighted the story of the D-day veteran and Florida Democratic congressman Sam Gibbons's response in 1994 to the House Republican leadership cutting off debate on Medicare reform: "You're a bunch of dictators, that's all you are. I had to fight you guys fifty years ago." And Spielberg stated that in addition to wanting to honor his father's generation, he made *Saving Private Ryan* to show warfare's "grimmest realities: fear, boredom, killing"— which he arguably did so effectively that he ended up making an antiwar statement. See Stephen E. Ambrose, *To America: Personal Reflections of an Historian* (New York: Simon & Schuster, 2002), pp. 126–47; Brokaw, *The Greatest Generation*, pp. xxiii–xxvi; and Steven Spielberg quote in Stephen J. Dubner, "Steven the Good," *The New York Times Magazine*, February 14, 1999, p. 42.

8. Chip Berlet, "Uniting to Defend the Four Freedoms," in Chip Berlet, ed., *Eyes Right! Challenging the Right Wing Backlash* (Boston: South End Press, 1995), pp. 357–60.

9. Lorrie Young, "Opinion: She Looked at a Rockwell Painting and Learned Something about Herself," *San Diego Union-Tribune*, November 22, 2000, p. B9.

10. Marcus Raskin and Robert Spero, *The Four Freedoms Under Siege: The Clear and Present Danger from Our National Security State* (Westport, CT: Praeger, 2007).

11. Wilson Carey McWilliams, "Memories and Heroes," *World View*, January 1984, p. 2.

Chapter One

1. Deborah Dash Moore, *GI Jews: How World War II Changed a Generation* (Cambridge, MA: Harvard University Press, 2004), pp. 18–19.

2. Leotha Hackshaw quoted in Ronald Takaki, *Double Victory: A Multicultural History of America in World War II* (Boston: Little, Brown and Company, 2000), pp. 47–48, and Walter Morris quoted in Tom Brokaw, *The Greatest Generation Speaks: Letters and Reflections* (New York: Random House, 1999), pp. 227–29. Actually, Morris and his comrades were fighting the Japanese, for the forest fires were ignited by Japanese balloon bombs that had come down in Washington State.

3. Lieutenant Zosel's letter is included in Bill Adler and Tracy Quinn McLennan, eds., *World War II Letters: A Glimpse into the Heart of the Second World War Through the Words of Those Who Were Fighting It* (New York: St. Martin's Press, 2002), pp. 77–78.

4. Harold E. Stearns, *America: A Re-appraisal* (New York: Hillman Curl, 1937), p. 11.

5. Joseph Alsop, *FDR, A Centenary Remembrance* (New York: Viking, 1982), pp. 11–13.

6. William Howard Taft (1924) quoted in Arthur Schlesinger, Jr., *The Crisis of the Old Order: The Age of Roosevelt, Volume 1, 1919–1933* (1957; New York: Houghton Mifflin, 2002 ed.), p. 60, and Harold Stearns, ed., *Civilization in the United States: An Inquiry by Thirty Americans* (New York: Harcourt, Brace, 1922), p. vii.

7. On "The Cult of Prosperity," see Merle Curti, *The Growth of American Thought* (New York: Harper & Row, 1964 ed.), pp. 678–84.

8. Irving Bernstein, *The Lean Years: A History of the American Worker, 1920–1933* (Boston: Houghton Mifflin, 1960), pp. 170–88.

9. Sidney Hillman (1914) quoted in Nelson Lichtenstein, "Great Expectations: The Promise of Industrial Jurisprudence and Its Demise, 1930–1960," in Nelson Lichtenstein and Howell John Harris, eds., *Industrial Democracy in America: The Ambiguous Promise* (New York: Cambridge University Press, 1993), p. 118, and Hillman (1918) quoted in Steven

Fraser, *Labor Will Rule: Sidney Hillman and the Rise of American Labor* (New York: Free Press, 1991), p. 144.

10. John Edgerton (1923) quoted in Bernstein, *The Lean Years*, p. 147. The fullest discussion of "Americanism" can be found in Gary Gerstle, *Working-Class Americanism* (Princeton, NJ: Princeton University Press, 2002 ed.).

11. On the American Plan and "Americanization," see Bernstein, *The Lean Years*, and Lizabeth Cohen, *Making a New Deal: Industrial Workers in Chicago, 1919–1939* (New York: Cambridge University Press, 1990), pp. 165, 175–83.

12. William Howard Taft quoted in Bernstein, *The Lean Years*, p. 191.

13. War Department, *Manual of Citizenship Training* (Washington: U.S. Government Printing Office, 1927), pp. 7–15. I was directed to the *Manual* by Christopher S. DeRosa, *Political Indoctrination in the US Army from World War II to the Vietnam War* (Lincoln: University of Nebraska, 2006), pp. 6–7. Also, see Joseph W. Bendersky, *"The Jewish Threat": Anti-Semitic Politics of the U.S. Army* (New York: Basic Books, 2000), pp. 121–225.

14. War Department, *Manual of Citizenship Training*, pp. 6, 16, 43–45 (italics added).

15. See, especially, John Egerton, *Speak Now Against the Day: The Generation Before the Civil Rights Movement in the South* (Chapel Hill: University of North Carolina Press, 1994), pp. 15–46.

16. James R. Barrett, "Americanization from the Bottom Up: Immigration and the Remaking of the Working Class in the United States, 1890–1930," *Journal of American History*, vol. 79, no. 3, December 1992, pp. 996–1020; Lawrence B. Glickman, *A Living Wage: American Workers and the Making of American Consumer Society* (Ithaca, NY: Cornell University Press, 1997), pp. 78–91; and Ron Rothbart, " 'Homes Are What Any Strike Is About': Immigrant Labor and the Family Wages," *Journal of Social History*, vol. 23, no. 2, Winter 1989, pp. 267–84.

17. Clayton Sinyai, *Schools Of Democracy: A Political History of the American Labor Movement* (Ithaca: Cornell University Press, 2006), esp. pp. 1–109; Eugene T. Sweeney, "The AFL's Good Citizen, 1920–1940," *Labor History*, vol. 13, no. 2, Spring 1972, pp. 200–216; Thomas Göbel, "Becoming American: Ethnic Workers and the Rise of the CIO," *Labor History*, vol. 29, no. 2, Spring 1988, pp. 174–75; and Cohen, *Making a New Deal*, pp. 47–48.

18. John L. Lewis, *The Miners' Fight for American Standards* (Indianapolis: Bell Publishing, 1925), pp. 11–13, 179.

19. A. Philip Randolph quoted in Beth Tompkins Bates, *Pullman Porters and the Rise of Protest Politics in Black America, 1925–1945* (Chapel Hill: University of North Carolina Press, 2001), p. 92.

20. June Granatir Alexander, *Ethnic Pride, American Patriotism: Slovaks and Other New Immigrants in the Interwar Era* (Philadelphia, PA: Temple Press, 2004), pp. 63–64, 161–62.

21. Charles and Mary Beard, *The Rise of American Civilization* (New York: Macmillan, 1927); Claude G. Bowers, *Jefferson and Hamilton: The Struggle for Democracy in America* (Boston: Houghton Mifflin, 1925); and Vernon Louis Parrington, *Main Currents in American Thought* (New York: Harcourt Brace, 1930 one-volume ed.). Quoted words are from Bowers, p. v, and Parrington, vol. 1, p. 285.

22. Blanche Wiesen Cook, *Eleanor Roosevelt: Volume One, 1884–1933* (New York: Penguin Books, 1992), pp. 258, 329ff.

23. Richard Lowitt, *George W. Norris: The Persistence of a Progressive, 1913–1933* (Urbana: University of Illinois Press, 1971); Patrick J. Maney, *Young Bob: A Biography of Robert M. La Follette, Jr.* (Madison: Wisconsin Historical Society Press, 2003); J. Joseph Huthmacher, *Senator Robert F. Wagner and the Rise of Urban Liberalism* (New York: Atheneum, 1968); and Christopher M. Finan, *Alfred E. Smith: The Happy Warrior* (New York: Hill and Wang, 2002).

24. Philip Abbott, *The Exemplary Presidency: Franklin D. Roosevelt and the American Political Tradition* (Amherst: University of Massachusetts Press, 1990), pp. 43–44.

25. Herbert Hoover, Speech in New York City, October 22, 1928, in *The New Day: Campaign Speeches of Herbert Hoover* (Palo Alto, CA: Stanford University Press, 1929), pp. 154–56, 168, 175.

Chapter Two

1. Herbert David Croly, *The Promise of American Life* (1909; New York: BiblioBazaar, 2006 ed.), pp. 11, 21.

2. Conrad Black, *Franklin Delano Roosevelt: Champion of Freedom* (New York: Public Affairs, 2003), p. 211; Robert S. McElvaine, *The Great Depression: America, 1929–1941* (New York: Three Rivers Press, 1993 ed.), esp. pp. 72–79; T. H. Watkins, *The Hungry Years: A Narrative His-*

tory of the Great Depression (New York: Henry Holt, 1999), pp. 3–131; and Studs Terkel, *Hard Times: An Oral History of the Great Depression* (New York: Pantheon, 1986 ed.), p. 390.

3. Zaragosa Varga, *Labor Rights Are Civil Rights: Mexican American Workers in Twentieth-Century America* (Princeton: Princeton University Press, 2005), p. 61.

4. Stephen Skowronek, *The Politics Presidents Make: Leadership from John Adams to George Bush* (Cambridge, MA: Harvard University Press, 1993), pp. 260–86.

5. T. H. Watkins, *The Great Depression: America in the 1930s* (Boston: Little, Brown and Company, 1993), esp. Chapter 3, "Shades of Revolution," pp. 76–107.

6. Paul Dickson and Thomas B. Allen, *The Bonus Army: An American Epic* (New York: Walker & Company, 2004), esp. pp. 153–83.

7. James J. Lorence, *Organizing the Unemployed: Community and Union Activists in the Industrial Heartland* (Albany: State University of New York Press, 1996), pp. 38–42, and Watkins, *The Hungry Years*, pp. 127–28.

8. Malcolm Cowley, *The Dream of the Golden Mountains: Remembering the 1930s* (New York: Viking, 1980), pp. 92–93.

9. *Vanity Fair*'s editors quoted in Frederic A. Ogg, "Does America Need a Dictator?" *Current History*, September 1932, pp. 641, 646, and 647.

10. Anne O'Hare McCormick, "America in a Mid-August Mood" (August 16, 1931), and "A New Americanism" (September 4, 1932), in Marion Turner Sheehan, ed., *The World at Home: Selections from the Writings of Anne O'Hare McCormick* (New York: Alfred A. Knopf, 1956), pp. 75, 116; and Gilbert Seldes, *The Years of the Locust (America, 1929–1932)* (New York: Little, Brown, 1933), p. 279.

11. McCormick, "A New Americanism," pp. 123–26; and McElvaine, *The Great Depression*, pp. 197–202.

12. Mary Heaton Vorse, "Rebellion in the Cornbelt: American Farmers Beat Their Plowshares into Swords," *Harper's*, December 1932, reprinted in David A. Shannon, ed., *The Great Depression* (Englewood Cliffs, NJ: Prentice-Hall, 1960), p. 127; Roy Rosenzweig, "Radicals and the Jobless: The Musteites and the Unemployed Leagues, 1932–1936," *Labor History*, vol. 16, Winter 1975, pp. 52–77; and Robert Cohen, *When the Old Left Was Young: Student Radicals and America's First Mass Student Movement, 1929–1941* (New York: Oxford University Press, 1993), p. 53.

13. In *Democracy at the Crossroads: A Symposium* (New York: Brewer, Warren & Putnam, 1932), see Ellis Meredith, "Foreword," p. 1; Robert F. Wagner, "The Right to Work," pp. 185–93; and Claude G. Bowers, "Democracy: Its Past and Future," pp. 246–61.

14. "Shacktown Pulls Through the Winter," *New York Times*, March 26, 1933, p. SM12.

15. McCormick, "A New Americanism," pp. 126–27.

16. Herbert Hoover, "Text of the President's Address," *New York Times*, November 1, 1932, p. 12. Also, see Donald A. Ritchie, *Electing FDR: The New Deal Campaign of 1932* (Lawrence: University Press of Kansas, 2007), esp. pp. 146–47.

17. Franklin D. Roosevelt, *Whither Bound?* (Boston: Houghton Mifflin, 1926), pp. 15–16; Rexford Tugwell, *The Democratic Roosevelt: A Biography of Franklin D. Roosevelt* (Baltimore, MD: Penguin Books, 1969 ed.), p. 197; and Roosevelt, "Democracy Is Not a Static Thing, It Is an Everlasting March" (October 1, 1935), in *PPAFDR—Volume Four: The Court Disapproves, 1935,* p. 403. In *Thomas Paine and the Promise of America* (New York: Hill and Wang, 2005), p. 211, I wrote, "Roosevelt was no radical." But as my lines here reveal, I have now come to view him rather differently.

18. McCormick, "A Little Left of Center" (November 25, 1934), in *The World at Home,* p. 249; Frances Perkins, *The Roosevelt I Knew* (New York: Viking, 1946), pp. 139–40, 330; Tugwell, *The Democratic Roosevelt,* p. 11; and Gary Scott Smith, *Faith and the Presidency* (New York: Oxford University Press, 2006), pp. 191–220.

19. Roosevelt, " 'I Pledge You, I Pledge Myself to a New Deal for the American People,' The Governor Accepts the Nomination for President" (July 2, 1932), in *PPAFDR—Volume One: The Genesis of the New Deal, 1928–1932,* p. 650, and Perkins, *The Roosevelt I Knew,* p. 330. On Roosevelt's ambitions to make the Democratic Party the party of progressive liberalism, see Samuel I. Rosenman, *Working with Roosevelt* (New York: Harper & Brothers, 1952), pp. 128, 162, 176–78, 463–70.

20. Roosevelt, "The First Inaugural Address as Governor" (January 21, 1929), in *PPAFDR—Volume One,* pp. 75–77.

21. Perkins, *The Roosevelt I Knew,* pp. 12–31.

22. Max Lerner, "Roosevelt and History" (1938), in Max Lerner, *Ideas Are Weapons: The History and Uses of Ideas* (New York: Viking, 1940), p. 247; Stanley High, *Roosevelt—And Then?* (New York: Harper and Broth-

ers, 1937), p. 63; and Frank Kingdon, *As FDR Said* (New York: Duell, Sloan, and Pearce, 1950), pp. 106–7.

23. Roosevelt, "Campaign Speech" (September 13, 1920), and "Speech Accepting the Democratic Vice Presidential Nomination" (August 9, 1920), in Basil Rauch, ed., *The Roosevelt Reader* (New York: Rinehart & Co., 1957), pp. 30, 37; and Tugwell, *The Democratic Roosevelt*, p. 140.

24. Roosevelt, "Is There a Jefferson on the Horizon?" (*New York Evening World*, December 3, 1925), in Rauch, ed., *The Roosevelt Reader*, pp. 44–47, and Roosevelt's Address to Jefferson Day Dinner (April 26, 1930), quoted in Black, *Franklin Delano Roosevelt*, p. 203.

25. Roosevelt, "Is There a Jefferson on the Horizon?" p. 47.

26. Roosevelt, "Message to the Congress Reviewing the Broad Objectives and Accomplishments of the Administration" (June 8, 1934), and "The First Fireside Chat of 1934—'Are You Better Off than You Were Last Year?'" (June 28, 1934), in *PPAFDR—Volume Three: The Advance of Recovery and Reform, 1934*, pp. 288, 317–18.

27. Roosevelt, "Radio Address on Brotherhood Day" (February 23, 1936), and "Address at the Dedication of a World War Memorial" (October 14, 1936), in *PPAFDR—Volume Five: The People Approve, 1936*, pp. 86, 475.

28. Roosevelt, "The 'Forgotten Man' Speech" (April 7, 1932), "The Country Needs, the Country Demands Bold, Persistent Experimentation" (May 22, 1932), "I Pledge You, I Pledge Myself to a New Deal for the American People" (July 2, 1932), "New Conditions Impose New Requirements . . ." (September 23, 1932), and "The Philosophy of Social Justice through Social Action" (October 2, 1932), in *PPAFDR—Volume One*, pp. 625, 645–46, 653–59, 747–54, 774.

29. Roosevelt, "I Pledge You, I Pledge Myself to a New Deal for the American People" (July 2, 1932), "The Philosophy of Social Justice," and "Campaign Address on the Eight Great Credit Groups of the Nation" (October 21, 1932), in *PPAFDR—Volume One*, pp. 659, 771–72, 777, 821–22. I would note that FDR's words in his acceptance speech echoed Moses' "Would that all the Lord's people were prophets" (Numbers 11:24–29).

30. On Lewis's and Hillman's support of FDR in 1932, see Melvin Dubofsky and Warren Van Tine, *John L. Lewis, A Biography* (New York: Times Books, 1977), p. 285, and Steven Fraser, *Labor Will Rule: Sidney Hillman and the Rise of American Labor* (New York: Free Press, 1991), p. 285.

Chapter Three

1. Roosevelt, "Inaugural Address" (March 4, 1933), in *PPAFDR—Volume Two: The Year of Crisis, 1933*, pp. 11, 12, 15.
2. Gardiner C. Means interview in Studs Terkel, *Hard Times: An Oral History of the Great Depression* (New York: Pantheon, 1986 edition), p. 248, and Edward M. Bernstein interview in Katie Louchheim, ed., *The Making of the New Deal: The Insiders Speak* (Cambridge, MA: Harvard Unversity Press, 1983), p. 274.
3. John Beecher interview in Terkel, *Hard Times*, p. 276.
4. On the New Deal, see William E. Leuchtenburg, *Franklin Roosevelt and the New Deal, 1932–1940* (New York: Harper & Row, 1963), and Anthony J. Badger, *The New Deal: The Depression Years, 1933–1940* (New York: Hill and Wang, 1989). And on the famous First Hundred Days specifically, see Jonathan Alter, *The Defining Moment: FDR's Hundred Days and the Triumph of Hope* (New York: Simon & Schuster, 2006), and Anthony J. Badger, *FDR: The First Hundred Days* (New York: Hill and Wang, 2008).
5. Roosevelt, "Presidential Statement on N.I.R.A." (June 16, 1933), in *PPAFDR—Volume Two*, p. 251 (italics added).
6. Irving Bernstein, *The Turbulent Years: A History of the American Worker, 1933–1941* (Boston: Houghton Mifflin, 1970), pp. 27–34.
7. Theodore Saloutos, *The American Farmer and the New Deal* (Ames: Iowa State University Press, 1982).
8. Eric Foner, *The Story of American Freedom* (New York: Norton, 1998), esp. pp. 195–218, and Cass Sunstein, *The Second Bill of Rights: FDR's Unfinished Revolution and Why We Need It More Than Ever* (New York: Basic Books, 2004), esp. pp. 61–95.
9. Roosevelt, "Message to the Congress . . ." (June 8, 1934), and "Second Fireside Chat of 1934—'We Are Moving Forward to Greater Freedom, to Greater Security for the Average Man'" (September 30, 1934), in *PPAFDR—Volume Three: The Advance of Recovery and Reform, 1934*, pp. 292, 422.
10. Jason Scott Smith, *Building New Deal Liberalism: The Political Economy of Public Works, 1933–1956* (New York: Cambridge University Press, 2006), pp. 88–98, 113, 121–34; Neil M. Maher, *Nature's New Deal: The Civilian Conservation Corps and the Roots of the American Environmental Movement* (New York: Oxford University Press, 2008), pp. 6, 13, 43–44, 54; Leuchtenburg, *Franklin Roosevelt and the New Deal*, p. 121;

Irving Bernstein, *A Caring Society: The New Deal, the Workers, and the Great Depression* (Boston: Houghton Mifflin, 1985), p. 174; and Sarah T. Phillips, *This Land, This Nation: Conservation, Rural America, and the New Deal* (New York: Cambridge University Press, 2007), pp. 75–148. Also see Nick Taylor, *American-Made: The Enduring Legacy of the WPA: When FDR Put the Nation to Work* (New York: Bantam Books, 2008); David E. Lilienthal, *TVA: Democracy on the March* (New York: Harper & Brothers, 1953 ed.); Phoebe Cutler, *The Public Landscape of the New Deal* (New Haven: Yale University Press, 1985); and Henry L. Henderson and David B. Woolner, eds., *FDR and the Environment* (New York: Palgrave, 2005).

11. Harvard Sitkoff, *A New Deal for Blacks: The Emergence of Civil Rights as a National Issue: The Depression Decade* (New York: Oxford University Press, 1978), esp. pp. 58–83.

12. Harry Hopkins, "Address at WPA Luncheon" (September 19, 1936), in Richard Polenberg, ed., *The Era of Franklin D. Roosevelt, 1933–1945* (Boston: Bedford Books, 2000), p. 86. Also, see Kirstin Downey, *The Woman Behind the New Deal: The Life and Legacy of Frances Perkins* (New York: Anchor Books, 2009); T. H. Watkins, *Righteous Pilgrim: The Life and Times of Harold L. Ickes, 1874–1952* (New York: Henry Holt, 1990); George McJimsey, *Harry Hopkins: Ally of the Poor and Defender of Democracy* (Cambridge, MA: Harvard University Press, 1987); Blanche Wiesen Cook, *Eleanor Roosevelt: The Defining Years, 1933–1938* (New York: Viking Penguin, 1999); Gary Gerstle, *American Crucible: Race and Nation in the Twentieth Century* (Princeton, NJ: Princeton University Press, 2001), pp. 154–55; and Peter H. Irons, *The New Deal Lawyers* (Princeton, NJ: Princeton University Press, 1982).

13. Roosevelt, "Radio Address on Brotherhood Day" (February 23, 1936), and "Address at the Dedication of the New Chemistry Building, Howard University, Washington, D.C. . . ." (October 26, 1936), in *PPAFDR— Volume Five: The People Approve, 1936*, pp. 85–86, 538–39.

14. John B. Kirby, *Black Americans in the Roosevelt Era: Liberalism and Race* (Knoxville: University of Tennessee Press, 1980), esp. pp. 97–151, and Sitkoff, *A New Deal for Blacks*, pp. 69–71.

15. Roosevelt, "Address before the Federal Council of Churches of Christ in America—'The Right to a More Abundant Life'" (December 6, 1933), in *PPAFDR—Volume Two*, pp. 517–20, and "Address at San Diego Exposition . . . "We Can Summon our Intelligence . . ." (October 2, 1935), in

PPAFDR—Volume Four: The Court Disapproves, 1935, p. 411; and FDR quoted in Frank Freidel, *Franklin D. Roosevelt: A Rendezvous with Destiny* (Little, Brown and Company, 1990), p. 4.

16. Roosevelt, "A Wider Opportunity for the Average Man—Address Delivered at Green Bay, Wisconsin" (August 9, 1934), in *PPAFDR—Volume Three*, pp. 370–72. On Roosevelt's "inclusive" rhetoric and narrative, see Mary E. Stuckey, *Defining Americans: The Presidency and National Identity* (Lawrence: University Press of Kansas, 2004), pp. 198–242.

17. Viola Elder quoted in Kenneth J. Bindas, *Remembering the Great Depression in the Rural South* (Gainesville: University Press of Florida, 2007), pp. 39–40; and Hortense Powdermaker, *After Freedom: A Cultural Study in the Deep South* (1939; New York: Atheneum, 1968 ed.), p. 139.

18. Joe Pullum, "CWA Blues" (1934), in Guido Van Rijn, *Roosevelt's Blues: African-American Blues and Gospel Songs on FDR* (Jackson: University Press of Mississippi, 1997), p. 69.

19. Bud Wilbur quoted in Renée Corona Kolvet and Victoria Ford, *The Civilian Conservation Corps in Nevada: From Boys to Men* (Reno: University of Nevada Press, 2006), p. 59; and James Danner quoted in James Bradley with Ron Powers, *Flags of Our Fathers* (New York: Bantam, 2000), p. 109, and Maher, *Nature's New Deal*, pp. 77–113.

20. Badger, *The New Deal*, p. 172; John Hope Franklin, *From Slavery to Freedom: A History of African Americans* (New York: Alfred A. Knopf, 2005 ed.), p. 433; Joseph Huthmacher, *Senator Robert F. Wagner and the Rise of Urban Liberalism* (New York: Atheneum, 1968), pp. 142–53; Meg Jacobs, *Pocketbook Politics: Economic Citizenship in Twentieth-Century America* (Princeton, NJ: Princeton University Press, 2005), pp. 111, 122–23; Rexford Tugwell, "Consumers and the New Deal" (1934), in Tugwell, *The Battle for Democracy* (New York: Columbia University Press, 1935), p. 286; and Roosevelt, "Annual Message to the Congress" (January 3, 1934), in *PPAFDR—Volume Three*, p. 13 (also quoted in Jacobs, *Pocketbook Politics*, p. 123), and "Address at San Diego Exposition . . . 'We Can Summon Our Intelligence'" (October 2, 1935), in *PPAFDR—Volume Four*, p. 409.

21. Bindas, *Remembering the Great Depression*, p. 38; Van Rijn, *Roosevelt's Blues*, pp. 32, 41; Nancy J. Weiss, *Farewell to the Party of Lincoln: Black Politics in the Age of FDR* (Princeton, NJ: Princeton University Press, 1983), pp. 218–19ff; and Bryant Simon, *A Fabric of Defeat: The Politics of South Carolina Millhands* (Chapel Hill: University of North Carolina Press, 1998), p. 82.

22. Rexford Tugwell, *The Democratic Roosevelt: A Biography of Franklin D. Roosevelt* (Baltimore, MD: Penguin Books, 1969 ed.), p. 52; Lawrence W. Levine and Cornelia R. Levine, *The People and The President: America's Conversation with FDR* (Boston: Beacon Press, 2002), p. 5; Leila A. Sussman, *Dear FDR: A Study of Political Letter-Writing* (Totowa, NJ: Bedminster Press, 1963), p. 141; Gerald Markowitz and David Rosner, *"Slaves of the Depression": Workers' Letters about Life on the Job* (Ithaca, NY: Cornell University Press, 1987), pp. 6, 15; Robert S. McElvaine, ed., *Down and Out in the Great Depression: Letters from the "Forgotten Man"* (Chapel Hill: University of North Carolina Press, 1983); and A. Philip Randolph, "The Crisis of the Negro and the Constitution" (1937), in August Meier, Elliott Rudwick, and Francis L. Broderick, eds., *Black Protest Thought in The Twentieth Century* (Indianapolis: Bobbs-Merrill, 1971 ed.), p. 206.

23. Edward Levinson, *Labor on the March* (1938; Ithaca, NY: Industrial Relations Press, 1995 ed.), pp. 52, 79; Thomas F. Burke quoted in Samuel G. Freedman, *The Inheritance: How Three Families and the American Political Majority Moved from Left to Right* (New York: Simon & Schuster, 1996), p. 103; and Rose Pesotta, *Bread upon the Waters* (1944; Ithaca, NY: Cornell University Press, 1987 ed.), p. 97.

24. Pesotta, *Bread upon the Waters*, esp. pp. 48, 98, 211–12.

25. Göbel, "Becoming American"; Gary Gerstle, *Working-Class Americanism* (Princeton, NJ: Princeton University Press, 2002 ed.), p. 126ff; Simon, *A Fabric of Defeat*, pp. 79–93; Beth Tompkins Bates, *Pullman Porters and the Rise of Protest Politics in Black America, 1925–1945* (Chapel Hill: University of North Carolina Press, 2001), p. 136; Pesotta, *Bread upon the Waters*, p. 26; and George Sanchez, *Becoming Mexican American: Ethnicity, Culture and Identity in Chicano Los Angeles, 1900–1945* (New York: Oxford University Press, 1993), p. 261.

26. Bernstein, *Turbulent Years*, pp. 39–41, and Milton Derber, *The American Idea of Industrial Democracy, 1865–1965* (Urbana: University of Illinois Press, 1970), p. 300.

27. Levinson, *Labor on the March*, esp. pp. 55–57; Bernstein, *Turbulent Years*, pp. 217–317; Simon, *A Fabric of Defeat*, pp. 90–108; Janet Irons, *Testing the New Deal: The General Strike of 1934 in the American South* (Chicago: University of Illinois Press, 2000); and Gerstle, *Working-Class Americanism*, pp. 127–37.

28. Cletus E. Daniel, *Bitter Harvest: A History of California Farmworkers* (Ithaca, NY: Cornell University Press, 1981); Vicki L. Ruiz, *Cannery*

Women, Cannery Lives: Mexican Women, Unionization, and the California Food Processing Industry, 1930–1950 (Albuquerque: University of New Mexico Press); Howard Kester, *Revolt Among the Sharecroppers* (1935; Knoxville: University of Tennessee Press, 1997); and Donald H. Grubbs, *Cry from the Cotton: The Southern Tenants Farmers' Union* (Chapel Hill: University of North Carolina Press, 1971).

29. James MacGregor Burns, *Roosevelt: The Lion and the Fox* (New York: Harcourt, Brace & World, 1956), pp. 200–202, and Doug Rossinow, *Visions of Progress: The Left-Liberal Tradition in America* (Philadelphia: University of Pennsylvania Press, 2008), pp. 103–42.

30. Landon R. Y. Storrs, *Civilizing Capitalism: The National Consumers' League, Women's Activism, and Labor Standards in the New Deal Era* (Chapel Hill: University of North Carolina Press, 2000), pp. 125–52; Annelise Orleck, *Common Sense and a Little Fire: Women and Working-Class Politics in the United States, 1900–1965* (Chapel Hill: University of North Carolina Press, 1995), pp. 229–40; and Jacobs, *Pocketbook Politics*, pp. 130–35.

31. Aaron Copland quoted in Elizabeth B. Crist, *Music for the Common Man: Aaron Copland During the Depression and War* (New York: Oxford University Press, 2005), p. 4; Alfred Kazin, *On Native Grounds: An Interpretation of Modern American Prose Literature* (1942; New York: Harcourt Brace Jovanovich, 1982 ed.), p. 489; Earl Browder, "Who Are the Americans?" (1935), in Earl Browder, *What Is Communism?* (New York: Workers Library Publishers, 1936), pp. 19–21; and Michael Denning, *The Cultural Front: The Laboring of American Culture in the Twentieth Century* (London: Verso, 1996).

32. Carl Sandburg, *The People, Yes* (New York: Harcourt, Brace, and Company, 1936).

33. Jonathan Scott Holloway, *Confronting the Veil: Abram Harris Jr., E. Franklin Frazier, and Ralph Bunche, 1919–1941* (Chapel Hill: University of North Carolina Press, 2002), pp. 1–34, and Beth Tompkins Bates, *Pullman Porters and the Rise of Protest Politics in Black America, 1925–1945*, pp. 126–47.

34. Patricia Sullivan, *Days of Hope: Race and Democracy in the New Deal Era* (Chapel Hill: University of North Carolina Press, 1996), pp. 3, 91, and Robin Kelley, *Hammer and Hoe: Alabama Communists During the Great Depression* (Chapel Hill: University of North Carolina Press, 1990).

35. Roosevelt, "A Radio Address to the Young Democratic Clubs of Amer-

ica" (August 24, 1935), in *PPAFDR—Volume Four*, p. 343, and Robert Cohen, *When the Old Left Was Young: Student Radicals and America's First Mass Student Movement, 1929–1941* (New York: Oxford University Press, 1993), pp. 141–42, 189–95.

Chapter Four

1. Anne O'Hare McCormick, "Roosevelt Surveys His Course" (July 8, 1934), in Marion Turner Sheehan, ed., *The World at Home: Selections from the Writings of Anne O'Hare McCormick* (New York: Alfred A. Knopf, 1956), p. 227; and I. F. Stone, "In Defense of Campus Radicals" (May 19, 1969), in Karl Weber, ed., *The Best of I. F. Stone* (New York: Public Affairs, 2006), p. 47.

2. Max Lerner, "Roosevelt and History" (1938), in Max Lerner, *Ideas Are Weapons: The History and Uses of Ideas* (New York: Viking, 1940), p. 245.

3. Herbert Hoover, *The Challenge to Liberty* (New York: Charles Scribner's Sons, 1935), pp. 9, 23–28, 109ff.

4. George Wolfskill, *The Revolt of the Conservatives: A History of the American Liberty League, 1934–1940* (Cambridge, MA: Houghton Mifflin, 1962); Frederick Rudolph, "The American Liberty League, 1934–1940," *American Historical Review*, vol. 56, no. 1, October 1950, pp. 19–33; and Raoul E. Desvernine, *Democratic Despotism* (New York: Dodd, Mead and Company, 1936).

5. Wolfskill, *Revolt*; Jerold S. Auerbach, *Labor and Liberty: The La Follette Committee and the New Deal* (Indianapolis, IN: Bobbs-Merrill, 1966), esp. pp. 97–130; Stuart Ewen, *PR! A Social History of Spin* (New York: Basic Books, 1996), pp. 288–336; and Richard S. Tedlow, "The National Association of Manufacturers and Public Relations During the New Deal," *Business History Review*, vol. 50, no. 1, Spring 1976, pp. 25–45.

6. Rudolph, "The American Liberty League," pp. 20–21, and Wolfskill, *Revolt*, esp. pp. 57–79.

7. Albert Fried, *FDR and His Enemies* (New York: Palgrave, 1999), pp. 1–144; Alan Brinkley, *Voices of Protest: Huey Long, Father Coughlin and the Great Depression* (New York: Alfred A. Knopf, 1982); Donald Warren, *Radio Priest: Charles Coughlin, The Father of Hate Radio* (New York: Free Press, 1996); and Edwin Amenta, *When Movements Matter: The Townsend Plan and the Rise of Social Security* (Princeton, NJ: Princeton University Press, 2006).

8. Francis Brown, "Three 'Pied Pipers' of the Depression," *New York Times Magazine*, March 17, 1935, in Carl Degler, ed., *The New Deal* (Chicago: Quadrangle Books, 1970), pp. 64–71, and Sinclair Lewis, *It Can't Happen Here* (1935; New York: Signet Classics, 2005).

9. Frances Perkins, *The Roosevelt I Knew* (New York: Viking, 1946), p. 283.

10. Roosevelt, "Annual Message to the Congress" (January 4, 1935), in *PPAFDR—Volume Four: The Court Disapproves, 1935*, pp. 16–22.

11. Irving Bernstein, *The Turbulent Years: A History of the American Worker, 1933–1941* (Boston: Houghton Mifflin, 1970), pp. 318–51.

12. Alfred Sloan quoted in Arthur Schlesinger, Jr., *The Coming of the New Deal—The Age of Roosevelt, Volume 2, 1933–1935* (1958; New York: Houghton Mifflin, 2003 ed.), pp. 311 and 405.

13. Robert Zieger, *The CIO, 1933–1935* (Chapel Hill: University of North Carolina Press, 1995), pp. 22–41; Robert Cohen, *When the Old Left Was Young: Student Radicals and America's First Mass Student Movement, 1929–1941* (New York: Oxford University Press, 1993), pp. 141–42; and John B. Kirby, *Black Americans in the Roosevelt Era: Liberalism and Race* (Knoxville: University of Tennessee Press, 1980), pp. 164–70.

14. Roger Kennedy and Nick Larson, *When Art Worked: The New Deal, Art and Democracy—An Illustrated Documentary* (New York: Rizzoli, 2009), p. 26; Nick Taylor, *American-Made: The Enduring Legacy of the WPA—When FDR Put the Nation to Work* (New York: Bantam Books, 2008), pp. 245–318; Jane De Hart Matthews, "Arts and the People: The New Deal Quest for Cultural Democracy," *Journal of American History*, vol. 62, no. 2, September 1975, pp. 316–39; Francis V. O'Connor, ed., *Art for the Millions: Essays from the 1930s by Artists and Administrators of the WPA Federal Art Project* (Greenwich, CT: New York Graphic Society, 1973); and Susan Quinn, *Furious Improvisation: How the WPA and a Cast of Thousands Made High Art Out of Desperate Times* (New York: Walker and Company, 2008).

15. Irving Bernstein, *A Caring Society: The New Deal, the Workers, and the Great Depression* (Boston: Houghton Mifflin, 1985), pp. 160–64; Harvard Sitkoff, *A New Deal for Blacks: The Emergence of Civil Rights as a National Issue—The Depression Decade* (New York: Oxford University Press, 1978), p. 73; Kriste Lindenmeyer, *The Greatest Generation Grows Up: American Childhood in the 1930s* (Chicago: Ivan R. Dee, 2005), pp. 18, 217–24; and Richard A. Reiman, *The New Deal & American Youth: Ideas & Ideals in a Depression Decade* (Athens: University of Georgia Press, 1992).

16. Roosevelt, "Annual Message to the Congress" (January 3, 1936), in *PPAFDR—Volume Five: The People Approve, 1936*, pp. 11–16.

17. Roosevelt, "We Are Fighting to Save a Great and Precious Form of Government for Ourselves and the World—Acceptance of the Renomination for the Presidency" (June 27, 1936), in *PPAFDR—Volume Five*, pp. 231–33.

18. Ibid.

19. Ibid., p. 234.

20. Ibid., p. 235.

21. Everett Carl Ladd, Jr., with Charles D. Hadley, *Transformations of the American Party System: Political Coalitions from the New Deal to the 1970s* (New York: W. W. Norton, 1975), pp. 42–87.

22. Roosevelt, "The United States Is Rising and Is Rebuilding on Sounder Lines," in *PPAFDR—1938 Volume: The Continuing Struggle for Liberalism*, pp. 167–68; Susan Dunn, *Roosevelt's Purge: How FDR Fought to Change the Democratic Party* (Cambridge, MA: Harvard University Press, 2010); and Patricia Sullivan, *Days of Hope: Race and Democracy in the New Deal Era* (Chapel Hill: University of North Carolina Press, 1996), pp. 61–66.

23. Florida workingman's letter quoted in William E. Leuchtenburg, *The White House Looks South* (Baton Rouge: Louisiana State University Press, 2005), p. 89; "Youth Vote Hitler 'Most Hated' Man," *New York Times*, January 27, 1939, p. 21; and James T. Patterson, *Congressional Conservatism and the New Deal* (Lexington: University of Kentucky Press, 1967).

24. Bernstein, *A Caring Society*, pp. 131–45.

25. Peter H. Irons, *A People's History of the Supreme Court* (New York: Penguin, 2006 ed.), pp. 318–33, and John Wertheimer, "A 'Switch in Time' Beyond the Nine: Civil Liberties and the 'Constitutional Revolution' of the 1930s" (Davidson College, unpublished paper, 1999).

26. Roosevelt, Introduction (1938) to *PPAFDR—Volume Two: The Year of Crisis, 1933*, p. 9.

27. Roosevelt, "All of Us, and You and I Especially" (April 21, 1938), and "A Greeting to the National Association for the Advancement of Colored People" (June 25, 1938), in *PPAFDR—1938 Volume*, pp. 259, 401.

28. Frank Murphy, *In Defense of Democracy* (Washington, DC: American Council on Public Affairs, 1940), pp. 14–15. On the creation of the Civil Liberties Unit/Civil Rights Section, see Kevin J. McMahon, *Reconsidering Roosevelt on Race: How the Presidency Paved the Road to Brown* (Chicago: University of Chicago Press, 2004), esp. pp. 144–45.

29. Sidney Fine, *Sit-Down: The General Motors Strike of 1936–1937* (Ann Arbor: University of Michigan Press, 1969).

30. Thomas Guglielmo, *White on Arrival: Italians, Race, Color, and Power in Chicago, 1890–1945* (New York: Oxford University Press, 2003), p. 139.

31. J. Morris Jones, *Americans All, Immigrants All* (Washington, DC: Federal Radio Education Committee, 1939); Diana Selig, *Americans All: The Cultural Gifts Movement* (Cambridge, MA: Harvard University Press, 2008), esp. pp. 243–49; and Barbara Diane Savage, *Broadcasting Freedom: Radio, War, and the Politics of Race, 1938–1948* (Chapel Hill: University of North Carolina Press, 1999), pp. 21–105.

32. Michael Denning, *The Cultural Front: The Laboring of American Culture in the Twentieth Century* (London: Verso, 1996), esp. pp. 115–18.

33. Sitkoff, *A New Deal for Blacks*, p. 258; Sullivan, *Days of Hope*, pp. 92–101; Thomas Krueger, *And Promises to Keep: The Southern Conference on Human Welfare, 1938–1948* (Nashville, TN: Vanderbilt University Press, 1967), pp. 16–59; and Irons, *A People's History of the Supreme Court*, pp. 370–71.

34. Lewis A. Erenberg, *Swingin' the Dream: Big Band Jazz and the Rebirth of American Culture* (Chicago: University of Chicago Press, 1998).

35. Raymond Arsenault, *The Sound of Freedom: Marian Anderson, the Lincoln Memorial, and the Concert That Awakened America* (New York: Bloomsbury Press, 2009), and "Public Approves Active First Lady," *New York Times*, January 16, 1939, p. 3, discussed in Blanche Wiesen Cook, *Eleanor Roosevelt: The Defining Years, 1933–1938* (New York: Viking Penguin, 1999), p. 574.

36. Charles F. McGovern, *Sold American: Consumption and Citizenship, 1890–1945* (Chapel Hill: University of North Carolina Press, 2006), pp. 262, 322, and Jacobs, *Pocketbook Politics*, pp. 172–73, 313–15.

37. Ewen, *PR!*, pp. 288–321, and Wendy L. Wall, *Inventing the "American Way": The Politics of Consensus from the New Deal to the Civil Rights Movement* (New York: Oxford University Press, 2008), pp. 48–55.

38. Dr. Ralph W. Robey, *Index of Abstracts of Social Science Textbooks* (National Association of Manufacturers, 1940); Joel Spring, *Educating the Consumer-Citizen: A History of the Marriage of Schools, Advertising and the Media* (Mahwah, NJ: Lawrence Erlbaum Publishers, 2003), pp. 125–35; William Pencak, *For God and Country: The American Legion, 1919–1941* (Boston: Northeastern University Press, 1989), pp. 272–73; and Gary B. Nash, Charlotte Crabtree, and Ross E. Dunn, *History on*

Trial: Culture Wars and the Teaching of the Past (New York: Alfred A. Knopf, 1997), pp. 40–45.

39. John Egerton, *Speak Now Against the Day: The Generation Before the Civil Rights Movement in the South* (Chapel Hill: University of North Carolina Press, 1994), pp. 173–74.

40. Roosevelt, "The Fight for Social Justice . . ." (November 4, 1938), in *PPAFDR—1938 Volume*, p. 586.

41. Arthur Garfield Hays, *Democracy Works* (New York: Random House, 1939), pp. 32, 56; Archibald MacLeish, *America Was Promises* (New York: Duell, Sloan & Pearce, 1939); and Chicago *Defender*, "Editorial" (July 22, 1939), quoted in Sitkoff, *A New Deal for Blacks*, p. 301.

42. George Sanchez, *Becoming Mexican American: Ethnicity, Culture and Identity in Chicano Los Angeles, 1900–1945*, (New York: Oxford University Press, 1993), pp. 247–49, and Mario T. García, *Mexican Americans: Leadership, Ideology, and Identity, 1930–1960* (New Haven, CT: Yale University Press, 1989), p. 166.

Chapter Five

1. Roosevelt, "The Annual Message to Congress" (January 6, 1941), *PPAFDR—1940 Volume: War and Aid to Democracies*, p. 663–72.

2. "The Presidency," *Time*, January 13, 1941, p. 9; Roosevelt, "There Can Be No Appeasement . . ." (December 29, 1940), in *PPAFDR—1940*, pp. 633–43; and Jerome S. Bruner, *Mandate from the People* (New York: Duell, Sloan and Pearce, 1944), p. 23.

3. Samuel I. Rosenman, *Working with Roosevelt* (New York: Harper & Brothers, 1952), p. 262.

4. Ibid., pp. 262–63.

5. "The Presidency," *Time*, January 13, 1941, p. 9.

6. Ibid.

7. "Roosevelt Rallies Democracy for Finish Fight on the Axis," *Newsweek*, January 13, 1941, pp. 13–14; "Our Purpose and Our Pledge," *New York Times*, January 7, 1941, p. 22; and Samuel Grafton, *An American Diary* (Garden City, NY: Doubleday, Doran and Company, 1943), p. 85.

8. Roosevelt's greatest lesson on Americans' isolationist feelings came in the wake of his famous 1937 "Quarantine Speech," wherein he proposed that "peace-loving nations" essentially corral the countries responsible for the "present reign of terror and international lawlessness." Which

seemed a reasonable proposal but, as he later noted, it "fell upon deaf ears—even hostile and resentful ears" and "became the subject of bitter attack." See Roosevelt, "The Will for Peace . . ." (October 5, 1937), in *PPAFDR—1937 Volume: The Constitution Prevails*, pp. 406–11; and for his reflective remarks, see his Introduction (1941) to *PPAFDR—1939 Volume: War—And Neutrality*, p. xxviii.

9. Robert Dallek, *Franklin D. Roosevelt and American Foreign Policy, 1932–1945* (New York: Oxford University Press, 1979), pp. 153–56.

10. Roosevelt, "A 'Fireside Chat'" (October 12, 1937), in *PPAFDR—1937*, p. 437, and "The Fight for Social Justice . . ." (November 4, 1938), in *PPAFDR—1938 Volume: The Continuing Struggle for Liberalism*, pp. 585–86; and on FDR's pedagogy on the threat of fascism and war, see Rosenman, *Working with Roosevelt*, pp. 171–80.

11. Roosevelt, "Dictatorships Do Not Grow Out of Strong and Successful Governments . . ." (April 14, 1938), and "If the Fires of Freedom . . ." (June 30, 1938), in *PPAFDR—1938*, pp. 242, 418.

12. Jerome S. Bruner, *Mandate from the People*, p. 19.

13. David F. Schmitz, *The Triumph of Internationalism: Franklin D. Roosevelt and a World in Crisis, 1933–1941* (Dulles, VA: Potomac Books, 2007), pp. 17–38; and David Kennedy, *Freedom from Fear: The American People in Depression and War, 1929–1945* (New York: Oxford University Press, 1999), pp. 387–88.

14. Donald Warren, *Radio Priest: Charles Coughlin, The Father of Hate Radio* (New York: Free Press, 1996), pp. 129–98; Neil Baldwin, *Henry Ford and the Jews: The Mass Production of Hate* (New York: Public Affairs, 2001); Doris Kearns Goodwin, *No Ordinary Time: Franklin and Eleanor—The Home Front in World War II* (New York: Simon & Schuster, 1994), pp. 172–76; Joseph W. Bendersky, *"The Jewish Threat": Anti-Semitic Politics of the U.S. Army* (New York: Basic Books, 2000), pp. 227–86; William Pencak, *For God and Country: The American Legion, 1919–1941* (Boston: Northeastern University Press, 1989), pp. 257–63; and Stephen H. Norwood, *The Third Reich in the Ivory Tower: Complicity and Conflict on American Campuses* (New York: Cambridge University Press, 2009).

15. Robert E. Sherwood, *Roosevelt and Hopkins: An Intimate History* (New York: Harper & Brothers, 1948), pp. 367–68; Allen J. Lichtman, *White Protestant Nation: The Rise of the Conservative Movement* (New York: Atlantic Monthly Press, 2008), p. 107; and for a contemporary exposé of

corporate collusion with German industry, see George Seldes, *Facts and Fascism* (New York: In Fact, 1943), pp. 11–104.

16. Peter Carroll, *The Odyssey of the Abraham Lincoln Brigade: Americans in the Spanish Civil War* (Palo Alto, CA: Stanford University Press, 1994).

17. Roosevelt, "I Have Seen War . . . I Hate War" (August 14, 1936), in *PPAFDR—Volume Five: The People Approve, 1936*, p. 289, and Dallek, *Franklin D. Roosevelt and American Foreign Policy*, pp. 102–21.

18. Robert Dallek, *Franklin D. Roosevelt and American Foreign Policy*, pp. 171–313; and Kennedy, *Freedom from Fear*, pp. 655–61. Regarding the refugee question, the United States did admit 105,000 refugees during the course of the 1930s—more than any other nation. But FDR's actions—or lack thereof—remain the subject of heated debate. See Richard Breitman and Allan J. Lichtman, *FDR and the Jews* (Cambridge, MA: Harvard University Press, 2013).

19. John Egerton, *Speak Now Against the Day: The Generation Before the Civil Rights Movement in the South* (Chapel Hill: University of North Carolina Press, 1994), p. 203; Geoffrey S. Smith, *To Save A Nation: American Countersubversives, the New Deal, and the Coming of World War II* (New York: Basic Books, 1973), pp. 152–53, 174–79; and for "A Cross-Section of Non-Interventionist Opinion," see Nancy Schoonmaker and Doris Fielding Reid, eds., *We Testify* (New York: Smith & Durrell, 1941).

20. Stephen Vincent Benét, "Democracy Is the Revolution" (November 20, 1940), in Benét, *A Summons to the Free* (New York: Farrar & Rienhart, 1941), p. 20.

21. Philip Gleason, "World War II and the Development of American Studies," *American Quarterly*, vol. 36, no. 3, September 1984, pp. 343–58; Harvey J. Kaye, *Thomas Paine and the Promise of America* (New York: Hill & Wang, 2005), pp. 216–18; Barry Schwartz, *Abraham Lincoln in the Post-Heroic Age: History and Memory in Late Twentieth-Century America* (Chicago: University of Chicago Press, 2008), pp. 57–66; Bernard Smith, ed., *The Democratic Spirit: A Collection of American Writings from the Earliest Times to the Present Day* (New York: Alfred A. Knopf, 1941); Norman Cousins, ed., *A Treasury of Democracy* (New York: Coward-McCann, 1942); Wallace P. Rusterholtz, *American Heretics and Saints* (Boston: Manthorne & Burack, 1938); Allan Seager, *They Worked for a Better World* (New York: Macmillan, 1939); Joseph H. Fichter, S.J., ed., *Roots of Change* (New York: D. Appleton–Century, 1939); Ralph Henry Gabriel, *The Course of American Democratic Thought* (New York: Ronald Press, 1940); George S. Counts, *The Prospects*

of Democracy (New York: John Day, 1938); Edward Bernays, *Speak Up for Democracy* (New York: Viking Press, 1940), pp. vii–viii; Perrett, *Days of Sadness*, p. 123; T. V. Smith and Robert A. Taft, "Forward America: A Debate" (May 16, 1939), in A. Craig Baird, ed., *Representative American Speeches: 1938–1939* (New York: H. W. Wilson Company, 1939), pp. 119–37; William T. Hutchinson, ed., *Democracy and National Unity* (Chicago: University of Chicago Press, 1941); Prudence Cutwright and W. W. Charters, eds., *Democracy Readers; A Series of Nine Books* (New York: Macmillan, 1940); Hilah Paulmier and Robert Haven Schauffler, eds., *Democracy Days* (New York: Dodd, Mead & Company, 1942); and Dramatists Play Services, *America in Action: Twelve One-Act Plays for Young People—Dealing With Freedom and Democracy* (New York: Thomas A. Crowell, 1941).

22. Paul Milkman, *PM: A New Deal in Journalism, 1940–1948* (New Brunswick, NJ: Rutgers University Press, 1997), pp. 12–13, 41, 59.

23. Richard W. Steele, "The War on Intolerance: The Reformulation of American Nationalism, 1939–1941," *Journal of American Ethnic History*, vol. 9, no. 1, September 1989, pp. 11–33; Wendy L. Wall, *Inventing the "American Way": The Politics of Consensus from the New Deal to the Civil Rights Movement* (New York: Oxford University Press, 2008), pp. 63–87; Louis Finkelstein, J. Elliot Ross, and William Adams Brown, *The Religions of Democracy* (New York: Devon-Adair, 1941); James Boyd, *The Free Company Presents . . .* (New York: Dodd, Mead & Company, 1941); Howard Blue, *Words at War: World War II Era Radio Drama and the Postwar Broadcasting Industry Blacklist* (Lanham, MD: Scarecrow Press, 2002), pp. 89–95; Albert Wertheim, *Staging the War: American Drama and World War II* (Bloomington: Indiana University Press, 2004), pp. 177–82; and J. Bradley Creed, "Freedom For and Freedom From: Baptists, Religious Liberty, and World War II," *Baptist History and Heritage*, vol. xxxvi, Summer/Fall 2001, no. 3, p. 38.

24. "I Hear America Singing," *Time*, July 8, 1940, and "American-Day Fete in Park Attracts Record City Crowd," *New York Times*, May 22, 1940, p. 1; and "Patriotic Display at the Fair Today," *New York Times*, October 15, 1940, p. 28.

25. Robert A. Divine, *The Reluctant Belligerent: American Entry into World War II* (New York: Alfred A. Knopf, 1979 ed.), pp. 86–96; William Allen White, ed., *Defense for America* (New York: Macmillan, 1940); "New Group Maps Democracy Drive," *New York Times*, October 10, 1940, p. 22; Michelle Hilmes, *Radio Voices: American Broadcasting, 1922–1952* (Minneapolis: University of Minnesota Press, 1997), pp. 238–39; and

Philip Seib, *Broadcasts from the Blitz: How Edward R. Murrow Helped Lead America Into War* (Washington, DC: Potomac Books, 2006).

26. Archibald MacLeish, "The American Cause" (1940—published as a book in 1941), in MacLeish, *A Time to Act: Selected Addresses* (Boston: Houghton Mifflin, 1943), p. 116; Lerner, *It Is Later Than You Think;* Lewis Mumford, *Men Must Act* (New York: Harcourt, Brace and Company, 1939); and Samuel Grafton, *All Out! How Democracy Will Defend America—Based on the French Failure, the English Stand, and the American Program* (New York: Simon and Schuster, 1940).

27. Robert H. Jackson, "The Call for a Liberal Bar" (1938), in Ann Fagan Ginger and Eugene Tobin, eds., *The National Lawyers Guild: From Roosevelt to Reagan* (Philadelphia: Temple University Press, 1988), pp. 23–24— also quoted and discussed in Kevin J. McMahon, *Reconsidering Roosevelt on Race: How the Presidency Paved the Road to Brown* (Chicago: University of Chicago Press, 2004), p. 137, and Risa L. Goluboff, *The Lost Promise of Civil Rights* (Cambridge, MA: Harvard University Press, 2007), p. 27.

28. "Mayor Dedicates Plaza of Freedom," *New York Times,* May 1, 1939, p. 4.

29. Charles E. Merriam, *What Is Democracy?* (Chicago: University of Chicago Press, 1941), pp. 77–80.

30. Eleanor Roosevelt, *The Moral Basis of Democracy* (New York: Howell, Soskin & Co., 1940), pp. 12, 24–37, 48, "Civil Liberties—The Individual and the Community" (1940), in Allida M. Black, *What I Hope to Leave Behind: The Essential Essays of Eleanor Roosevelt* (New York: Carlson Publishing, 1995), p. 153; "The Four Equalities," *The New Threshold,* no. 1, August 1934, pp. 4, 34; and Diane M. Blair, "We Go Ahead Together or We Go Down Together: The Civil Rights Rhetoric of Eleanor Roosevelt," in James Arnt Aune and Enrique D. Rigsby, eds. *Civil Rights Rhetoric and the American Presidency* (College Station: Texas A&M University Press, 2005), pp. 62–82.

31. Roosevelt, "Campaign Address at Cleveland, Ohio" (November 2, 1940), in *PPAFDR—1940,* pp. 547–52.

32. Roosevelt, "Campaign Address at Boston" (October 30, 1940), in ibid., p. 517.

33. Stephen Vincent Benét, "The Power of the Written Word" (November 14, 1940), in Benét, *A Summons to the Free,* pp. 10–12.

34. Eliot Janeway, "The Four Freedoms vs. 'The New Order,'" in Edward Taylor, Edgar Snow, and Eliot Janeway, *Smash Hitler's International: The Strategy of a Political Offensive Against the Axis* (New York: Greystone Press, 1941), pp. 72–96, and William Allen White quoted in William

J. vanden Heuvel, "The Four Freedoms," in Stuart Murray and James McCabe, *Norman Rockwell's Four Freedoms* (New York: Gramercy Books, 1993), p. 108.

35. Divine, *The Reluctant Belligerent*, pp. 149–50; Bruner, *Mandate from the People*, p. 21; Lee Kennett, *G.I.: The American Soldier in World War II* (Norman: University of Oklahoma Press, 1997 ed.), p. 6; and Dallek, *Franklin D. Roosevelt and American Foreign Policy*, p. 302.

36. Philip Abbott, *The Exemplary Presidency: Franklin D. Roosevelt and the American Political Tradition* (Amherst: University of Massachusetts Press, 1990), esp. pp. 152–80, and Alfred Haworth Jones, *Roosevelt's Image Brokers: Poets, Playwrights, and the Use of the Lincoln Symbol* (Port Washington, NY: Kennikat Press, 1974).

37. James MacGregor Burns, *Roosevelt: The Soldier of Freedom, 1940–1945* (New York: Harcourt Brace Jovanovich, 1970), pp. 132–33; Ian Kershaw, *Fateful Choices: Ten Decisions That Changed the World, 1940–1941* (London: Penguin Books, 2008), pp. 184–242, 298–330; and Roosevelt and Churchill, "The Atlantic Charter" (August 14, 1941), in *PPAFDR—1941 Volume: The Call to Battle Stations*, pp. 314–15.

38. Elizabeth Borgwardt, *A New Deal for the World: America's Vision for Human Rights* (Cambridge, MA: Harvard University Press, 2005), esp. pp. 1–4, 21–28.

39. Meg Jacobs, *Pocketbook Politics: Economic Citizenship in Twentieth-Century America* (Princeton, NJ: Princeton University Press, 2005), pp. 182–89.

40. Julia M. Seibel, "Soldiers on the Homefront: Protecting the Four Freedoms through the Office of Civilian Defense," in Thomas C. Howard and William D. Pederson, eds., *Franklin D. Roosevelt and the Formation of the Modern World* (New York: M. E. Sharpe, 2003), pp. 169–72.

41. Seibel, in ibid., pp. 173–87, and Matthew Dallek, "Civic Security," *Democracy*, no. 7, Winter 2008, p. 14.

42. John Wertheimer, "A 'Switch in Time' Beyond the Nine: Civil Liberties and the 'Constitutional Revolution' of the 1930s" (Davidson College, unpublished paper, 1999), pp. 31–41; Mary Anderson, "The Four Freedoms," and A. Philip Randolph, "Chart and Compass," in John Waterman Wise, ed., *Our Bill of Rights: What It Means to Me—A National Symposium* (New York: Bill of Rights Sesqui-Centennial Committee, 1941), pp. 15–18, 112–13; and Norman Corwin, *We Hold These Truths* (1941), in *More by Corwin: 16 Radio Dramas by Norman Corwin* (New York: Henry Holt, 1944), p. 85—a recording of which is available at http://www.youtube.com/watch?v=6f6LIfSnctY.

43. Lawrence R. Samuel, *Pledging Allegiance: American Identity and the Bond Drive of World War II* (Washington, DC: Smithsonian Institution Press, 1997), esp. pp. 13–19, 31–35, and William A. Bacher, ed., *The Treasury Star Parade* (New York: Farrar & Rinehart, 1942).

44. Sherwood, *Roosevelt and Hopkins*, p. 266.

45. I. F. Stone, "Aviation's Sitdown Strike" (August 17, 1940), in I. F. Stone, *A Nonconformist History of Our Times: The War Years, 1939–1945* (Boston: Little, Brown and Company, 1988), pp. 17–23; Nelson Lichtenstein, *Labor's War at Home: The CIO in World War II* (New York: Cambridge University Press, 1982), p. 31; Henry Stimson quoted in Brian Waddell, *The War Against the New Deal: World War II and American Democracy* (DeKalb: Northern Illinois University Press, 2001), p. 54; and Bruce Catton, *The War Lords of Washington* (New York: Harcourt, Brace and Company, 1948), pp. 28–40.

46. Neil A. Wynn, *The Afro-American and the Second World War* (New York: Holmes & Meier, 1993 rev. ed.), pp. 21–23.

47. Frank A. Warren, *Noble Abstractions: American Liberal Intellectuals and World War II* (Columbus: Ohio State University Press, 1999), pp. 108–10.

48. Milton Derber, *The American Idea of Industrial Democracy, 1865–1965* (Urbana: University of Illinois Press, 1970), pp. 158–63ff, 368–82; Walter P. Reuther, "500 Planes a Day" (December 23, 1940), in Henry M. Christman, ed., *Walter P. Reuther Selected Papers* (New York: Macmillan, 1961), pp. 1–12; and Nelson Lichtenstein, *Walter Reuther: The Most Dangerous Man in Detroit* (New York: Basic Books, 1995), pp. 161–70.

49. Robert H. Zieger, *The CIO, 1935–1955* (Chapel Hill: University of North Carolina Press, 1995), pp. 111–20.

50. Lichtenstein, *Labor's War at Home*, pp. 60–63.

51. Glenda Elizabeth Gilmore, *Defying Dixie: The Radical Roots of Civil Rights, 1919–1950* (New York: W. W. Norton & Company, 2008), pp. 7, 158, 358; A. Philip Randolph, "Call to the March" (January 1941), in August Meier, Elliott Rudwick, and Francis L. Broderick, *Black Protest Thought in the Twentieth Century* (Indianapolis: Bobbs-Merrill, 1971 ed.), pp. 221–24; and Lucy G. Barber, *Marching on Washington: The Forging of an American Political Tradition* (Berkeley: University of California Press, 2002), p. 121.

52. Gilmore, *Defying Dixie*, pp. 360–61; Barber, *Marching on Washington*, pp. 126–34; and David Brody, "The New Deal and World War II," in

John Braeman, Robert H. Bremner, and David Brody, eds., *The New Deal: The National Level* (Columbus: Ohio State University Press, 1975), p. 275.

53. Patricia Sullivan, *Days of Hope: Race and Democracy in the New Deal Era* (Chapel Hill: University of North Carolina Press, 1996), pp. 114–15ff, and Barbara Diane Savage, *Broadcasting Freedom: Radio, War, and the Politics of Race, 1938–1948* (Chapel Hill: University of North Carolina Press, 1999), pp. 63–76.

54. "The Sun: Its Credo," *Chicago Sun*, December 4, 1941—on which see "New Chicago Sun Begins Career," *New York Times*, December 4, 1941, p. 27.

Chapter Six

1. Joseph Goebbels quoted in Glenda Elizabeth Gilmore, *Defying Dixie: The Radical Roots of Civil Rights, 1919–1950* (New York: W. W. Norton & Company, 2008), p. 170.

2. For America's production figures, see John Keegan, ed., *Oxford Companion to World War II* (Oxford: Oxford University Press, 2001 ed.); Gerald Nash, *The Great Depression and World War II: Organizing America* (New York: St. Martin's, 1979), p. 135; and David Kennedy, *Freedom from Fear: The American People in Depression and War, 1929–1945* (New York: Oxford University Press, 1999), p. 655.

3. Emily Yellin, *Our Mothers' War: American Women at Home and at the Front During World War II* (New York: Free Press, 2004), pp. 167–74.

4. Samuel Hynes, Introduction to *Reporting World War II: American Journalism, 1938–1946* (New York: Library of America, 2001 ed.), p. xix, and Ernest Montoya quoted in Maggie Rivas-Rodriguez et al., eds., *A Legacy Greater Than Words: Stories of U.S. Latinos & Latinas of the World War II Generation* (Austin, TX: U.S. Latino & Latina Oral History Project, 2006), p. xxvii.

5. Hadley Cantril, "The Mood of the Nation," *New York Times*, September 27, 1942, p. SM18; Selden Menefee, *Assignment: U.S.A.* (New York: Reynal & Hitchcock, 1943), p. 3; and Daniel Inouye's "memoir" in Tom Brokaw, *The Greatest Generation* (New York: Random House, 1998), p. 356.

6. Nelson Lichtenstein, *Labor's War at Home: The CIO in World War II* (New York: Cambridge University Press, 1982), pp. 67–109, and Andrew

E. Kersten, *Labor's Home Front: The American Federation of Labor During World War II* (New York: New York University Press, 2006), pp. 102–3.

7. Meg Jacobs, *Pocketbook Politics: Economic Citizenship in Twentieth-Century America* (Princeton, NJ: Princeton University Press, 2005), pp. 191–95, and Nelson Lichtenstein, *Walter Reuther: The Most Dangerous Man in Detroit* (Urbana: University of Illinois Press, 1995), p. 176.

8. John Bush Jones, *The Songs that Fought the War: Popular Music and the Home Front: 1939–1945* (Waltham, MA: Brandeis University Press, 2006), p. 45; Ronald Takaki, *Double Victory: A Multicultural History of America in World War II* (Boston: Little, Brown and Company, 2000), p. 20; Gilmore, *Defying Dixie*, pp. 370, 386; Patricia Sullivan, *Lift Every Voice: The NAACP and the Making of the Civil Rights Movement* (New York: New Press, 2009), p. 267; and Harvard Sitkoff, "African American Militancy in the World War II South: Another Perspective," in Neil R. McMillen, ed., *Remaking Dixie: The Impact of World War II on the South* (Jackson: University Press of Mississippi, 1997), pp. 76–77.

9. Kevin J. McMahon, *Reconsidering Roosevelt on Race: How the Presidency Paved the Road to* Brown (Chicago: University of Chicago Press, 2004), pp. 144–76; Risa L. Goluboff, *The Lost Promise of Civil Rights* (Cambridge, MA: Harvard University Press, 2007), pp. 51–80; Michael Anderson, "Politics, Patriotism, and the State: The Fight over the Soldier Vote, 1942–1944," in Andrew E. Kersten and Kriste Lindenmeyer, eds., *Politics and Progress: American Society and State since 1865* (Westport, CT: Praeger, 2001), pp. 85–100; and Alexander Keyssar, *The Right to Vote: The Contested History of Democracy in the United States* (New York: Basic Books, 2000), pp. 246–47.

10. Francis Biddle, *Democratic Thinking: The William H. White Lectures at the University of Virginia [1942–1943]* (New York: Charles Scribner's Sons, 1944), p. 10.

11. Thomas J. Wallner quoted in Catton, *The War Lords of Washington*, pp. 180–81, and W. P. Witherow quoted in John MacCormac, *This Time for Keeps* (New York: Viking Press, 1943), p. 146.

12. Representatives Gifford and Cox quoted in Lawrence W. Levine and Cornelia R. Levine, eds., *The People and the President: America's Conversation with FDR* (Boston: Beacon Press, 2002), p. 523, and Max Lerner, "Stand and Fight" (July 7, 1943), in *Public Journal: Marginal Notes on Wartime America* (New York: Viking Press, 1945), pp. 170–71.

13. Richard Polenberg, *One Nation Divisible: Class, Race, and Ethnicity in the*

United States Since 1938 (New York: Penguin Books, 1980), pp. 67–85; Richard Steele, "Violence in Los Angeles: Sleepy Lagoon, the Zoot-Suit Riots, and the Liberal Response," in Richard Griswold del Castillo, ed., *World War II and Mexican American Civil Rights* (Austin: University of Texas Press, 2008), pp. 41–48; and Neil A. Wynn, *The Afro-American and the Second World War* (New York: Holmes & Meier, 1993 rev. ed.), pp. 68–71.

14. Max Lerner, "Against the Police State" (April 6, 1944), in *Public Journal*, p. 81, and Roger Daniels, *Prisoners Without Trial: Japanese Americans in World War II* (New York: Hill and Wang, 2004 ed.), pp. 22–48.

15. Archibald MacLeish, "The Image of Victory" (May 15, 1942), in *A Time to Act: Selected Addresses* (Boston: Houghton Mifflin, 1943), p. 183.

16. John Mason Brown, *To All Hands: An Amphibious Adventure* (New York: Whittlesey House, 1943), p. 224.

17. Ibid., p. 224.

18. Max Lerner, *It Is Later Than You Think: The Need for a Militant Democracy* (New York: Viking, 1943 ed.), p. xxxii.

19. Hadley Cantril, ed., *Public Opinion 1935–1946* (Princeton, NJ: Princeton University Press, 1951), p. 1062.

20. Jerome S. Bruner, *Mandate from the People* (New York: Duell, Sloan and Pearce, 1944), pp. 27–28, and "I Married My Soldier Anyway," *Good Housekeeping*, June 1942, p. 74, quoted in Yellin, *Our Mothers' War*, pp. 5–6.

21. Paul Fussell, *The Boys' Crusade: The American Infantry in Northwestern Europe, 1944–1945* (New York: Modern Library, 2003), p. 8; Peter Schrijvers, *The Crash of Ruin: American Combat Soldiers During World War II* (New York: New York University Press, 1998), pp. 223–59; Peter Schrijvers, *The GI War Against Japan: American Soldiers in Asia and the Pacific During World War II* (New York: New York University Press, 2005); Lee Kennett, *G.I.: The American Soldier in World War II* (Norman: University of Oklahoma Press, 1997 ed.), p. 184; and Brown, *To All Hands*, pp. 51, 62–64.

22. Christopher S. DeRosa, *Political Indoctrination in the U.S. Army from World War II to the Vietnam War* (Lincoln: University of Nebraska Press, 2006), pp. 19–22, and Benjamin L. Alpers, "This Is the Army: Imagining a Democratic Military in World War II," *Journal of American History*, vol. 85, June 1998, esp. pp. 153–56.

23. War Department, *Manual of Citizenship Training* (Washington, DC: U.S.

Government Printing Office, 1927); Colonel Clayton E. Wheat, ed., *The Democratic Tradition in America* (Boston: Ginn and Company, 1943); and the Director of Morale Services Division quoted in Charles G. Bolte, *The New Veteran* (New York: Reynal & Hitchcock, 1945), p. 86.

24. Deborah Dash Moore, *GI Jews: How World War II Changed a Generation* (Cambridge, MA: Harvard University Press, 2004), pp. 118–23, and Dan Kurzman, *No Greater Glory: The Four Immortal Chaplains and the Sinking of the Dorchester in World War II* (New York: Random House, 2004), p. ix.

25. Samuel A. Stouffer et al., *The American Soldier* (Princeton: Princeton University Press, 1949), vol. I, pp. 431–37.

26. Ibid., p. 508, and vol. II, p. 151; and Captain Tania M. Chacho, "Why Did They Fight? American Airborne Units in World War II," *Defence Studies*, vol. 1, no. 3, Autumn 2001, p. 70.

27. Bill Mauldin, *Up Front* (1945; New York: W. W. Norton & Company, 2000 ed.), p. 50; E. B. Sledge, *With the Old Breed at Peleliu and Okinawa* (1981; New York: Presidio Press, 2007 ed.), pp. 39–40; Margaret Bourke-White, *"The Purple Heart Valley": A Combat Chronicle of the War in Italy* (New York: Simon & Schuster, 1944), pp. 78–79; Schrijvers, *The Crash of Ruin*, p. 56; Samuel Hynes, *The Soldiers' Tale: Bearing Witness to Modern War* (New York: Viking Penguin, 1997), p. 163; Ernie Pyle quoted in Fussell, *The Boys' Crusade*, p. 23; and Kennett, *G.I.*, p. 83.

28. Donald L. Miller, *Masters of the Air: America's Bomber Boys Who Fought the Air War Against Nazi Germany* (New York: Simon & Schuster, 2006), pp. 167–68.

29. Stanley Silverman quoted in I. Kaufman, *American Jews in World War II: The Story of 550,000 Fighters for Freedom* (New York: Dial Press, 1947), pp. 55–56.

30. Gary Gerstle, *American Crucible: Race and Nation in the Twentieth Century* (Princeton, NJ: Princeton University Press, 2001), p. 227; Donald L. Miller, *The Story of World War II* (New York: Touchstone, 2001 ed.), pp. 331–32, 474–78; Wynn, *The Afro-American and the Second World War*, pp. 35–37; and the Memoir of Commander Ethan A. Hurd, in Carol Adele Kelly, ed., *Voices of My Comrades: America's Reserve Officers Remember World War II* (New York: Fordham University Press, 2007), pp. 204–5.

31. Frederick Lewis Allen, "Three Years of It: America at War, 1941–1944," *Harper's Magazine*, December 1944, p. 13.

32. Takaki, *Double Victory*, p. 182.

33. Chaplain Albert S. Goldstein, "Faith and the Army: Part Two," *The Jewish Layman*, November 1943, p. 22; Miller, *Masters of the Air*, p. 13; and Kaufman, *American Jews in World War II*, pp. 18–41, 206–27.

34. Raul Morin, *Among the Valiant: Mexican Americans in WWII and Korea* (Alhambra, CA: Borden Publishing, 1966), p. 24, and Richard Griswold del Castillo, "The War and Changing Identities: Personal Transformations," in Griswold del Castillo, ed., *World War II and Mexican American Civil Rights*, pp. 49–73.

35. Mas Takahashi quoted in Michael Takiff, *Brave Men, Gentle Heroes: American Fathers and Sons in World War II and Vietnam* (New York: Harper, 2004), p. 456, and Robert Asahina, *Just Americans: How Japanese Americans Won a War at Home and Abroad—The Story of the 100th Battalion/442d Regimental Combat Team in World War II* (New York: Gotham Books, 2006).

36. Raymond Nakai quoted in Jere Franco, *Crossing the Pond: The Native American Effort in World War II* (Denton: University of North Texas Press, p. 61. See also Kenneth William Townsend, *World War II and the American Indian* (Albuquerque: University of New Mexico Press, 2000), esp. pp. 61–80, 125–50.

37. Al Banker quoted in Melton A. McLaurin, *The Marines of Montford Point: America's First Black Marines* (Chapel Hill: University of North Carolina Press, 2007), p. 23; Elaine Bennett quoted in Brenda L. Moore, *To Serve My Country, to Serve My Race* (New York: New York University Press, 1996), p. 9; and May Miller quoted in Yellin, *Our Mothers' War*, p. 208.

38. Private Williams's letter (1942?) quoted in Leon F. Litwack, *How Free is FREE?: The Long Death of Jim Crow* (Cambridge, MA: Harvard University Press, 2009), p. 55; Maggi M. Morehouse, *Fighting in the Jim Crow Army: Black Men and Women Remember World War II* (Lanham, MD: Rowman & Littlefield, 2000), pp. 99–108; Wynn, *The Afro-American and the Second World War*, pp. 28–29; Walter White, *A Rising Wind* (Garden City, NY: Doubleday, Doran, and Company, 1945), p. 34; Neil R. McMillen, "Fighting for What We Didn't Have: How Mississippi's Black Veterans Remember World War," in Neil R. McMillen, ed., *Remaking Dixie*, pp. 93–110; Miller, *The Story of World War II*, pp. 246–50; McLaurin, *The Marines of Montford Point*, pp. 118–55; and Robert F. Jefferson, *Fighting for Hope: African American Troops of the 93rd Division in World*

War II and Postwar America (Baltimore, MD: Johns Hopkins University Press, 2008).

39. John Hersey, *Into the Valley: A Skirmish of the Marines* (1943; New York: Schocken, 1989 ed.), pp. 59–60.

40. Miller, *The Story of World War II*, pp. 297–98, 503; Moore, *GI Jews*, pp. 179–82; and Stephen Ambrose, *Citizen Soldiers* (New York: Simon & Schuster, 1997), p. 473.

41. Rene Gagnon letter quoted in James Bradley with Ron Powers, *Flags of Our Fathers* (New York: Bantam Books, 2000), p. 217, and Lieutenant Shannon's letter is in Bill Adler and Tracy Quinn McLennan, eds., *World War II Letters: A Glimpse into the Heart of the Second World War Through the Words of Those Who Were Fighting It* (New York: St. Martin's Press, 2002), p. 83.

42. Archibald MacLeish note to FDR quoted in John Morton Blum, *V Was for Victory: Politics and American Culture During World War II* (New York: Harcourt Brace, 1976), p. 29, and Roosevelt, "The Peoples of All United Nations . . ." (February 12, 1943), in *PPAFDR—1943 Volume: The Tide Turns*, pp. 73–74.

43. Richard W. Steele, "The Pulse of the People: Franklin D. Roosevelt and the Gauging of American Public Opinion," *Journal of Contemporary History*, vol. 9, no. 4, October 1974, pp. 207–15.

44. MacCormac, *This Time for Keeps*; Herbert Agar, *A Time for Greatness* (Boston: Little, Brown and Company, 1942), p. 145; and Biddle, *Democratic Thinking*, p. 6.

45. Henry A. Wallace, "The Price of Free World Victory" (May 8, 1942), in Henry A. Wallace, *The Century of the Common Man: Selected from Recent Public Papers* (New York: Reynal & Hitchcock, 1943), pp. 14–23; Max Lerner, "The People's Century" (1941), in Max Lerner, *Ideas for the Ice Age: Studies in a Revolutionary Era* (New York: Viking Press, 1941), p. 57; Henry R. Luce, *The American Century* (New York: Farrar & Rienhart, 1941); and Norman D. Markowitz, *The Rise and Fall of the People's Century: Henry A. Wallace and American Liberalism, 1941–1948* (New York: Free Press, 1973), pp. 49–52.

46. Eleanor Roosevelt, "Race, Religion, and Prejudice" (*New Republic*, May 11, 1942), in Allida M. Black, ed., *What I Hope to Leave Behind: The Essential Essays of Eleanor Roosevelt* (New York: Carlson Publishing, 1995), p. 159.

47. Norman Corwin et al., *This Is War!: A Collection of Plays About Amer-*

ica on the March (New York: Dodd, Mead & Company, 1942); William L. Bird, Jr., and Harry B. Rubinstein, *Design for Victory: World War II Posters on the American Home Front* (New York: Princeton Architectural Press, 1998), p. 27; and Office of War Information, *The United Nations Fight for the Four Freedoms* (Washington, DC, 1942).

48. Ellen G. Landau, *Artists for Victory: An Exhibition Catalog* (Washington, DC: Library of Congress, 1983); Robert O. Ballou and Irene Rakosky, *A History of the Council on Books in Wartime, 1942–1946* (New York, 1946); Arch Oboler and Stephen Longstreet, eds., *Free World Theater: Nineteen New Radio Plays* (New York: Random House, 1944); Elizabeth B. Crist, *Music for the Common Man: Aaron Copland During the Depression and World War II* (New York: Oxford University Press, 2005); and Edwin McNeill Poteat, *Four Freedoms and God* (New York: Harper & Brothers, 1943).

Chapter Seven

1. Norman Corwin, *A Moment of the Nation's Time* (1943) in *More by Corwin: 16 Radio Dramas by Norman Corwin* (New York: Henry Holt, 1944), pp. 359–63, and Ellen G. Landau, *Artists for Victory: An Exhibition Catalog* (Washington, DC: Library of Congress, 1983), pp. 2–3, 36–37, 38–39, 55.

2. Wendell Willkie, *One World* (1943), full text included in *Prefaces to Peace* (New York: Books in Wartime/Cooperatively published by Simon & Schuster et al., 1943), pp. 138, 121; and Ellsworth Barnard, *Wendell Willkie, Fighter for Freedom* (Marquette: Northern Michigan University Press, 1966), p. 412.

3. Norman Rockwell's Four Freedoms, *Saturday Evening Post, Freedom of Speech*, February 20, *Freedom of Worship*, February 27, *Freedom from Want*, March 6, and *Freedom from Fear*, March 13; Stuart Murray and James McCabe, eds., *Norman Rockwell's Four Freedoms* (New York: Gramercy Books, 1993), pp. 61–69; and Carlos Bulosan, "Freedom from Want" (*Saturday Evening Post*, March 6, 1943), reprinted in Murray and McCabe, op. cit., pp. 131–34.

4. Lawrence R. Samuel, *Pledging Allegiance: American Identity and the Bond Drive of World War II* (Washington, DC: Smithsonian Institution Press, 1997), pp. 68–69, and Murray and McCabe, *Norman Rockwell's Four Freedoms*, pp. 71–91.

5. Private Albert B. Gerber, "What I Am Fighting For," *Saturday Evening Post*, July 24, 1943, p. 25. The complete series of four essays ran in the magazine from July 10 through July 31, 1943.

6. Editorial, "The Four Freedoms Are an Ideal," *Saturday Evening Post*, September 25, 1943, p. 112.

7. Four Freedoms on the Home Front, Inc., *Freedom from Racketeering Labor Leaders* (Washington Crossing, NJ, 1944), p. 8.

8. "Fuller Warns Bankers," *New York Times*, May 21, 1942, p. 31.

9. Sydney Weinberg, "What to Tell America: The Writers' Quarrel in the Office of War Information," *Journal of American History*, vol. 55, June 1968, pp. 84–86; Allan W. Winkler, *The Politics of Propaganda: The Office of War Information, 1942–1945* (New Haven, CT: Yale University Press, 1978), pp. 63–65ff; and Frank W. Fox, *Madison Avenue Goes to War: The Strange Military Career of American Advertising, 1941–1945* (Provo, UT: Brigham Young University Press, 1975).

10. John Bush Jones, *All-Out for Victory! Magazine Advertising and the World War II Home Front* (Waltham, MA: Brandeis University Press, 2009), pp. 5, 46–48.

11. "Urges Fifth Freedom," *New York Times*, August 15, 1943, p. 30; Nicholas Murray Butler, "What Does Freedom Mean?" (September 5, 1943), in *Vital Speeches of the Day*, September 15, 1943, p. 711; Eric Foner, *The Story of American Freedom* (New York: W. W. Norton & Company, 1998), p. 230; and Rep. Edith Norse Rodgers's letter to *The Saturday Evening Post* in Murray and McCabe, *Norman Rockwell's Four Freedoms*, p. 65.

12. Caroline F. Ware, *The Consumer Goes to War: A Guide to Victory on the Home Front* (New York: Funk & Wagnalls, 1942), pp. 193–93ff, 196–99, 226, and Michael Kazin, "America's Labor Day: The Dilemma of a Workers' Celebration," *Journal of American History*, vol. 78, no. 4, March 1992, p. 1319.

13. Langston Hughes, "How About It, Dixie" (October 1942), in Arnold Rampersad, ed., *The Collected Poems of Langston Hughes* (New York: Alfred A. Knopf, 1994), p. 291, and Selden Menefee, *Assignment: U.S.A.* (New York: Reynal & Hitchcock, 1943), pp. 170–71.

14. Richard Gosser quoted in Nelson Lichtenstein, *Walter Reuther: The Most Dangerous Man in Detroit* (New York: Basic Books, 1995), p. 199; Nelson Lichtenstein, *Labor's War at Home: The CIO in World War II* (New York: Cambridge University Press, 1982), pp. 89ff, 117–35; Robert Zieger,

The CIO, 1933–1935 (Chapel Hill: University of North Carolina Press, 1995), pp. 150–73; and James B. Atleson, *Labor and the Wartime State: Labor Relations and Law During World War II* (Urbana: University of Illinois Press, 1998), pp. 130–57.

15. Max Lerner, "Who Are the Strikers?" (December 29, 1943), in *Public Journal: Marginal Notes on Wartime America* (New York: Viking Press, 1945), p. 189.

16. Roi Ottley, *"New World A-Coming": Inside Black America* (Boston: Houghton Mifflin, 1943), p. 307; Mabel K. Staupers quoted in Emily Yellin, *Our Mothers' War: American Women at Home and at the Front During World War II* (New York: Free Press, 2004), p. 209; and Glenda Elizabeth Gilmore, *Defying Dixie: The Radical Roots of Civil Rights, 1919–1950* (New York: W. W. Norton & Company, 2008), p. 389.

17. Mary McLeod Bethune, "'Certain Unalienable Rights,'" in Rayford W. Logan, ed., *What the Negro Wants* (1943; South Bend, IN: University of Notre Dame Press, 2001 ed.), pp. 248–49; and Robert J. Norrell, *The House I Live In: Race in the American Century* (New York: Oxford University Press, 2005), p. 127.

18. Neil A. Wynn, *The Afro-American and the Second World War* (New York: Holmes & Meier, 1993 rev. ed.), p. 108.

19. Roosevelt, "Address to the Congress on the State of the Union" (January 7, 1943), and "Message to Congress Transmitting . . ." (March 10, 1943), in *PPAFDR—1943 Volume: The Tide Turns*, pp. 30–31, 122–23; Arthur J. Altmeyer, *The Formative Years of Social Security: A Chronicle of Social Security Legislation and Administration* (Madison: University of Wisconsin Press, 1968), p. 146; "New Bill of Rights Is Urged for Peace," *New York Times*, November 15, 1942; Marion Clawson, *New Deal Planning: The National Resources Planning Board* (Baltimore, MD: Johns Hopkins University Press, 1981), p. 137; National Resources Planning Board, *Security, Work, and Relief Policies*; and *National Resources Development Report for 1943*.

20. *National Resources Development Report for 1943*, p. 3, and National Resources Planning Board, *Security, Work, and Relief Policies*, p. 1.

21. John Morton Blum, *V Was for Victory: Politics and American Culture During World War II* (New York: Harcourt Brace, 1976), pp. 238–39; Editorial, "Post-War Planning," *New York Times*, March 12, 1943, p. 16; and National Association of Manufacturers, *JOBS—FREEDOM—OPPORTUNITY in the Postwar Years* (New York, March 1943).

22. Twentieth Century Fund, *Wartime Facts and Postwar Problems: A Study and Discussion Manual* (New York: Twentieth Century Fund, 1943), pp. iv, 4.

23. I. F. Stone, "Planning and Politics" (March 20, 1943), in I. F. Stone, *A Nonconformist History of Our Times: The War Years, 1939–1945* (Boston: Little, Brown and Company, 1988), pp. 159–63. Also, see Bruce Bliven, Max Lerner, and George Soule, "Charter for America," *New Republic*, April 19, 1943, p. 542.

24. Jerome S. Bruner, *Mandate from the People* (New York: Duell, Sloan and Pearce, 1944), pp. 153–59, 256–57.

25. Ibid., pp. 170–79, 188–91.

26. Ibid., p. 174, and Hadley Cantril, ed., *Public Opinion 1935–1946* (Princeton, NJ: Princeton University Press, 1951), p. 200.

27. Roosevelt, "The Massed, Angered Forces of Common Humanity Are on the March . . ." (July 28, 1943), in *PPAFDR—1943 Volume*, pp. 333–34; Samuel I. Rosenman, *Working with Roosevelt* (New York: Harper & Brothers, 1952), p. 395, and Glenn C. Altschuler and Stuart M. Blumin, *The G.I. Bill: A New Deal for Veterans* (New York: Oxford University Press, 2009), pp. 44–45.

28. Beardsley Ruml, "A Fighting Creed for America," *New York Times*, June 20, 1943, p. SM8, and *Unfinished Business* (New York: J. J. Little and Ives, 1943); and "First Lady Adds to Four Freedoms," *New York Times*, July 15, 1943, p. 13 (referring to Eleanor Roosevelt, "The Four Equalities," *The New Threshold*, no. 1, August 1943, pp. 4, 34).

29. J. Joseph Huthmacher, *Senator Robert F. Wagner and the Rise of Urban Liberalism* (New York: Atheneum, 1968), pp. 292–93, and Andrew E. Kersten, *Labor's Home Front: The American Federation of Labor During World War II* (New York: New York University Press, 2006), pp. 189–215.

30. Zieger, *The CIO*, pp. 181–83.

31. Office of War Information, *Battle Stations for All: The Story of the Fight to Control Living Costs* (Washington, DC: Office of War Information, February 1943), pp. 7, 46, 53, 100, and Meg Jacobs, *Pocketbook Politics: Economic Citizenship in Twentieth-Century America* (Princeton, NJ: Princeton University Press, 2005), pp. 197, 200, 202–3.

32. Andrew Kersten, *A. Philip Randolph: A Life in the Vanguard* (Lanham, MD: Rowman & Littlefield, 2007), pp. 64–65.

33. Christopher Paul Moore, *Fighting for America: Black Soldiers—The Unsung Heroes of World War II* (New York: Ballantine Books, 2005), p. 132; and Thomas Cripps and David Culbert, "The Negro Soldier (1944):

Film Propaganda in Black and White," *American Quarterly*, vol. 31, no. 5, Winter 1979, pp. 616–40.

34. Anderson, "Politics, Patriotism, and the State," pp. 91–95, and Max Lerner, "The Betrayal of Ten Million" (December 6, 1943), in *Public Journal*, pp. 172–73.

35. Margaret Bourke-White, *"The Purple Heart Valley"*: *A Combat Chronicle of the War in Italy* (New York: Simon & Schuster, 1944), p. 74.

36. Private Herrett S. Wilson quoted in Judy Barrett Litoff and David C. Smith, eds., *Since You Went Away: World War II Letters from American Women on the Home Front* (Lawrence: University Press of Kansas, 1991), p. 267.

37. Charles G. Bolte, *The New Veteran* (New York: Reynal & Hitchcock, 1945), pp. 34–35; Bill Mauldin, *Up Front* (1945; New York: W. W. Norton & Company, 2000 ed.), p. 130; and Kersten, *Labor's Home Front*, p. 62. Bolte, an American, was wounded while serving in the British Army. Determined to fight the Nazis, he and a number of other Yanks had volunteered to do so before the United States entered the war—on which, see Rachel S. Cox, *Into Dust and Fire: Five Young Americans Who Went First to Fight the Nazi Army* (New York: New American Library, 2012).

38. John Steinbeck, "The Shape of the World" (July 16, 1943), in Steinbeck, *Once There Was a War* (1958; New York: Penguin Books, 2007 ed.), pp. 68–70.

39. Ibid.

40. Roosevelt, "The Nine Hundred and Twenty-ninth Press Conference (Excerpts)" (December 28, 1943), in *PPAFDR—1943 Volume*, p. 573.

Chapter Eight

1. For a video of FDR pronouncing the Second Bill of Rights, see http://www.youtube.com/watch?v=3EZ5bx9AyI4&feature=related.

2. Roosevelt, "Unless There Is Security at Home, There Cannot Be Lasting Peace in the World—Message to the Congress on the State of the Union" (January 11, 1944), in *PPAFDR—1944-45, Volume: Victory and the Threshold of Peace*, pp. 32–37.

3. Ibid., p. 37.

4. "The Soldiers' President?" *Time*, January 24, 1941, pp. 11–12.

5. Roosevelt, "Unless There Is Security at Home," p. 40, and Cass R. Sunstein, *The Second Bill of Rights: FDR's Unfinished Revolution and Why We Need It More Than Ever* (New York: Basic Books, 2004).

6. Roosevelt, "Unless There Is Security at Home," pp. 40–41.

7. Ibid., p. 42.

8. Roosevelt, "The President Vetoes a Revenue Bill . . ." (February 22, 1944); "Message to the Congress on Soldier Vote Legislation" (January 25, 1944); and "Statement of the President on Allowing Soldier Vote Bill to Become Law Without His Signature," pp. 111–16, in *PPAFDR—1944–45 Volume.*

9. David B. Ross, *Preparing for Ulysses: Politics and Veterans During World War II* (New York: Columbia University Press, 1969), pp. 77–103; Glenn C. Altschuler and Stuart M. Blumin, *The G.I. Bill: A New Deal for Veterans* (New York: Oxford University Press, 2009), pp. 58–64ff; and Suzanne Mettler, "The Creation of the G.I. Bill of Rights in 1944: Melding Social and Participatory Citizenship Ideals," *Journal of Policy History,* vol. 17, no. 4, 2005, pp. 360–67.

10. Roosevelt, "The President Signs the G.I. Bill of Rights" (June 22, 1944), in *PPAFDR—1944–45 Volume,* p. 182; Ross, *Preparing for Ulysses,* pp. 103–24; Altschuler and Blumin, *The G.I. Bill,* pp. 8, 64–71; and Edward Humes, *Over Here: How the G.I. Bill Transformed the American Dream* (Orlando, FL: Harcourt, 2006), esp. pp. 4–5.

11. Doris Kearns Goodwin, *No Ordinary Time: Franklin and Eleanor—The Home Front in World War II* (New York: Simon & Schuster, 1994), pp. 491–501.

12. *The People's Program* (1944) reprinted in Joseph Gaer, *The First Round: The Story of the CIO Political Action Committee* (New York: Duell, Sloan and Pearce, 1944), pp. 185–212; Robert H. Zieger, *The CIO, 1935–1955* (Chapel Hill: University of North Carolina Press, 1995), pp. 181–85; and Steven Fraser, *Labor Will Rule: Sidney Hillman and the Rise of American Labor* (New York: Free Press, 1991), pp. 502–16.

13. Zieger, *The CIO;* Fraser, *Labor Will Rule;* CIO-PAC, *Full Employment: Proceedings of the Conference on Full Employment* (New York: CIO Political Action Committee, January 15, 1944); and Gaer, *The First Round,* which provides a full collection of CIO-PAC pamphlets.

14. *This Is Your America* (1944) in Gaer, *The First Round,* pp. 17–47; Zieger, *The CIO,* pp. 183–84.

15. American Federation of Labor, *Post-War Program* (April 12, 1944), pp. 3, 19–20, and Andrew E. Kersten, *Labor's Home Front: The American Federation of Labor During World War II* (New York: New York University Press, 2006), p. 209.

16. James B. Atleson, *Labor and the Wartime State: Labor Relations and Law During World War II* (Urbana: University of Illinois Press, 1998), p. 141.

17. Meg Jacobs, *Pocketbook Politics: Economic Citizenship in Twentieth-Century America* (Princeton, NJ: Princeton University Press, 2005), p. 212.

18. Zieger, *The CIO*, p. 150.

19. "American-Day Fete in Park Attracts Record City Crowd," *New York Times*, May 22, 1944, p. 1, and Rev. Brendan Larnen, *The Four Freedoms* (Washington, DC: National Council of Catholic Men, 1944), pp. 5, 15–16.

20. Walter White et al., "A Declaration by Negro Voters" (January 1944), in August Meier, Elliott Rudwick, and Francis L. Broderick, eds., *Black Protest Thought in the Twentieth Century* (Indianapolis, IN: Bobbs-Merrill, 1971 ed.), p. 267.

21. Gunnar Myrdal, *An American Dilemma: The Negro Problem and Modern Democracy* (New York: Harper & Brothers, 1944), pp. xlviii, 5, 1019, 1021.

22. Michael J. Klarman, *From Jim Crow to Civil Rights: The Supreme Court and the Struggle for Racial Equality* (New York: Oxford University Press, 2004), pp. 137–41, 236–48; Osceola McKaine quoted in Patricia Sullivan, *Days of Hope: Race and Democracy in the New Deal Era* (Chapel Hill: University of North Carolina Press, 1996), pp. 189–91; John Egerton, *Speak Now Against the Day: The Generation Before the Civil Rights Movement in the South* (Chapel Hill: University of North Carolina Press, 1994), pp. 227–28; and Neil A. Wynn, *The Afro-American and the Second World War* (New York: Holmes & Meier, 1993 rev. ed.), p. 37.

23. Jules Witcover, *Party of the People: A History of the Democrats* (New York: Random House, 2003), pp. 401–8; "Democratic Platform of 1944," in Donald Bruce Johnson, ed., *National Party Platforms: Volume 1, 1840–1956* (Urbana: University of Illinois Press, 1978 ed.), pp. 402–4; and Susan Dunn, *Roosevelt's Purge: How FDR Fought to Change the Democratic Party* (Cambridge, MA: Harvard University Press, 2010), pp. 231–35. Roosevelt also secretly reached out to Wendell Willkie to explore the possibility of bringing together all liberals and progressives in a single party and leaving conservative Democrats and Republicans to do whatever they wished. Willkie himself liked the idea, for his increasingly liberal views were alienating him from his own party. However, he insisted that the two of them wait until after the November elections to move on it—which would turn out to be too late, for Willkie, who was only fifty-two at the time, died suddenly that October (Samuel I. Rosenman, *Working with Roosevelt* [New York: Harper & Brothers, 1952], pp. 445–54, 463–70).

24. Lewis Gould, *Grand Old Party: A History of the Republicans* (New York: Random House, 2003), pp. 295–99, and Joseph P. Kamp, *VOTE CIO . . . And Get a Soviet America* (New York: Constitutional Educational League, 1944).

25. "Republican Platform of 1944," in Donald Bruce Johnson, ed., *National Party Platforms: Volume 1*, pp. 407–13; and Thomas E. Dewey quoted in Carol P. Kaplan and Lawrence Kaplan, "Public Opinion and the 'Economic Bill of Rights,'" *Journal of Progressive Human Services*, vol. 4, no. 1, 1993, p. 49.

26. Roosevelt, "'We Are Not Going to Turn Back the Clock'—Campaign Address at Soldiers' Field, Chicago" (October 28, 1944), in *PPAFDR—1944–45 Volume*, p. 371, and Rosenman, *Working with Roosevelt*, pp. 471–506.

27. Roosevelt, "'As for Myself . . .' —Campaign Address at Fenway Park, Boston" (November 4, 1944), in *PPAFDR—1944–45 Volume*, p. 398.

28. Michael Anderson, "Politics, Patriotism, and the State: The Fight over the Soldier Vote, 1942–1944," in Andrew E. Kersten and Kriste Lindenmeyer, eds., *Politics and Progress: American Society and State since 1865* (Westport, CT: Praeger, 2001), p. 95.

29. Robert Emmett Sherwood (on FDR's passing), April 13, 1945, in Donald Porter Geddes, *Franklin Delano Roosevelt—A Memorial* (New York: Pitman Publishing, 1945), pp. 48, 52–53.

30. Detroit woman quoted in James Agee, "A Soldier Died Today" *Time*, April 23, 1945, in Samuel Hynes, *The Soldiers' Tale: Bearing Witness to Modern War* (New York: Viking Penguin, 1997), pp. 623–24; Private First Class Lester Rebuck quoted in Debs Myers, Jonathan Kilbourn, and Richard Harrity, eds., *Yank—The GI Story of the War* (New York: Duell, Sloan & Pearce, 1947), p. 229.

31. Rebuck quote in *Yank*; editors of *Yank* also quoted in *Yank*, p. 225; and I. F. Stone, "Farewell to F.D.R." (April 21, 1945), in I. F. Stone, *A Nonconformist History of Our Times: The War Years, 1939–1945* (Boston: Little, Brown and Company, 1988), pp. 272–74.

32. Norman Corwin, "On a Note of Triumph" (1945), in Corwin, *Untitled and Other Radio Dramas* (New York: Henry Holt and Company, 1947), p. 441.

33. Harvey J. Kaye, "Celebrating the Vets of World War II Without Betraying the Sixties," January 13, 2000, http://www.tompaine.com/Archive/scontent/2661.html, reprinted in Kaye, *Are We Good Citizens?* (New York: Teachers College Press, 2001), pp. 84–86.

34. The line "file away the Four Freedoms with the Ten Commandments" is drawn from Edward Newhouse, "The Four Freedoms—A Short Story," *New Yorker*, February 10, 1945, pp. 236ff.

35. Norman Corwin, "14 August" (1945), in Corwin, *Untitled and Other Radio Dramas*, pp. 503–4.

Chapter Nine

1. William Harlan Hale, *The March of Freedom: A Layman's History of the American People* (New York: Harper & Brothers Publishers, 1947), pp. 277–78.

2. Ibid.

3. Frank Donovan, *Mr. Roosevelt's Four Freedoms: The Story Behind the United Nations Charter* (New York: Dodd, Mead & Company, 1966), and Elizabeth Borgwardt, *A New Deal for the World: America's Vision for Human Rights* (Cambridge, MA: Harvard University Press, 2005), esp. pp. 184–93.

4. Walter Reuther, "Our Fear of Abundance," *New York Times Magazine*, September 16, 1945, reprinted in Henry M. Christman, ed., *Walter P. Reuther: Selected Papers* (New York: Macmillan, 1961), pp. 13–21, and Jack Metzgar, *Striking Steel: Solidarity Remembered* (Philadelphia: Temple University Press, 2000), p. 227.

5. Harry Truman, "Special Message to the Congress Presenting a 21-Point Program for the Reconversion Period," September 6, 1945, The American Presidency Project: http://www.presidency.ucsb.edu/ws/index.php?pid=12359&st=&st1=#axzz1SOJJ7v72.

6. Stuart Chase, *For This We Fought: Guide Lines to America's Future* (New York: Twentieth Century Fund, 1946), pp. 124–25ff; Henry A. Wallace, *Sixty Million Jobs* (New York: Simon & Schuster, 1945); and Chester Bowles, *Tomorrow Without Fear* (New York: Simon & Schuster, 1946).

7. Walter P. Reuther, "This is Your Fight!" *Nation*, January 12, 1946, pp. 35–36.

8. Robert H. Zieger, *The CIO, 1935–1955* (Chapel Hill: University of North Carolina Press, 1995), p. 243; Kevin Boyle, *The UAW and the Heyday of American Liberalism, 1945–1968* (Ithaca, NY: Cornell University Press, 1995), p. 25; Nelson Lichtenstein, "From Corporatism to Collective Bargaining: Organized Labor and the Eclipse of Social Democracy in the Postwar Era," in Steve Fraser and Gary Gerstle, eds., *The Rise and Fall of the New Deal Order, 1930–1980* (Princeton, NJ: Princeton Uni-

versity Press, 1989), p. 126ff; George Lipsitz, *Rainbow at Midnight: Labor and Culture in the 1940s* (Urbana: University of Illinois Press, 1994), esp. pp. 99–154 (Robert Taft quoted on p. 172); and Metzgar, *Striking Steel*, pp. 28–29.

9. CIO Political Action Committee, *The People's Program for 1946: Pamphlet of the Month No. 11* (New York, 1946); Barbara S. Griffith, *The Crisis of American Labor: Operation Dixie and the Defeat of the CIO* (Philadelphia: Temple University Press, 1988); Timothy J. Minchin, *What Do We Need a Union For? The TWUA in the South, 1945–1955* (Chapel Hill: University of North Carolina Press, 1997), pp. 26–47; and F. Ray Marshall, *Labor in the South* (Cambridge, MA: Harvard University Press, 1967), pp. 246–69.

10. Stephen F. Lawson, *Running for Freedom: Civil Rights and Black Politics in America Since 1941* (New York: McGraw-Hill, 1997 ed.), pp. 21–26; John Dittmer, *Local People: The Struggle for Civil Rights in Mississippi* (Urbana, IL: University of Illinois Press, 1994), p. 9; Jennifer E. Brooks, *Defining the Peace: World War II Veterans, Race, and the Remaking of Southern Political Tradition* (Chapel Hill: University of North Carolina Press, 2004), pp. 28–29; Robert J. Norrell, *The House I Live In: Race in the American Century* (New York: Oxford University Press, 2005), p. 138; Robert J. Saxe, *Settling Down: World War II Veterans' Challenge to the Postwar Consensus* (New York: Palgrave Macmillan, 2007), pp. 155–90; and Harvard Sitkoff, *The Struggle for Black Equality* (New York: Hill and Wang, 2008 ed.), p. 13.

11. Robert F. Jefferson, *Fighting for Hope: African American Troops of the 93rd Infantry Division in World War II and Postwar America* (Baltimore, MD: Johns Hopkins University Press, 2008), pp. 231–35; Thomas J. Sugrue, *Sweet Land of Liberty: The Forgotten Struggle for Civil Rights in the North* (New York: Random House, 2008), pp. 96–112; Patricia Sullivan, *Lift Every Voice: The NAACP and the Making of the Civil Rights Movement* (New York: New Press, 2009), pp. 293–311, 323; and Michael J. Klarman, *From Jim Crow to Civil Rights: The Supreme Court and the Struggle for Racial Equality* (New York: Oxford University Press, 2004), pp. 236–89.

12. NFLU supporters' statement (May 14, 1948) quoted in Raphael Rajendra, "Hopeless Struggle: The National Farm Labor Union's Attempt to Organize Farm Workers in California, 1947–1950," Senior Thesis, Columbia University, Spring 2003, pp. 39–40. See also Shana Bernstein, "Interracial Activism in the Los Angeles Community Service Organi-

zation: Linking the World War II and Civil Rights Eras," *Pacific Historical Review*, vol. 80, no. 2, May 2011, pp. 231–67; Richard Griswold del Castillo and Richard A. Garcia, *César Chávez: A Triumph of Spirit* (Norman: University of Oklahoma Press, 1995), p. 16; Henry A. J. Ramos, *The American G.I. Forum: In Pursuit of the American Dream, 1948–1983* (Houston, TX: Arte Publico Press, 1998), esp. pp. 1–85, and Richard Griswold del Castillo, "Epilogue: Civil Rights on the Home Front—Leaders and Organizations," in Richard Griswold del Castillo, ed., *World War II and Mexican American Civil Rights* (Austin: University of Texas Press, 2008), pp. 95–107.

13. Saxe, *Settling Down*, pp. 19–53; Michael Gambone, *The Greatest Generation Comes Home: The Veterans in American Society* (College Station: Texas A&M University Press, 2005); and Michael Kazin, *The Populist Persuasion: An American History* (New York: Basic Books, 1995), pp. 197–99ff.

14. Mark D. Van Ells, *To Hear Only Thunder Again: America's World War II Veterans Come Home* (Lanham, MD: Lexington Books, 2001), pp. 86–87, and Suzanne Mettler, *Soldiers to Citizens: The G.I. Bill and the Making of the Greatest Generation* (New York: Oxford University Press, 2005), p. 132.

15. Saxe, *Settling Down*, pp. 123–30, and Charles G. Bolte, *The New Veteran* (New York: Reynal & Hitchcock, 1945), p. 173.

16. Max Lerner, "Roosevelt and History" (1938), in Max Lerner, *Ideas Are Weapons: The History and Uses of Ideas* (New York: Viking, 1940), p. 245; William Leuchtenburg, *In the Shadow of FDR: From Harry Truman to Barack Obama* (Ithaca, NY: Cornell University Press, 2009 ed.), pp. 1–40; and Nelson Lichtenstein, "Politicized Unions and the New Deal Model: Labor, Business, and Taft-Hartley," in Sidney M. Milkis and Jerome M. Mileur, eds., *The New Deal and the Triumph of Liberalism* (Amherst: University of Massachusetts Press, 2002), p. 151.

17. Mary Sperling McAuliffe, *Crisis on the Left: Cold War Politics and American Liberals, 1947–1954* (Amherst: University of Massachusetts Press, 1978); Stephen M. Gillon, *Politics and Vision: The ADA and American Liberalism, 1947–1985* (New York: Oxford University Press, 1987), pp. 1–32; and Zieger, *The CIO*, pp. 253–93.

18. Patrick Renshaw, *American Labor and Consensus Capitalism, 1935–1990* (Jackson: University Press of Mississippi, 1991), pp. 48–49; Griffith, *The Crisis of American Labor*, pp. 62–87; Patricia Sullivan, *Days of Hope: Race*

and Democracy in the New Deal Era (Chapel Hill: University of North Carolina Press, 1996), pp. 207–9; and William Powell Jones, " 'Simple Truths of Democracy': African Americans and Organized Labor in the Post–World War II South," in Eric Arnesen, ed., *The Black Worker: Race, Labor and Civil Rights Since Emancipation* (Urbana: University of Illinois Press, 2007), pp. 254–56ff.

19. Max Lerner, "The Waste of History" (July 13, 1948), in Max Lerner, *Actions and Passions: Notes on the Multiple Revolutions of Our Time* (New York: Simon & Schuster, 1949), p. 213.

20. Tracy Roof, *American Labor, Congress, and the Welfare State, 1935–2010* (Baltimore, MD: Johns Hopkins University Press, 2011), esp. pp. 52–64.

21. Alonzo Hamby, *Beyond the New Deal: Harry S. Truman and American Liberalism* (New York: Columbia University Press, 1973), esp. pp. 87–120, 169–94, 403–22, and Nicolaus Mills, *Winning the Peace: The Marshall Plan and America's Coming of Age as a Superpower* (Hoboken, NJ: John Wiley & Sons, 2008).

22. "Executive Order on Loyalty" (November 25, 1946), in Barton J. Bernstein and Allen J. Matusow, eds., *The Truman Administration: A Documentary History* (New York: Harper & Row, 1966), pp. 357–66.

23. Max Lerner, "The Muzzling of the Movies" (October 22, 1947), in *Actions and Passions*, p. 76; Ellen Schrecker, *Many Are the Crimes: McCarthyism in America* (Boston: Little, Brown and Company, 1998); and Ellen Schrecker, ed., *The Age of McCarthyism: A Brief History with Documents* (Boston: Bedford Books, 1994). Strangely enough, Joseph McCarthy would say that he had taken up the anti-Communist crusade because the Truman administration had made a "hollow mockery" of FDR's Four Freedoms (Arthur Herman, *Joseph McCarthy: Reexamining the Life and Legacy of America's Most Hated Senator* [New York: Free Press, 2000], p. 37).

24. On the details of the Payne case, see Jack E. Davis, " 'Whitewash' in Florida: The Lynching of Jesse James Payne and Its Aftermath," *Florida Historical Quarterly*, vol. 68, no. 3, January 1990, pp. 277–98.

25. John Egerton, *Speak Now Against the Day: The Generation Before the Civil Rights Movement in the South* (Chapel Hill: University of North Carolina Press, 1994), pp. 359–65.

26. Meg Jacobs, *Pocketbook Politics: Economic Citizenship in Twentieth-Century America* (Princeton, NJ: Princeton University Press, 2005), pp. 226–30, and Robert Griffith, "Forging America's Postwar Order: Domestic Poli-

tics and Political Economy in the Age of Truman," in Michael J. Lacey, ed., *The Truman Presidency* (New York: Cambridge University Press, 1989), p. 64.

27. Peter H. Irons, "American Business and the Origins of McCarthyism: The Cold War Crusade of the United States Chamber of Commerce," in Robert Griffith and Athan Theokaris, eds., *The Specter: Original Essays on the Cold War and the Origins of McCarthyism* (New York: New Viewpoints, 1974), p. 77, and Colin Gordon, *Dead on Arrival: The Politics of Health Care in Twentieth-Century America* (Princeton, NJ: Princeton University Press, 2004), p. 140.

28. Alfred Sloan quoted in Jacobs, *Pocketbook Politics*, p. 221.

29. Elizabeth A. Fones-Wolf, *Selling Free Enterprise: The Business Assault on Labor and Liberalism, 1945–60* (Urbana: University of Illinois Press, 1994), p. 43; Howell John Harris, *The Right to Manage: Industrial Relations Policies of American Business in the 1940s* (Madison: University of Wisconsin Press, 1982), esp. pp. 120–21; Robert Zieger, *American Workers, American Unions* (Baltimore, MD: Johns Hopkins, 1994 ed.), pp. 108–14; National Association of Manufacturers, *Now . . . Let's Build America: Industry's Recommendations to the 80th Congress* (Washington, DC, 1946); Stephen Amberg, *The Union Inspiration in American Politics: The Autoworkers and the Making of a Liberal Industrial Order* (Philadelphia: Temple University Press, 1994), p. 145; and Jefferson Cowie, *Capital Moves: RCA's Seventy-Year Quest for Cheap Labor* (New York: New Press, 1999), esp. pp. 1–72.

30. Robert Griffith, "The Selling of America: The Advertising Council and American Politics, 1942–1960," in *Business History Review*, vol. 57, no. 3, Autumn 1983, p. 392, and Fones-Wolf, *Selling Free Enterprise*.

31. Attorney General Tom C. Clark is quoted in Michael Kammen, *Mystic Chords of Memory: The Transformation of Tradition in American Culture* (New York: Alfred A. Knopf, 1991), p. 574. On the story of the Freedom Train, see Stuart J. Little, "The Freedom Train: Citizenship and Postwar Culture, 1946–1949," *American Studies*, vol. 34, no. 1, 1993, pp. 35–67, and Wendy L. Wall, *Inventing the "American Way": The Politics of Consensus from the New Deal to the Civil Rights Movement* (New York: Oxford University Press, 2008), pp. 201–40.

32. Wall, ibid., pp. 221–22.

33. Ibid., p. 212; American Heritage Foundation, *The Documents on the Freedom Train* (New York, 1947); American Heritage Foundation

and the Advertising Council, *Good Citizen: The Rights and Duties of an American* (New York, 1947), pp. 16, 60; and Richard M. Fried, *The Russians Are Coming! The Russians Are Coming!: Pageantry and Patriotism in Cold-War America* (New York: Oxford University Press, 1998), pp. 36–37.

34. Little, "The Freedom Train," p. 51.

35. Ibid., p. 54.

36. William E. Leuchtenburg, "New Faces of 1946," *Smithsonian Magazine*, November 2006, http://www.smithsonianmag.com/history-archaeology /newfaces.html.

37. Steven F. Lawson, ed., *To Secure These Rights: The Report of President Harry S. Truman's Committee on Civil Rights* (Boston: Bedford/St. Martin's, 2004), Introduction, p. 14, and "To Secure These Rights," pp. 43, 51–54; and Harry S. Truman, "Address Before the National Association for the Advancement of Colored People," June 29 1947, The American Presidency Project: http://www.presidency.ucsb.edu/ws/index .php?pid=12686&st=&st1=#axzz1XNCHVTNn.

38. "A. Philip Randolph Urges Civil Disobedience Against a Jim Crow Army," in August Meier, Elliott Rudwick, and Francis L. Broderick, *Black Protest Thought in the Twentieth Century* (Indianapolis, IN: Bobbs-Merrill, 1971 ed.), pp. 274–80.

39. Harry Truman, "Address at the Gilmore Stadium in Los Angeles," September 23, 1948, The American Presidency Project: http://www.presidency .ucsb.edu/ws/index.php?pid=13012&st=&st1=#axzz1XNCHVTNn.

40. Kevin J. McMahon, *Reconsidering Roosevelt on Race: How the Presidency Paved the Road to Brown* (Chicago: University of Chicago Press, 2004), pp. 177–96, and Kim McQuaid, *Uneasy Partners: Big Business in American Politics, 1945–1990* (Baltimore, MD: Johns Hopkins University Press, 1994), pp. 85–86.

41. Robert A. Taft, "The Fair Deal Is Creeping Socialism" (1950), in Alonzo M. Hamby, ed., *Harry S. Truman and the Fair Deal* (Lexington, MA: D. C. Heath and Company, 1974), p. 42.

42. "Fuller Warns Bankers," *New York Times*, May 21, 1942, p. 31.

43. Wall, *Inventing the "American Way,"* pp. 194–97; Fones-Wolf, *Selling Free Enterprise*, pp. 50–53; and Griffith, "The Selling of America," pp. 399–403.

44. Alton Ketchum, *The Miracle of America* (New York: Advertising Council, 1948).

45. Michael K. Brown, "Bargaining for Social Rights: Unions and the Reemergence of Welfare Capitalism, 1945–1952," *Political Science Quarterly*, vol. 112, no. 4, 1997–98, p. 653—Walter Reuther quoted on p. 646; Nelson Lichtenstein, *Walter Reuther: The Most Dangerous Man in Detroit* (New York: Basic Books, 1995), pp. 276–79; and Nelson Lichtenstein, *State of the Union: A Century of American Labor* (Princeton, NJ: Princeton University Press, 2002), pp. 122–28.

46. Lichtenstein, *State of the Union*, pp. 122–28; Alan Derickson, "Health Security for All? Social Unionism and Universal Health Insurance, 1935–1958," *Journal of American History*, vol. 80, no. 4, March 1994, pp. 1341–43, 1346–54; and Jennifer Klein, *For All These Rights: Business, Labor, and the Shaping of America's Public-Private Welfare State* (Princeton, NJ: Princeton University Press, 2003), esp. pp. 204–57.

47. On several Left intellectuals who traveled from far left to far right see John P. Diggines, *Up from Communism: Conservative Odysseys in American Intellectual History* (New York: Harper & Row, 1975).

48. Reinhold Niebuhr, *The Irony of American History* (1952; Chicago: University of Chicago Press, 2008 ed.); Arthur M. Schlesinger, Jr., *The Vital Center: The Politics of Freedom* (1949; New Brunswick, NJ: Transaction Publishers, 1998 ed.); John Kenneth Galbraith, *American Capitalism: The Concept of Countervailing Power* (1952), included in Galbraith, *The Affluent Society and Other Writings, 1952–1967* (New York: Library of America, 2010), pp. 1–175; and McAuliffe, *Crisis on the Left*, pp. 63–74. Other ADA co-founders included Eleanor Roosevelt, Walter Reuther, the Minnesota Democrat and future vice president Hubert Humphrey, and the ILGWU leader David Dubinsky.

49. Donald Montgomery quoted in Boyle, *The UAW*, p. 47; McAuliffe, *Crisis on the Left*; Hamby, *Beyond the New Deal*, pp. 278–84; and Kevin Mattson, *When America Was Great: The Fighting Faith of Postwar Liberalism* (New York: Routledge, 2004).

50. Zieger, *The CIO*, pp. 253–93; Glenda Elizabeth Gilmore, *Defying Dixie: The Radical Roots of Civil Rights, 1919–1950* (New York: W. W. Norton & Company, 2008), pp. 414–20ff; Thomas Krueger, *And Promises to Keep: The Southern Conference on Human Welfare, 1938–1948* (Nashville, TN: Vanderbilt University Press, 1967), pp. 159–91; Saxe, *Settling Down*, pp. 137–53; and *Life's Picture History of World War II* (New York: Time Incorporated, 1950), p. 267.

51. "Republican Platform of 1952," in Donald Bruce Johnson, ed., *National*

Party Platforms: Volume 1, 1840–1956 (Urbana: University of Illinois Press, 1978 ed.), pp. 496–97; Lichtenstein, *Walter Reuther*, p. 320; and Gillon, *Politics and Vision*, pp. 83–85.

52. Clinton Rossiter, "The Shaping of the American Tradition," *William and Mary Quarterly*, 3rd ser., vol. 11, no. 4, October 1954, p. 519, and "Democrats: Voice of Opposition," *Time*, December 21, 1953, http://www.time.com/time/magazine/article/0,9171,890795,00.html.

Chapter Ten

1. President Eisenhower (August 1, 1954) quoted in Tom Wicker, *Dwight D. Eisenhower* (New York: Henry Holt and Company, 2002), p. 3; Eisenhower, "Personal and confidential to Edgar Newton Eisenhower (November 8, 1954), in *The Papers of Dwight David Eisenhower* (Baltimore, MD: Johns Hopkins University Press, 1996), Doc. 1147, http://www.eisenhowermemorial.org/presidential-papers/first-term/documents/1147.cfm; and Rick Atkinson, *The Day of Battle: The War in Sicily and Italy, 1943–1944* (New York: Henry Holt and Company, 2007), pp. 36–37.

2. Jim Newton, *Eisenhower: The White House Years* (New York: Doubleday, 2011), pp. 102–8, 162–69.

3. Robert Griffith, "Dwight D. Eisenhower and the Corporate Commonwealth," *American Historical Review*, vol. 87, no. 1, February 1982, pp. 87–122, and Newton, *Eisenhower*, esp. pp. 209–11, 247–53.

4. Stella Suberman, *The GI Bill Boys—A Memoir* (Knoxville: University of Tennessee Press, 2012), p. 201; Edward Humes, *Over Here: How the G.I. Bill Transformed the American Dream* (Orlando, FL: Harcourt, 2006); Claudia Goldin and Robert A. Margo, "The Great Compression: The Wage Structure in the United States at Mid-Century," *Quarterly Journal of Economics*, vol. 107, February 1992, no. 1, pp. 1–34; and Paul Krugman, *The Conscience of a Liberal* (New York: W. W. Norton & Company, 2007), pp. 37–56.

5. J. Ronald Oakley, *God's Country: America in the Fifties* (New York: Barricade Books, 1990), pp. 112–14.

6. James Reston, "Our History Suggests a Remedy," in John Jessup, ed., *The National Purpose* (New York: Time, Inc./Holt, Rinehart and Winston, 1960), pp. 114–15, and for the 1950s polls see Samuel A. Stouffer, *Communism, Conformity, and Civil Liberties: A Cross-Section of the Nation Speaks Its Mind* (Garden City, NY: Doubleday, 1955).

7. Joseph Brodsky, "The U.S. a Strong and Stable Land: Progressive Conservatism Is Its Mood," *Time*, September 14, 1953; John Bodnar, *The "Good War" in American Memory* (Baltimore, MD: Johns Hopkins University Press, 2010), pp. 95–98; Robert Putnam, *Bowling Alone: The Collapse and Revival of American Community* (New York: Simon & Schuster, 2000), pp. 17–18ff; Suzanne Mettler, *Soldiers to Citizens: The G.I. Bill and the Making of the Greatest Generation* (New York: Oxford University Press, 2005), pp. 123–31; and Oakley, *God's Country*, pp. 115–17.

8. Richard F. Hamilton, *Class and Politics in the United States* (New York: John Wiley & Sons, 1972), esp. pp. 87–90; Nelson Lichtenstein, *State of the Union: A Century of American Labor* (Princeton, NJ: Princeton University Press, 2002), pp. 98–140; and Jack Metzgar, *Striking Steel: Solidarity Remembered* (Philadelphia: Temple University Press, 2000).

9. Robert J. Norrell, *The House I Live In: Race in the American Century* (New York: Oxford University Press, 2005), p. 156, and Thomas J. Sugrue, *Sweet Land of Liberty: The Forgotten Struggle for Civil Rights Up North* (New York: Random House, 2008), pp. 111–21.

10. Aaron Henry quoted in Stephen Tuck, *We Ain't What We Ought to Be: The Black Freedom Struggle from Emancipation to Obama* (Cambridge, MA: Harvard University Press, 2010), p. 256; Charles M. Payne, *I've Got the Light of Freedom: The Organizing Tradition and the Mississippi Freedom Struggle* (Berkeley: University of California Press, 2007 ed.), pp. 29–66; Norrell, *The House I Live In*, pp. 148–85; Numan V. Bartley, *The Rise of Massive Resistance: Race and Politics in the South During the 1950's* (Baton Rouge: Louisiana State University Press, 1969); and Pete Daniel, *Lost Revolutions: The South in the 1950s* (Chapel Hill: University of North Carolina Press, 2000), pp. 209–27.

11. Harvard Sitkoff, *The Struggle for Black Equality* (New York: Hill and Wang, 2008 ed.), pp. 37–56.

12. "Parnassus, Coast to Coast," *Time*, June 11, 1956, p. 2; Jules Witcover, *The Party of the People: A History of the Democrats* (New York: Random House, 2003), pp. 457–74; Daniel Bell, ed., *The New American Right* (New York: Criterion Books, 1955); Seymour Martin Lipset, *Political Man: The Social Bases of Politics* (Garden City, NY: Doubleday and Company, 1960), esp. pp. 87–126; and Walter A. Jackson, "White Liberals, Civil Rights and Gradualism, 1954–1960," in Brian Ward and Tony Badger, eds., *The Making of Martin Luther King and the Civil Rights Movement* (New York: New York University Press, 1996), esp. pp. 103–4. It should

be noted regarding the working class of the 1950s that while workers expressed support for Senator Joe McCarthy *in* polls, they did not turn out for him *at the* polls. In Milwaukee, his strongest support came from the city's upper-middle-class suburbs. See Hamilton, *Class and Politics in the United States*, pp. 115–16ff.

13. George Meany, "What Labor Means by 'More,'" in Editors of *Fortune*, eds., *The Fabulous Future: America in 1980* (New York: E. P. Dutton & Co., 1956), p. 50; Robert H. Zieger, "George Meany: Labor's Organization Man," in Melvin Dubofsky and Warren Van Tine, eds., *Labor Leaders in America* (Urbana: University of Illinois Press, 1987), pp. 324–49; and Joshua Freeman, *Working-Class New York: Life and Labor Since World War II* (New York: New Press, 2000), esp. pp. 1–176.

14. C. Wright Mills, *The Sociological Imagination* (New York: Oxford University Press, 1959), pp. 171–76; Reston, "Our History Suggests a Remedy," p. 115; and on the social critics, see Richard H. Pells, *The Liberal Mind in a Conservative Age: American Intellectuals in the 1940s and 1950s* (Hanover, NH: Wesleyan University Press, 1989 ed.), pp. 183–261.

15. Kim Phillips-Fein, *Invisible Hands: The Businessmen's Crusade Against the New Deal* (New York: W. W. Norton, 2009), esp. pp. 1–130; David Farber, *The Rise and Fall of Modern American Conservatism: A Short History* (Princeton, NJ: Princeton University Press, 2010), pp. 39–76; and Allan J. Lichtman, *White Protestant Nation: The Rise of the American Conservative Movement* (New York: Atlantic Monthly Press, 2008), pp. 207–23. Notably, NAM went after "statism" and the Four Freedoms in a widely distributed full-color comic book, *Fight for Freedom!* (1951).

16. C. Wright Mills, *The Power Elite* (New York: Oxford University Press, 1956), and the American Round Table, *People's Capitalism*, sponsored by Yale University and the Advertising Council (New York: Advertising Council, 1956), p. 3. For a full discussion of the Ad Council's campaigns, see Wendy L. Wall, *Inventing the "American Way": The Politics of Consensus from the New Deal to the Civil Rights Movement* (New York: Oxford University Press, 2008), pp. 172–77ff.

17. Arthur Goodfriend, *What Is America?* (New York: Simon & Schuster, 1954).

18. Ibid., esp. pp. 59, 82, 88, 89, 94.

19. The American Round Table, *People's Capitalism*, p. 44.

20. Max Lerner, *The Unfinished Country: A Book of American Symbols* (New York: Simon & Schuster, 1959), p. xxiv.

21. Mary Dudziak, *Cold War Civil Rights: Race and the Image of American Democracy* (Princeton, NJ: Princeton University Press, 2000), pp. 79–151.

22. Jack Metzgar, *Striking Steel: Solidarity Remembered* (Philadelphia: Temple University Press, 2000), esp. pp. 85–92; Elizabeth Tandy Shermer, " 'Is Freedom of the Individual Un-American?' Right-to-Work Campaigns and Anti-Union Conservatism, 1943–1958," in Nelson Lichtenstein and Elizabeth Tandy Shermer, eds., *The Right and Labor in America: Politics, Ideology, and Imagination* (Philadelphia: University of Pennsylvania Press, 2012), esp. pp. 130–36; and Mike Davis, *Prisoners of the American Dream: Politics and Economy in the History of the U.S. Working Class* (New York: Verso, 1986), pp. 121–24.

23. G. Calvin Mackenzie and Robert Weisbrot, *The Liberal Hour: Washington and the Politics of Change in the 1960s* (New York: Penguin Press, 2008), pp. 57–59.

24. Davis, *Prisoners of the American Dream*, pp. 123–24; Metzgar, *Striking Steel*, pp. 85–92; and Joseph E. Slater, *Public Workers: Government Employee Unions, the Law, and the State, 1900–1962* (Ithaca, NY: Cornell University Press/ILR, 2004), esp. pp. 158–80.

25. Sitkoff, *The Struggle for Black Equality*, pp. 32–33, 37–56.

26. *Prospect for America: The Rockefeller Panel Reports* (Garden City, NY: Rockefeller Brothers Fund, 1961); John K. Jessup, ed., *The National Purpose: America in Crisis—An Urgent Summons* (New York: Time/Holt, Rinehart and Winston, 1960); *Goals for Americans: The Report of the President's Commission on National Goals—Programs for Action in the Sixties* (New York: American Assembly/Prentice Hall, 1960); John W. Jeffries, "The 'Quest for National Purpose' of 1960," *American Quarterly*, vol. 30, no. 4, Autumn 1978, pp. 451–70; and Robert M. Collins, "Growth Liberalism in the Sixties: Great Societies at Home and Grand Designs Abroad," in David Farber, ed., *The Sixties . . . From Memory to History* (Chapel Hill: University of North Carolina Press, 1994), pp. 16–17.

27. Arthur Schlesinger, Jr., "The New Mood in Politics" (1960), reprinted in *The Politics of Hope* and *The Bitter Heritage* (Princeton, NJ: Princeton University Press, 2008), p. 106; Archibald MacLeish, "We Have Purpose . . . We All Know It," in Jessup, ed., *The National Purpose*, pp. 38, 47; Andrew B. Lewis, *The Shadows of Youth: The Remarkable Journey of the Civil Rights Generation* (New York: Hill and Wang, 2009), pp. 1–112; and

Frederick A. Manchester, "The Tricky Four Freedoms," *Freeman: Ideas on Liberty*, vol. 10, no. 4, April 1960, pp. 25–36.

28. "Democratic Platform 1960" and "Republican Platform 1960," in Donald Bruce Johnson, ed., *National Party Platforms: Volume II, 1960–1976* (Urbana: University of Illinois Press, 1978), pp. 574–600, 604–21. On polls showing Americans leaning left, see Hamilton, *Class and Politics in the United States*, pp. 89–90, 130–34; and on the drafting of the Democratic platform, see Chester Bowles, *Promises to Keep: My Years in Public Life, 1941–1969* (New York: Harper & Row, 1971), pp. 289–92.

29. James MacGregor Burns, *Running Alone: Presidential Leadership—JFK to Bush II* (New York: Basic Books, 2006), pp. 31–42, and Mackenzie and Weisbrot, *The Liberal Hour*, pp. 72–79, 364–69. Kennedy himself had insisted he was no liberal, saying, "I never joined Americans for Democratic Action or the American Veterans Committee" (Chris Matthews, *Jack Kennedy: Elusive Hero* [New York: Simon & Schuster, 2012], p. 226).

30. Sitkoff, *The Struggle for Black Equality*, pp. 61–183.

31. Richard Harrity, ed., *Yank—The GI Story of the War* (New York: Duell, Sloan & Pearce, 1947), p. 225; Lewis, *The Shadows of Youth*; James Miller, *Democracy Is in the Streets: From Port Huron to the Siege of Chicago* (Cambridge, MA: Harvard University Press, 1994 ed.); Robert Cohen and Reginald Zelnick, eds., *The Free Speech Movement: Reflections on Berkeley in the 1960s* (Berkeley: University of California Press, 2000).

32. John F. Kennedy, "Inaugural Address" (January 20, 1961), The American Presidency Project: http://www.presidency.ucsb.edu/ws/index .php?pid=8032&st=&st1=. See also Kennedy, "Accepting the Democratic Party Nomination for the Presidency of the United States" (July 15, 1960); "Speech Accepting New York Liberal Party Nomination" (September 14, 1960); and "Speech . . . to National Conference on Constitutional Rights and American Freedom" (October 12, 1960), The American Presidency Project: http://www.presidency.ucsb.edu/ws/index.php?pid =25966&st=&st1=; http://www.presidency.ucsb.edu/ws/index.php?pid =74012&st=&st1=; and http://www.presidency.ucsb.edu/ws/index.php ?pid=25783&st=&st1=. And regarding the former AVC members of Kennedy's cabinet, see Joseph C. Goulden, *The Best Years, 1945–1950* (New York: Athenuem, 1976), pp. 61–62.

33. Burns, *Running Alone*, pp. 57–58, and Kim McQuaid, *Uneasy Partners: Big Business in American Politics* (Baltimore, MD: Johns Hopkins University Press, 1994), pp. 113–24.

34. Four Freedoms, Inc., *A Story That Must Be Told . . .* (New York: Four Freedoms, Inc., 1963), and Edward M. Kennedy, "The Immigration Act of 1965," *Annals of the American Academy of Political and Social Science*, vol. 367, September 1966, pp. 137–49. See also John F. Kennedy, *A Nation of Immigrants* (New York: Harper & Row, 1964), in which JFK spoke of immigration in terms of the pursuit of the Four Freedoms, esp. pp. 6–7ff.

35. Dolores Huerta quoted in Richard Griswold del Castillo and Richard A. Garcia, *César Chávez: A Triumph of Spirit* (Norman: University of Oklahoma Press, 1995), p. 72; Andrew E. Kersten, *A. Philip Randolph: A Life in the Vanguard* (Lanham, MD: Rowman & Littlefield, 2007), p. 89; Frank Bardacke, *Trampling Out the Vintage: César Chávez and the Two Souls of the United Farm Workers* (New York: Verso, 2011); Leon Fink, *Upheaval in the Quiet Zone: A History of Hospital Workers' Union, Local 1199* (Urbana: University of Illinois Press, 1989); Richard D. Kahlenberg, *Tough Liberal: Albert Shanker and the Battle over Schools, Unions, Race, and Democracy* (New York: Columbia University Press, 2007), pp. 4–51; Kevin Boyle, *The UAW and the Heyday of American Liberalism, 1945–1968* (Ithaca, NY: Cornell University Press, 1995), p. 159; and Tom Hayden, *The Port Huron Statement: The Visionary Call of the 1960s Revolution* (New York: Thunder's Mouth Press, 2005).

36. Sitkoff, *The Struggle for Black Equality*, pp. 89–103. And on the respective leaders, see Roy Wilkins, *Standing Fast: The Autobiography of Roy Wilkins* (New York: Da Capo Press, 1994); Nancy J. Weiss, *Whitney M. Young, Jr., and the Struggle for Civil Rights* (Princeton, NJ: Princeton University Press, 1989); James Farmer, *Lay Bare the Heart: An Autobiography of the Civil Rights Movement* (New York: Arbor House, 1985); Thomas F. Jackson, *From Civil Rights to Human Rights: Martin Luther King, Jr., and the Struggle for Economic Justice* (Philadelphia: University of Pennsylvania Press, 2007), esp. pp. 26–41; Harvard Sitkoff, *King: Pilgrimage to the Mountaintop* (New York: Hill and Wang, 2008); and Barbara Ransby, *Ella Baker and the Black Freedom Movement: A Radical Democratic Vision* (Chapel Hill: University of North Carolina Press, 2003).

37. Cynthia E. Harrison, "A 'New Frontier' for Women: The Public Policy of the Kennedy Administration," *Journal of American History*, vol. 67, no.

3, December 1980, pp. 630–746; Betty Friedan, *The Feminine Mystique* (1963; New York: W. W. Norton, 2001 ed.); Daniel Horowitz, *Betty Friedan and the Making of the Feminine Mystique: The American Left, the Cold War, and Modern Feminism* (Amherst: University of Massachusetts Press, 1998); and Stephanie Coontz, *A Strange Stirring: The Feminine Mystique and American Women at the Dawn of the 1960s* (New York: Basic Books, 2011).

38. Rachel Carson, *Silent Spring* (Boston: Houghton Mifflin, 1962); Michael Egan, *Barry Commoner and the Science of Survival: The Remaking of American Environmentalism* (Cambridge, MA: MIT Press, 2009); and Michael Harrington, *The Other America: Poverty in the United States* (New York: Macmillan, 1962).

39. John F. Kennedy, "Special Message to the Congress on Protecting the Consumer Interest" (March 15, 1962), The American Presidency Project: http://www.presidency.ucsb.edu/ws/?pid=9108, and "Radio and Television Report to the American People on Civil Rights" (June 11, 1963), The American Presidency Project: http://www.presidency.ucsb.edu/ws/index.php?pid=9271. Also, see Lizabeth Cohen, *A Consumers' Republic: The Politics of Mass Consumption in Postwar America* (New York: Alfred A. Knopf, 2003), pp. 349–54ff; Peter Irons, *A People's History of the Supreme Court* (New York: Penguin Books, 2006 ed.), pp. 410–20; and Sitkoff, *The Struggle for Black Equality*, pp. 120–37.

40. Sitkoff, ibid.

41. Ibid., pp. 147–53.

42. Bill Moyers's recollection of Lyndon Johnson's words quoted in Randall B. Woods, *LBJ: Architect of American Ambition* (New York: Free Press, 2006), p. 561.

43. Ibid.; Nick Kotz, *Judgment Days: Lyndon Baines Johnson, Martin Luther King, Jr., and the Laws That Changed America* (Boston: Houghton Mifflin, 2005), pp. 22–32; Doris Kearns Goodwin, *Lyndon Johnson and the American Dream* (New York: St. Martin's Griffin, 1991 ed.), pp. 19–101; and Robert A. Caro, *Master of the Senate: The Years of Lyndon Johnson* (New York: Knopf, 2002).

44. Lyndon Johnson, "Annual Message to the Congress on the State of the Union" (January 8, 1964), The American Presidency Project: http://www.presidency.ucsb.edu/ws/index.php?pid=26787&st=&st1=; "Special Message to the Congress Proposing a Nationwide War on the Sources of Poverty" (March 16, 1964), The American Presidency Project: http://

www.presidency.ucsb.edu/ws/index.php?pid=26109&st=economic+
opportunity+act&st1=; "Remarks at the University of Michigan" (May
22, 1964), The American Presidency Project: http://www.presidency.ucsb
.edu/ws/index.php?pid=26262; "Television Address to the American People" (October 7, 1964), The American Presidency Project: http://www
.presidency.ucsb.edu/ws/index.php?pid=26574; "Toasts of the President
and President Segni" (January 14, 1964), The American Presidency Project: http://www.presidency.ucsb.edu/ws/index.php?pid=25980.

45. Woods, LBJ, p. 563; Martin Luther King, Jr., Why We Can't Wait (New
York: Signet Classics, 2000 ed.), pp. 170–74; and Kotz, Judgment Days,
pp. 182–85.

46. Bruce Watson, Freedom Summer (New York: Penguin Books, 2010);
Robert Cohen, Freedom's Orator: Mario Savio and the Radical Legacy of
the 1960s (New York: Oxford University Press, 2009); and Cohen and
Zelnick, eds., The Free Speech Movement.

47. Ronald Reagan, "A Time for Choosing" (aka "The Speech"), October 27,
1964, http://www.reagan.utexas.edu/archives/reference/timechoosing.html.

48. William E. Leuchtenburg, In the Shadow of FDR: From Harry Truman to
Barack Obama (Ithaca, NY: Cornell University Press, 2009 ed.), p. 140.

49. Lyndon B. Johnson, "Annual Message to the Congress on the State of
the Union" (January 4, 1965), The American Presidency Project: http://
www.presidency.ucsb.edu/ws/index.php?pid=26907.

50. Tracy Roof, American Labor, Congress, and the Welfare State, 1935–2010
(Baltimore, MD: Johns Hopkins University Presss, 2011), pp. 92–99, and
Jerry Wurf, Labor's Last Angry Man (New York: Atheneum, 1982).

51. Kotz, Judgment Days, pp. 250–337; Lyndon B. Johnson, "Special Message
to the Congress: The American Promise" (March 15, 1965), The Amer-
ican Presidency Project: http://www.presidency.ucsb.edu/ws/?pid=26805;
Annelise Orelick, "Introduction: The War on Poverty from the Grass
Roots Up," in Annelise Orelick and Lisa Gayle Hazirijian, eds., The War
on Poverty: A New Grassroots History, 1964–1980 (Athens: University of
Georgia Press, 2011), pp. 1–28; Report of the White House Conference "To
Fulfill The Rights"—June 1–2, 1966 (Washington, DC: U.S. Government
Printing Office, 1966); A. Philip Randolph Institute, A "Freedom Budget
for All Americans" (New York: October 1966); and Andrew E. Kersten,
A. Philip Randolph: A Life in the Vanguard (Lanham, MD: Rowman &
Littlefield, 2007), pp. 88–112.

52. David Vogel, Fluctuating Fortunes: The Political Power of Business in Amer-

ica (New York: Basic Books, 1989), pp. 38–58; Ralph Nader, *Unsafe at Any Speed: The Designed-in Dangers of the American Automobile* (New York: Grossman Publishers, 1965); Les Leopold, *The Man Who Hated Work and Loved Labor: The Life and Times of Tony Mazzocchi* (White River Junction, VT: Chelsea Green Publishing, 2007); and Horowitz, *Betty Friedan*, pp. 227–29.

53. Young Americans for Freedom, "The Sharon Statement" (1960), in *The Rise of Conservatism in America, 1945–2000: A Brief History with Documents* (Boston: Bedford/St. Martin's, 2008), pp. 64–65, and John A. Andrew III, *The Other Side of the Sixties: Young Americans for Freedom and the Rise of Conservative Politics* (New Brunswick, NJ: Rutgers University Press, 1997).

54. Lyndon Johnson, "Remarks in New York City Upon Receiving the National Freedom Award" (February 23, 1966), The American Presidency Project: http://www.presidency.ucsb.edu/ws/?pid=28101.

55. "Johnson Denies 'Blind Escalation' in Vietnam War," *New York Times*, February 24, 1966, p. A1, and Lyndon Johnson, "Annual Message to the Congress on the State of the Union" (January 12, 1966), The American Presidency Project: http://www.presidency.ucsb.edu/ws/index.php?pid=28015.

56. Woods, *LBJ*, p. 451; Goodwin, *Lyndon Johnson*, p. 92; Haynes Johnson and Nick Kotz, *The Unions* (New York: Pocket Books, 1972), pp. 112–29; and Gilbert J. Gall, *The Politics of Right to Work: The Labor Federations as Special Interests, 1943–1979* (New York: Greenwood Press, 1988), pp. 169–79.

57. Collins, "Growth Liberalism in the Sixties," esp. pp. 23–25.

58. Maurice Isserman and Michael Kazin, *America Divided: The Civil War of the 1960s* (New York: Oxford University Press, 2000), esp. pp. 147–221, and James T. Patterson, *The Eve of Destruction: How 1965 Transformed America* (New York: Basic Books, 2012), pp. 89–219.

59. Dan T. Carter, *The Politics of Rage: George Wallace, the Origins of the New Conservatism, and the Transformation of American Politics* (Baton Rouge: Louisiana State University Press, 2000 ed.), esp. pp. 294–323; Dominic Sandbrook, *Mad as Hell: The Crisis of the 1970s and the Rise of the Populist Right* (New York: Alfred A. Knopf, 2011), p. 243; Hamilton, *Class and Politics in the United States*, pp. 132–33; Lichtenstein, *State of the Union*, p. 185; Thomas Ferguson and Joel Rogers, *Right Turn: The Decline of the Democrats and the Future of American Politics* (New York: Hill and Wang, 1986), pp. 13–15; and Vogel, *Fluctuating Fortunes*, pp. 59–112.

60. Isserman and Kazin, *America Divided*, pp. 221–40.

61. Richard Nixon interview in David Frost, *The Presidential Debate, 1968* (New York: Stein and Day, 1968), p. 11.

62. Richard Nixon, "Address Accepting the Presidential Nomination at the Republican National Convention in Miami Beach, Florida" (August 8, 1968), The American Presidency Project: http://www.presidency.ucsb.edu/ws/index.php?pid=25968.

63. Robert Mason, *Richard Nixon and the Quest for a New Majority* (Chapel Hill: University of North Carolina Press, 2004), and Kevin Phillips, *The Emerging Republican Majority* (New Rochelle, NY: Arlington House, 1969).

64. Mason, *Richard Nixon and the Quest for a New Majority*, pp. 56–61; Albert H. Cantril and Charles W. Roll, Jr., *Hopes and Fears of the American People* (New York: Universe Books, 1971); Vogel, *Fluctuating Fortunes*, pp. 60–64; and Jill Quadagno, *One Nation Uninsured: Why the U.S. Has No National Health Insurance* (New York: Oxford University Press, 2005), pp. 109–23.

65. Mason, *Richard Nixon*, pp. 161–78, and Bruce Miroff, *The Liberals' Moment: The McGovern Insurgency and the Identity Crisis of the Democratic Party* (Lawrence: University Press of Kansas, 2007). It should also be noted that McGovern, who hailed from a right-to-work state, had failed to vote against shutting down the filibuster protecting the Taft-Hartley Act in 1965.

66. Michael Harrington, *The Twilight of Capitalism* (New York: Simon & Schuster, 1976), and Robert A. Nisbet, *Twilight of Authority* (New York: Oxford University Press, 1975).

67. *Time* quote (November 9, 1970) in Jefferson Cowie, *Stayin' Alive: The 1970s and the Last Days of the Working Class* (New York: New Press, 2010), p. 2, and Ferguson and Rogers, *Right Turn*, pp. 34–35ff.

68. Cowie, *Stayin' Alive*, p. 236, and Steven M. Gillon, "The Travail of the Democrats: Search for a New Majority," in Peter B. Kovler, ed., *Democrats and the American Idea: A Bicentennial Appraisal* (Lanham, MD: Center for National Policy Press, 1992), esp. pp. 290–95.

69. Meany quoted in Kim Moody, *An Injury to All: The Decline of American Unionism* (New York: Verso, 1988), p. 125.

70. David Rockefeller (January 1971) quoted in Terry H. Anderson, "The New American Revolution: The Movement and Business," in Farber, ed., *The Sixties*, p. 187.

71. Lewis F. Powell, Jr., "Attack on American Free Enterprise System," Con-

fidential Memorandum of August 23, 1971, http://www.pbs.org/wnet /supremecourt/personality/sources_document13.html.

72. Vogel, *Fluctuating Fortunes*, pp. 113–240.

73. Samuel P. Huntington, "The United States," in Michael Crozier, Samuel Huntington, and Joji Watanuki, *The Crisis of Democracy: Report on the Governability of Democracies to the Trilateral Commission* (New York: New York University Press, 1975), pp. 59, 102, 113–14.

74. Cowie, *Stayin' Alive*, pp. 231–35, and Joseph McCartin, "Turnabout Years: Public Sector Unionism and the Fiscal Crisis," in Bruce J. Schulman and Julian E. Zelizer, eds., *Rightward Bound: Making America Conservative in the 1970s* (Cambridge, MA: Harvard University Press, 2008), 128–47.

75. Alice O'Connor, "Financing the Counterrevolution," in Schulman and Zelizer, eds., *Rightward Bound*, pp. 148–68.

76. Lane Kenworthy, Sondra Barringer, Daniel Duer, and Garrett Andrew Schneider, "The Democrats and Working-Class Whites," June 10, 2007, http://www.u.arizona.edu/~lkenwor/thedemocratsandworkingclasswhites.pdf.

77. John Bodnar, *The "Good War" in American Memory* (Baltimore, MD: Johns Hopkins University Press, 2010), photo set between pp. 84 and 85.

78. Jimmy Carter, "My Name Is Jimmy Carter and I'm Running for President" (July 15, 1976), in *A Government as Good as Its People* (New York: Simon & Schuster, 1977), pp. 125–28.

79. Douglas Fraser, "Resignation Letter" (July 19, 1978), in Howard Zinn and Anthony Arnove, eds., *Voices of a People's History* (New York: Seven Stories Press, 2004), 530–33; Sandbrook, *Mad as Hell*, pp. 238–40ff; Vogel, *Fluctuating Fortunes*, pp. 148–92; and on "Carterland," see Jacob S. Hacker and Paul Pierson, *Winner-Take-All Politics: How Washington Made the Rich Richer and Turned Its Back on the Middle Class* (New York: Simon & Schuster, 2010), pp. 98–132.

80. Michael Lind, *Land of Promise: An Economic History of the United States* (New York: HarperCollins, 2012), pp. 381–86; Leonard Silk (1980) quoted in Leuchtenburg, *In the Shadow of FDR*, p. 208; and Jeff Madrick, *Age of Greed: The Triumph of Finance and the Decline of America, 1970 to the Present* (New York: Alfred A. Knopf, 2011), pp. 150–51ff.

81. Jimmy Carter, "The State of the Union Address" (January 19, 1978), The American Presidency Project: http://www.presidency.ucsb.edu/ws /index.php?pid=30856&st=&st1=.

82. Jimmy Carter, "Anti-Inflation Program Address to the Nation" (Octo-

ber 24, 1978), The American Presidency Project: http://www.presidency
.ucsb.edu/ws/index.php?pid=30040&st=&st1=, and "The State of the
Union Address Delivered Before a Joint Session of the Congress" (January 23, 1979), The American Presidency Project: http://www.presidency
.ucsb.edu/ws/index.php?pid=32657&st=&st1=.

83. Jimmy Carter, "Address to the Nation on Energy and National Goals:
'The Malaise Speech'" (July 15, 1979), The American Presidency Project: http://www.presidency.ucsb.edu/ws/index.php?pid=32596.

84. Ronald Reagan, "Remarks at a Ceremony Commemorating the 40th
Anniversary of the Normandy Invasion, D-Day" (June 6, 1984), The
American Presidency Project: http://www.presidency.ucsb.edu/ws/index
.php?pid=40018&st=&st1=#axzz1M9GTGSDu.

85. Douglas Brinkley, *The Boys of Pointe Du Hoc: Ronald Reagan, D-Day, and
the U.S. Army 2nd Ranger Battalion* (New York: HarperCollins, 2005),
pp. 5–10.

86. Jimmy Carter, "The State of the Union Address" (January 19, 1978), and
"Anti-Inflation Program Address to the Nation" (October 24, 1978),
The American Presidency Project: http://www.presidency.ucsb.edu
/ws/?pid=30040; and "Address to the Nation on Energy and National Goals:
'The Malaise Speech'" (July 15, 1979), The American Presidency Project:
http://www.presidency.ucsb.edu/ws/index.php?pid=32596&st=&st1=; and
Stephen F. Hayward, *The Age of Reagan: The Fall of the Old Liberal Order,
1964–1980* (Roseville, CA: Forum, 2001), pp. 535–608.

87. Ronald Reagan, "Remarks and a Question-and-Answer Session With
Regional Editors and Broadcasters," February 10, 1986, The American
Presidency Project: http://www.presidency.ucsb.edu/ws/index.php?pid
=36859&st=&st1=#axzz1Ob58d2de. On Reagan's political and ideological vision by someone who campaigned with and worked for him, see
Martin Anderson, *Revolution: The Reagan Legacy* (Stanford, CA: Hoover
Institution Press, 1990 expanded ed.), esp. pp. xxvi–xxvii.

88. Garry Wills, *Reagan's America* (New York: Penguin Books, 2000), and
Thomas W. Evans, *The Education of Ronald Reagan: The General Electric
Years and the Untold Story of His Conversion to Conservatism* (New York:
Columbia University Press, 2006).

89. Reagan did occasionally slip up regarding FDR and the New Deal, as in
1976, when he told an interviewer, "Fascism was really the basis for the
New Deal" (Ronald Reagan, "Interview: I've Had a Bum Rap," *Time*, May
17, 1976, http://www.time.com/time/magazine/article/0,9171,945592,00

.html), and again in 1981 ("Reagan Says Many New Dealers Wanted Fascism," *New York Times*, December 23, 1981, p. A12).

90. Ronald Reagan, "Address Accepting the Presidential Nomination at the Republican National Convention" (July 17, 1980), The American Presidency Project: http://www.presidency.ucsb.edu/ws/index .php?pid=25970#axzz1M9GTGSDu; Bernard von Bothmer, *Framing the Sixties: The Use and Abuse of a Decade from Ronald Reagan to George W. Bush* (Amherst: University of Massachusetts Press, 2010), esp. pp. 28–44, 56–58; and Harvey J. Kaye, *The Powers of the Past* (Minneapolis: University of Minnesota Press, 1991), esp. pp. 96–105, and *Thomas Paine and the Promise of America* (New York: Hill and Wang, 2005), esp. pp. 3–4, 222–26.

91. Ronald Reagan, "Remarks Announcing America's Economic Bill of Rights" (July 3, 1987), The American Presidency Project: http://www .presidency.ucsb.edu/ws/index.php?pid=34512&st=&st1=#axzz1Mv4Kwlfp, and Anderson, *Revolution*, pp. 113–21, 186–87. Reagan also revealed his ambitions in 1986 when, after lying to reporters about the "failure" of the War on Poverty, he spoke longingly of the 1920s as a time when "values of the individual, the family, and the community commanded the day . . . Taxes . . . were low . . . regulation of the economy was slight . . . [C]aricatured as a time of cultural intolerance, immigrants actually made tremendous advances in all walks of American life." Reagan, "Remarks and a Question-and-Answer Session with Regional Editors and Broadcasters."

92. Ronald Reagan, "Farewell Address to the Nation" (January 11, 1989), The American Presidency Project: http://www.presidency.ucsb.edu/ws /index.php?pid=29650#axzz1Mv4Kwlfp.

Chapter Eleven

1. Barack Obama, *The Audacity of Hope: Thoughts on Reclaiming the American Dream* (New York: Three Rivers Press, 2006), and "Remarks to the Detroit Economic Club" (May 7, 2007), The American Presidency Project: http://www.presidency.ucsb.edu/ws/index.php?pid=77000.

2. Scott Yenor, "A New Deal for Roosevelt," *Claremont Review of Books*, Winter 2006, pp. 65–66; Barack Obama, "Remarks in Denver: 'The Past Versus the Future'" (January 30, 2008), The American Presidency Project: http://www.presidency.ucsb.edu/ws/index.php?pid=77031, "Keynote Address at the 2004 Democratic National Convention" (July 27, 2004),

The American Presidency Project: http://www.presidency.ucsb.edu/ws/index.php?pid=76988, and "Remarks in Janesville, Wisconsin: 'Keeping America's Promise'" (February 13, 2008), The American Presidency Project: http://www.presidency.ucsb.edu/ws/index.php?pid=77032; *Time*, November 24, 2008; and Harvey J. Kaye, "On Hearing Obama Speak Paine's Words," *History News Network*, January 26, 2009, and "Americans Should Embrace Their Radical History," *History News Network*, March 9, 2009.

3. Jon Meacham, "It's Not Easy Bein' Blue," *Newsweek/Daily Beast*, October 17, 2008; Amity Shlaes, "A Chilling Uncertainty," *Washington Post*, December 31, 2008; Patrick Perry, "Norman Rockwell's Four Freedoms," *Saturday Evening Post*, January 1, 2009; and Jim DeMint, *Saving Freedom: We Can Stop America's Slide into Socialism* (Nashville, TN: Fidelis Books, 2009), p. 8.

4. For a most generous view of Obama's first-term accomplishments, see Michael Grunwald, *The New New Deal: The Hidden Story of Change in the Obama Era* (New York: Simon & Schuster, 2012).

5. Theda Skocpol and Vanessa Williamson, *The Tea Party and the Remaking of Republican Conservatism* (New York: Oxford University Press, 2012), p. 4, and Ronald P. Formisano, *The Tea Party: A Brief History* (Baltimore, MD: Johns Hopkins University Press, 2012).

6. Barack Obama, "Remarks on Signing an Executive Order Establishing the National Commission on Fiscal Responsibility and Reform and an Exchange With Reporters" (February 18, 2010), The American Presidency Project: http://www.presidency.ucsb.edu/ws/index.php?pid=87564&st=&st1=; Jonathan Alter, *The Promise: President Obama, Year One* (New York: Simon & Schuster, 2010), p. xv; John Judis, "The Unnecessary Fall," *New Republic*, September 2, 2010, pp. 12–15; and Michael Tomasky, "The Elections: How Bad for Democrats?" *New York Review of Books*, October 28, 2010, p. 6.

7. John Nichols, *Uprising* (New York: Nation Books, 2012).

8. Barack Obama, "Remarks at George Washington University" (April 13, 2011), The American Presidency Project: http://www.presidency.ucsb.edu/ws/?pid=90246; Barack Obama, "The President's Weekly Address" (July 2, 2011), The American Presidency Project: http://www.presidency.ucsb.edu/ws/index.php?pid=90588&st=&st1=; and Lori Montgomery, "In Debt Talks, Obama Offers Social Security Cuts," *Washington Post*, July 6, 2011.

9. Todd Gitlin, *Occupy Nation: The Roots, the Spirit, and the Promise of Occupy Wall Street* (New York: HarperCollins, 2012).

10. Max Lerner, "The Waste of History" (July 13, 1948), in Max Lerner, *Actions and Passions: Notes on the Multiple Revolutions of Our Time* (New York: Simon & Schuster, 1949), p. 213.

11. Franklin D. Roosevelt letter of 1930 quoted in Rexford Tugwell, *The Democratic Roosevelt: A Biography of Franklin D. Roosevelt* (Baltimore, MD: Penguin Books, 1969 ed.), p. 197.

INDEX